Encounters
with **Babaji**
Master of the Himalayas

RENATA CADDY, born in Munich in 1941, grew up in a culturally and spiritually very open family. She studied painting, graphics and sculpture in Munich, Berlin and Paris. She explored important questions like the meaning of life early on, and this found expression in her artistic and literary work. Her paintings were exhibited on numerous occasions and she gave a number of readings of her own texts and poems.

In 1978 she first met Babaji in Herakhan, India. After that she visited him regularly until he left his body in 1984. In 1979 she began to create a "garden of heaven" from what had been a wilderness at her house on Lake Constance, Germany. She did this with the blessing and inspiration of Babaji. The garden is called "Nandan Van"; regular meditations and the eight solar festivals are held there. Her husband Peter Caddy, the co-founder of the Findhorn Community, played a prominent part in its creation. Inspired by Babaji, Renata Caddy has been offering seminars and creatively intense workshops on finding yourself, self-realization and true happiness.

BABAJI is recognized as a mahavatar, a manifestation of Shiva, who is able to appear in a human form. At the beginning of the 19th century Babji emerged from a ball of light as a young man of between 20 and 25 years who remained on earth until 1922. As had been predicted, he again appeared in 1970 in a cave in the Herakhan valley in the foothills of Mt. Kailash in India. People from all over the world, whom he had called in dreams and visions, came to him and thus an ashram grew up under his leadership.

Renata Caddy visited Babaji for the first time in 1978. This book is a collection of those overwhelming experiences with Babaji in India and later also in Tibet. The profound emotion elicited by the encounters with Babaji, his work and teachings, can be felt in each story.

This very inspiring and healing book can be a substantial aid in the spiritual development of anyone, no matter what their religious background, especially now that Babaji has taken on his new human form on the material plane.

Encounters with Babaji

Master of the Himalayas

RENATA CADDY

FINDHORN PRESS

© 2010 Schirner Verlag, Darmstadt, Germany
Original Title: *Segen von Babaji: Begegnung mit dem Meister vom Himalaya*

English edition © 2012 Findhorn Press Ltd.
Published under licence from Schirner Verlag, Darmstadt, Germany.

The right of Renata Caddy to be identified as the author
of this work has been asserted by her in accordance
with the Copyright, Designs and Patents Act 1998.

ISBN 978-1-84409-574-2

A CIP record for this title is available from the British Library.

Translated by Krishna Viswanathan and Richard Freeman
Edited by Tony Mitton
Cover by Murat Karaçay, adapted by Thierry Bogliolo
Interior design by Damian Keenan

Digital Imaging: Martin Bichler, Meersburg
Photographs on pages 139, 178, 181, 185 by Martin Bichler
Printed and bound in the EU

1 2 3 4 5 6 7 8 9 17 16 15 14 13 12

Published by
Findhorn Press
117-121 High Street,
Forres IV36 1AB,
Scotland, UK

t +44 (0)1309 690582
f +44 (0)131 777 2711
e info@findhornpress.com
www.findhornpress.com

Contents

This book
is dedicated to the Divine Flame
in everyone

Young Babaji, giving a blessing (1970)

Foreword
by Ruth Maria Kubitschek

I know Renata Caddy as a highly gifted painter. Her powerful pictures, their explosions of colour and light, touch the heart and emit a strong healing power and radiance.

In the same way, I know Renata Caddy's garden which she created together with her husband, Peter Caddy, the co-founder of the Findhorn community in the north of Scotland.

Renata has intuitively conceived this garden, which she calls a "Garden of Heaven." When one wanders through it, its beauty and wonderful vibrations touch the heart and senses – healing, as with her pictures.

Now I have come to know her as a writer and I have read her book with bated breath. She has carried me along with her extraordinary visions, which lead to Babaji: there, I lived and learned – so powerfully does she describe life with this great master, his works, his life and the deep meaning these have for our time.

A fiery vivaciousness shines from every sentence, and from the pictures that she unfolds before us. It is a book of tremendous depth, of unusual thoughts and events into which she courageously moves following an inner calling. In the midst of a Tibet occupied by the Chinese, on the Holy Mt. Kailash and around Lake Manasarovar, she dares to carry out healing fire ceremonies in complete faith in God, in order to help heal the deep wounds that have been inflicted everywhere.

I have the greatest respect for Renata Caddy, whose work and influence extend way beyond this book.

RUTH MARIA KUBITSCHEK is a well-known actress in German theatre and television. She has written several books, engages in painting and leading meditations, and in her love for the Earth has created a wonderful and very special garden.

Introduction

The One without colour appears
By the manifold application of his power
With many colours of his hidden purpose

May the being of splendour
In which the world dissolves
And from whom it rises
Grant us clear understanding

SVETASHVATARA UPANISHAD

This is a book about Babaji. It is about encounters with him, his teachings and his work, especially his work of transformation at this time as it approaches its end, and it is about his seed for the light-filled New, which is coming.

Baba means father, Babaji: revered father.
Babaji is seen as an Avatar – an embodiment of the Divine, as Shiva Mahavatar: as Lord Shiva in human form.

As such, Babaji created a human form for himself without passing through the portal of birth and according to Shri Muniraj, who has deep vision, this physical form of Babaji has existed for many thousands of years.

Mostly working out of sight, he also steps into view now and again. Babaji is able to appear in several places at once, either in a single or in various human forms, just as he wishes and according to the demands of his work.

Many people, myself included, were able to witness this on several occasions. What to us seems unbelievable is normal for him who operates from the love, the light and the power of divine awareness.

In the West, Babaji became known through Paramahansa Yogananda's *Autobiography of a Yogi*, which speaks of him as the great hidden leader of mankind.

Babaji has appeared again and again over the millennia, and in public too. For instance, about 500 years ago he appeared as Lama Baba in Tibet.

Old Herakhan-Baba (1911)

Here is a short summary of recorded experiences:[1]

At the beginning of the 19th century he materialized in physical form at the top of Mt. Kailash in the Kumaon region in the foothills of the Indian Himalayas. Mt. Kailash has been known from time immemorial as the seat of Lord Shiva.

At first Babaji showed himself above Kailash as a radiant light, which came and went. When the villagers saw it, they gathered there singing and praying. On the third day, a being, Babaji, appeared out of the ball of light, radiant and about 20 to 25 years old.

During the period of his physical presence, from the start of the 19th century until 1922, Babaji was seen by many people in a wide variety of locations. He appeared to people who revered him in dreams, visions, in his light form or in physical form and he helped them in times of need. Mainly he appeared to individual people, sometimes also to families. He never stayed long in one place; he disappeared and reappeared somewhere else. Thus it was not easy to encounter him. Whenever a larger number of people gathered around him, his presence turned into a celebration. He was there to serve all beings.

In the Kumaon region Babaji was known and revered as Herakhan Baba for his numerous healings and raisings from the dead. In August 1922, while crossing the river on foot at the place where the Kali and Gauri streams meet, he dissolved his form into light before the eyes of those accompanying him. Beforehand, he had promised to return as a blessing to the world.

In the period between 1922 and 1970 Babaji continued to bless people in dreams and visions or he appeared to them physically, as was the case with Mahendra Baba who announced Babaji's public return and spread the news.

In June 1970, Babaji appeared in a cave at the foot of Mt. Kailash. He was in the same body, now newly transformed into a divinely beautiful youth. This time he would undertake wider work in public.

In the cave he showed himself to a person whom he had called through a dream, first in his earlier form as the old Herakhan Baba and shortly thereafter in his new young form. To others who came, he also showed both bodies alternately in order to make his identity known.

From 1970, Babaji lived amongst the people. In the previous century he had arranged for a small temple to be built, high up near the little village of Herakhan opposite Mt. Kailash. That is where he stayed. An ashram grew up around the temple. Using that as his base, he was extremely active until, in 1984, to everyone's great surprise, he left his human form. This time he did not dematerialize as before, but allowed it to go through "death."

This event has deep meaning for our time. In this human form he had borne and transformed an immeasurable amount of suffering. This was precious for the Earth. That is obviously why he gave this substance to the Earth, by giving her his body that had passed through death.

In this context, a story is told of Babaji in his previous form as the old Herakhan Baba:

He was travelling with a devotee to Badrinarayam Dham, when the devotee fell ill with cholera. As his limbs became cold and he felt death drawing close,

Beautiful young Babaji in meditation (1970)

the devotee began crying bitterly at the thought of his wife and children. The old Herakhan Baba then said: "You have a family. I will give up my body in your place." As he said this, the devotee was instantaneously freed of his illness, which passed to the master. Babaji gave his devotee instructions to cremate his body after his death and to give the ashes to the holy waters of the Ganges. In deep sorrow at the death of the master the devotee carried out the rites as he had been instructed.

When, after a month of deep grief, he came to Almora, he heard that the old Herakhan Baba was alive and well in the house of one of his followers. The devotee could not believe it. When he went there and saw his revered master sitting there in exactly the same body, he was at first completely at a loss. Then, after a while, his state of mind changed to profound gratitude and joy.

This story was told to me by the great seer and sage Shastriji Acharya Vishnu Datt Mishra, who was almost always with Babaji.

After we had given his human form to the Earth in Herakhan, Babaji continued to appear to people in various forms. "It is always the same body" said Shastriji.

For example, my husband Peter Caddy and I met him in the valley of Herakhan; also, I met him several times later on three pilgrimages to Mt. Kailash in Tibet. This is covered, among other things, in this book – how Babaji called me, my first twelve days with him, and especially the astounding way in which Babaji led and taught those who came to him.

Babaji said: "I have come to bring the light, to lead you beyond all limitations and attachments to the freedom of Oneness, the Oneness with the Divine Spirit and with everything that is!"

Babaji is a being of pure love.
  "I am you. Give me your problems; I will bear your burden!"
  "I am here to help you, to guide you!"
  "Repeat God's name continuously!"
  "I am in each of your breaths!"

His central question, to which he repeatedly returned, was:
  "Are you happy?
  When you are happy, I am happy.
  When I am happy, the whole world is happy.
  Be happy!"

"There is only one religion, and that is humanity.

Be fully human! To serve mankind is to serve God."

As early as February 1983, on Shivaratri, Babaji had given his blessing to this book, which at that time was still mainly in the heavens. I delayed writing it for a long time. It became three volumes: "*Love of the Heart.*"

I wish you much joy in reading this first volume: "*Encounter with Babaji, the master of the Himalayas: A poem of love.*"

1. *A Poem of Love*

Encounters with Babaji between 1978 and 1984,
his Teachings and Legacy

The first 12 days with Babaji

Out of blue I dreamed red
In red I fell into black
Through black I won gold
In gold I knew white
In white I recognized You
Then I awoke

"Oh daughter of the Himalayas!" I heard a gentle voice inside of me singing, again and again.

I sat in the plane to India on my way to Babaji who had appeared in a cave in Herakhan in 1970. Herakhan lies some 10 hours to the northeast of Delhi.

It was January 15, 1978. I was in my 36th year. If someone had told me at Christmas time, that three weeks later I would be sitting in a plane to India on the way to Babaji, I would not have believed it and would have considered it impossible. How did it come to pass?

Despite years of dedicated spiritual training, I had reached a point of deep internal crisis. As a result of difficult life circumstances, I felt myself somehow at a loss. From the depths of my heart I implored God: "Please help me!" – that is when Babaji appeared!

Two years previously, in 1975, I had already heard of Babaji through a friend, Gabriele Wosien. At that time I was somehow sceptical when I was told: "The Babaji who Paramahansa Yogananda wrote about in his *Autobiography of a Yogi* has appeared again, and this time he is there for the public."

Of how many people has it been claimed that they are the legendary Babaji?

But when I saw a photo of him shortly after his public appearance, I was deeply moved. Whilst I breathed his name up through my spine, an intense light arose! Still the time was not yet ripe. After the death of the « Mother », the partner of Shri Aurobindo who had guided me from within since 1968, I no longer wanted an external spiritual teacher.

I was not really open, but I fixed his photo on the wall in my studio beside the other great teachers from east and west whom I had encountered either inwardly or outwardly and whom I revered.

Two years later when, together with my friend Marcel,[2] I met Gabriele Wosien by chance again in Munich and took her back to our home, she told us during the car journey about Babaji while the thick snow fell outside. We were totally surrounded in white.

"His teaching is so simple. He teaches truth, simplicity and love, and that it is important to continually repeat God's name!"

All of this now reached a wide-open heart.

On the night of New Year's Eve, she showed us and a group of friends some pictures of Babaji – at that time there were not many photos. Each one of them was more moving than the last. My eyes fell on one picture that gave me a real shock. It showed the old Herakhan Baba, of whom it is said that he is Babaji in an earlier form. His gaze was so stern and penetrating that he really frightened me: "Oh no, he cannot be that strict with me!" I thought.

The next morning, the morning of New Year's Day, I awoke beaming from a dream about a white field of snow, with the happily satisfying inner knowledge that I would immediately be flying to Babaji.

A friend of ours planned to fly to a solar energy congress in Delhi in the middle of January and I knew spontaneously that I would be travelling with him. I had never been in the north of India before.

Then the stern picture of Herakhan Baba came to my mind again, so that I asked Gabriele Wosien: "Please show me that awe-inspiring photo once again!"

Whether I liked it or not, Babaji began to look at me and to work with me just through this picture. He made me conscious of everything in me that was not in harmony with the Divine. I truly got frightened. But it was clear for me that I definitely did not want to fly to Babaji with fear!

Various aspects within me said: "Why the haste? You can go to Babaji later as well, for example in the autumn." But the innermost within me knew: "Now or never!"

I went into seclusion and from deep within I asked Babaji: "Please help me!" But no direction came, no dream. I was simply being processed. Finally, in the evening dusk of the third day, as I made a small ritual fire ceremony and once again looked deeply into the picture of the Old Herakhan Baba, infinite love came towards me, love and nothing but love! Overwhelming and completely wonderful: I felt the presence in the room of the young Babaji who said to me: "Now you can come."

Now that it was clear that I would make the flight and not before, now at last he gave me a dream. I call it "the little dream," despite the fact that it was significant and later provided me with the central key for understanding Babaji's current appearance.

The Mandala Dream

I saw the creation pictured in the form of five giant three-dimensional mandalas. Each one superseded the next. They were of themselves very dynamic, moving around a still centre, an empty but seemingly breathing circle. In the middle, coming from an entirely other dimension far away, a being slowly came into appearance.

At times I only saw his face, at others he sat in the lotus position, different and new in each of the mandalas but always giving the impression of asceticism. It was Babaji. I knew; he is the Lord of the mandalas.

At the last mandala he, the Lord of the mandalas, who had always been in the middle, now danced from the outside right into his own mandala. At first I saw him in profile. A soft young profile. But then he turned his face towards me, laughing, having become quite rounded.

I awoke with a great shock and thumping heart: Shocked because he had laughed, shocked because he, the sublime Lord of the mandala, who is always in the centre, was now also dancing from the outer right side into his own mandala. Thereby he changed his form greatly, growing significantly in volume and weight.

The Great Light Experience

Once I had actually got the charter ticket in my hand, there happened the most indescribable and greatest inner event of my life up until then. It was the night of the full moon, from January 9 to 10, 1978. What started in sleep carried over into a waking state and continued in that state.

Babaji was there. He stood in front of a wall of light and nothingness. It was the threshold to another dimension.

Looking at this spiritual threshold, I saw myself as if I had landed underwater, was walking under water. I appeared to belong to him, and Babaji, who was observing from above, looked down and seemed to be startled that I had come into Samsara, the world of illusion. I saw him watchfully following from above each of my steps. Like a finger of light, his gaze marked a point of light on the surface of the water where, under the water, I should take a step. The point of light above and the step below then fell together. I saw myself wandering under the water, led by the ray of light from his gaze.

Was it he who ultimately was responsible for me?
Did he want to raise me up again into his realm?
How had he raised me up through the water?
Indescribable!
I was with him.

Now he gave me a book. It was the book of all my lives. Outside, it was coloured red, the pages within white, with larger initial letters like those found in medieval books. On every page and always in the same letters there stood writing meaning: "So it was!" And in these large letters the events of each single life were finely drawn. Babaji turned the pages one after another and thanks to his presence I was able to understand what I saw. Then he raised me up on high. Truly unbelievable, beyond words and any means of expression, I was close to him. Unconditionally, completely heartfelt, breathless, I became one with him in the Light of Love beyond words.

In the light of love – forever one.
I knew: He is my highest self.
I knew: This is the Lord!
Not just the teacher of all my lives.

In this state I had no wish ever to be in a body again. Was it that I could not keep a hold on this high dimension of being one with him in light? I knew only one thing. That if I was ever again to be in a body, then I could only bear the knowledge of this love, this light, by bowing deeply down before him, down through the ground.

That same night, he brought me back into my body. This was not easy for me, maybe because I would have loved to stay with him. During the entire time, I had been sitting physically upright in bed.

Later, as I lay awake and the tears of emotion flowed, my heart and soul were still full with his sweetness beyond time. For quite a while my room was bathed in a gentle, almost breathing, vibrating white light, full of peace. Slowly I found my way back into the night and to sleep.

This night, I had not only met Babaji as a great teacher, but experienced him as the Lord. This was something truly overwhelming.

When I had seen pictures of him, I had not the slightest notion of this. Not even when the photo of the Old Herakhan Baba had begun to speak with me. I simply thought that Babaji is a great teacher in the Himalayas. But now I had come to know who He is. And I knew that nothing on earth would be able to take this knowledge away from me, even if I myself was still unable to grasp it completely.

On the Way to Babaji

With this knowledge I flew to India. I needed a few days to acclimatize in Delhi and make a renewed inner preparation. In this process, I had got a sore throat and fever. Finally, on Friday, January 20, 1978 I set off for Herakhan.

At 7 a.m. the bus left Delhi. We had boarded a rattly old Indian bus; at each stop one had to check whether the luggage was still on the roof. At 2 p.m. we were at Haldwani. To my astonishment there were two people accompanying me on my journey to Babaji: Vijay, a very fine Indian, and David, a young American doctor.

In Haldwani we drove in rickshaws to Patel-Chowk, where we sought out a tall, rather Tibetan good-looking Indian, Shri Trilok Singh, referred to as Muniraj. I had been told that he would arrange for a jeep for the onward journey.

As we were leaving, I saw Muniraj standing tall on a stone step in front of his shop and I suddenly realized who he was. Standing there in silent majesty was a king of wide lands and realms of light!

My love for him was awoken.

In the jeep we went to Damside, a tiny place with a couple of Chai shops. From there we started on a beautiful 2½ hour river walk, which crossed through the Gautam Ganga River some 20 times. Our luggage was transported by Indian mountain people or on little Himalayan horses.

Arrival in Herakhan

Oh Herakhan Valley!
We arrived in the sun-flooded light of evening.
What a valley, so full of living stones, so woven with light, so deeply familiar,
so highly secret.
What a valley! How holy it is!
And what mountains are these?
Everything wondrous, so very alive, deeply touching.

Below to the left, in a great wild mountain, lay the cave where Babaji had appeared and over to the right, high up on the hill like a small fortress, his temple-ashram. 108 steps led us up into the singing of the songs, Kirtan of the evening. Thus I came into the sanctum of Babaji.

We could hear the tones of "OM namah Shivay – Shivaye namah OM!" as we went towards Babaji in greeting, just as we were, in jeans and pullovers.

My heart was beating wildly.

Oh how alive he sat there!

Silent, happy and moved, I bowed to him and took my place in the group, waiting and listening.

He called me to him.

"Where do you come from? What is your name?"

I looked at him.

His gaze is unforgettable for me, multilayered, knowing, deeply welcoming and extremely serious. He pervaded my being totally to the core, body and soul.

I answered with a smile as if to say to him. "But you know me!" Also in order to find the one I knew, to find the one who had called me here.

"Why do you smile?" he asked me.

For a moment my breathing stopped. I felt the depth of his earnestness and truth.

"There was a dream. You know!" I answered him.

Without going into the matter any further he put a candy in my hand.

"Do you want anything? Tea?" he then asked and then arranged that all of us who had just arrived were brought tea from outside, whilst inside the singing continued.

Soon they all came out, and my travelling companions and I were greeted by a number of truly wonderful people, full of joy, as if we were old friends. They also came from the west, several from America. One of them was Leonhard Orr.

In the meantime it had become dark and all the bells of the temple of Herakhan were ringing, calling to the evening Arati, which is the evening ritual, followed by devotional songs.

I was given a room with two others, David and Govindi, in the only larger house that was built at that time. I quickly searched for my gift for Babaji and brought it to him. Again: How he looked! So penetrating, but somehow milder now. Without opening it he placed my gift beside himself.

"Your name is Nila!"

Now he smiled.

"Nila means blue. Your soul is blue like sky."

He looked at me once again.

"I met you. I came to you in Germany."

Yes, thanks to God that he said this!

Babaji at the roots of the Satikund
tree in the valley of Herakhan

Now he no longer looked so deeply stern, but rather alert and loving. After a while he sent for me again. "What do you do?" "I paint and also attempt thereby to create a therapy for others." "Then you treat me!" he said. I had brought paints for him with me. "Shall I fetch them?" "Yes!"

And while they all sat there and sang, I brought my large empty book and coloured pencils. He opened it and immediately painted a big OM right at the top of the first page.

He sat there in the candlelight on his simple throne, a podium with a dark red velvet seat on it, in front of which were three steps. As he spontaneously painted, me standing at his side, I felt how through the simple act of painting a very understanding and loving bond came into being between us.

But then he, who sat there, was at first in no way familiar to me in this form, in no way easy to comprehend – only his eyes, which led into profound depths, were anciently familiar. I still did not understand: Why had he become so rounded, completely different from the photos of his first appearance.

In the first night in the ashram, I saw on the wall in front of me a huge image of a face in profile, which then turned and laughed, although it did not laugh.

It was Babaji's profile as he now looked. It was the same profile that I had seen in my mandala dream, when the Lord of the mandala suddenly danced into his mandala from outside on the right, and had turned and laughed, and which had given me such a great shock: He was no longer ascetic, but had become rounded. It began to dawn on me that Babaji's physical transformation was connected with something immensely deep.

Saturday, January 21, 1978 — My first day at the Ashram

Up at 3 a.m., I was instructed. 4 a.m. at the latest! Down to the river! As cold as it was wonderful! No hesitation and submerse oneself! At first it is a matter of courage, thereafter simply beautiful! Beneath this crystal starry sky, stars shining white in the night, and bathing in the totally pure, flowing waters of the Gautam Ganga. What a sense of freedom!

Then, between 4 and 7 a.m. meditation. Each one as they will and where they will. Fixed though is the morning Arati at 7 a.m., the ritual devotion. For this everyone comes to the temple in the middle of the ashram to ring bells and sing together.

The first day, which began in the starlit night, grew long with clouds and wind. It began to blow a gale and to rain and it became very cold.

In the morning, I visited Fakiranand, Babaji's secretary – an elderly, attentive, friendly person. He lived in a tiny room, in the lobby of which the library of the ashram was housed. What had brought me here, he wanted to know.

I told him of my great light experience. He understood. Yes, he himself had had such an experience a few years earlier, just here, where he now sat – seven hours long.

I proceeded to describe how the Old Herakhan Baba had moved me so deeply, and that then Babaji came in his young appearance, but that Babaji's current round appearance puzzled me.

Fakiranand understood this well: every time over the last two years that he had been asked about his great physical change, Babaji had answered, "Don't look at the shape." Fakiranand also made the comment that clairvoyant people had repeatedly been able to perceive the form of the previous Babaji through his current form.

In truth, it was crucial for me to experience the identity of the current Babaji, whose appearance was so very different from the Old Herakhan Baba. Meanwhile others had gathered by Fakiranand and had shifted the discussion to the world situation and what awaited mankind. Only those who held God at the centre of their lives, only those would be protected when the worldwide revolution predicted by Babaji took place.

TRUTH, SIMPLICITY and LOVE, that is the core of Babaji's teaching – and repeating the mantra **"OM NAMAH SHIVAY,"** [3] day and night without ceasing.

It was time for the midday meal. I heard drums. It was raining cats and dogs as I went up from Fakiranand. A figure was standing there in the rain: "Ay, come"! It was Babaji himself, dressed in a long fire-red cloth and a light blue pullover. With this exclamation, he sprang at me like a Red Indian, grabbed my wrist and led me to a particular place.

Everyone else was already assembled for the meal. Not as usual under the open sky, but because of the rain, under the roof around the small temple which formed the centre of the ashram. I knew neither what nor who was honoured inside. Babaji had placed me right in front of its door, at its threshold. After the meal Babaji said to me, "Now, you take rest!". And indeed I slept very deeply.

At 5 p.m. in the afternoon we were all gathered together again to sing mantras and songs of devotion.

« OM NAMAH SHIVAY – SHIVAYE NAMAH OM »

After a while, Babaji appeared in the middle of the Bhajan singing and, as always, took his place on his small throne at the front. Each of those present, when they felt the moment right, went to him to greet and bow to him. Strange, some of them were dancing towards him to the rhythm of the songs!

I was amazed that that was allowed here.

"Are you happy?" Babaji asked me. "Do you like it here?" "…yes," I replied somewhat hesitantly. And once again, as on almost every opportunity in these first few days, he placed a large candy in my hand for me to eat while he gazed at me with an indescribable look. Oh, I realized: he has put a special energy into these candies and I am expected – and graced – to eat all of this.

"What is your name?" he asked me repeatedly – "Renata!" – "What is your name?" – "Ah, Nila" I answered eventually – it took me a while to comprehend that I should now leave behind me all the other names which had been given me up till now, and simply be Nila: Blue like the sky.

The evening Arati came – in the temple, Puja, a service for the Divine, was cel-ebrated mornings and evenings. Thereby some twelve bells were rung continu-ously for about half an hour, which sounded beautiful. There was drumming at the same time. Then the Divine was honoured in the heart of the temple with flames on a small Arati holder.[4] The light was passed around, whereby each sym-bolically took the light of the flame with his hands to his heart and head.
At the close everyone sung a ritual prayer that contained, among others, the Tarak mantra, the highest mantra with the 108 names of Shiva. Babaji himself was pres-ent. At the beginning, when he entered, he always sat some ten minutes in si-lence, draped in his cloth. Only his face remained visible. Oh, how I liked him, as he sat, still and erect, tall and powerfully in meditation in front of us. How beautiful he was.

« OM HARIYAKHANDI – HARIYAKHANDI OM »[5]

Was this a name? – Every time that this word was sung, a mysterious longing and a shiver went through me. Although I did not understand, these words felt con-nected with the one who sat in silence in front of us. Was this mantra his name?

Now the Saturday evening: Babaji turned it into a celebration. In fact in front of us, on his seat, he began to sway as if in a dance and encouraged us to follow his example! I remembered Shiva Nataraja, the dancing Shiva. In truth, there was dancing in Babaji's presence! Some of those present stood up and also began to dance, others remained seated, singing, drumming and shaking rattles in rhythm.

I also could no longer remain in my seat and began to try to find my own dance. No, the dance found me and we all danced and danced…

Babaji looked on – he was happy! At the end we all bowed where we were, danced and sang right in front of him – and as I then bowed down in front of him, he pulled me up by the parting in my hair, powerfully, but very lovingly. A blessed feeling!

The valley of Herakhan between Kailash and Siddheswar

Oh, how I wanted to discover whether he was the Herakhan Baba of my picture and I drew it out of my pocket, in order to ask him personally as he left. But he went quickly past me. His back instead now towered powerfully in front of me. He paused in front of the door to the innermost part of the temple, which was now opened, and disappeared abruptly and in silence.

Now the view of the temple, the centre of the ashram, was clear, and what did I see? Lovingly decorated, the statue of the Old Herakhan Baba sat there. Ah, this is how Babaji has given me the answer to my question. There was indeed a deep bond between the two. It was wonderful to see that the Old Herakhan Baba statue was honoured in the centre of the ashram, but still the identity of the young Babaji as it related to the older one was not clear to me.

Sunday, January 22, 1978 —
My second day at the Ashram

My second day in the ashram: Chandan. I heard that at 5 a.m. we would be allowed to go to Babaji for Chandan and afterwards go to his fire.

Chandan means that Babaji draws three strokes across your forehead as the sign of Shiva and adds a red dot between your eyebrows.

It felt truly impressive to walk in the darkness along a steep slope to get to Babaji's small room, a room which felt as precious as an emerald – and to see him sitting there dressed in white, serious, silent and totally aware of everything. With one hand he held each person's head as with the other he stroked a wonderful gold-yellow fluid paint across their forehead and at the end set the red point in the middle of their brow. It felt so good. – Apparently he blessed us in this way, imparting peace to our restless minds.

Then all of us who had been invited to Chandan assembled in a semi-circle around the fire, which burnt in the dark outside Babaji's room, under a magnificent great tree.

A large bowl of rice mixed with sesame, barley and sugar, which as I later learnt was to be offered by him, had been already prepared beside his seat. Babaji came and sat down on his seat close to the fire and began to carry out the holy, sacrificial ritual. It was simple and deeply impressive. He was so completely composed!

With his eyes shut most of the time, he threw one handful after another into the fire – pausing every now and then as if he was entering another level of consciousness. His holy fire! – Sometimes he looked at one or other of us before throwing another handful of the offering into the fire. As he did so, his gaze was penetrating and indescribably deep.

After Chandan, those who had participated were expected to remain awake and do something useful, or at best meditate – in any case not to sleep. I came to know about this only after I had blissfully fallen asleep during my attempted meditation in my room following my first Chandan. Indeed, I was simply not accustomed to getting up this early and then meditating.

Babaji seemed to know all this, because that morning he was fairly indifferent to me as I bowed before him. It began to dawn on me that he apparently knew what one did, or indeed did not do. In actual fact he knew what was happening within each one of us. Thus it came about that a very nice American doctor was publicly and very humorously accused of either not washing himself at all, or only with a cat's lick. We should take a complete bath, especially when we intended afterwards to go to Chandan.

It was Sunday. After a wild morning wind and a sky heavy with rain, the sun came out, precisely in time for us to leave.

The day was inviting, fresh and sunny. All residents of the ashram were to walk with Babaji to Damside, where he planned to hold a fire ceremony. Damside – that meant wading through the water 20 times, just like on the way to Herakhan, through this so eloquent valley of the stones! Now I was full of anticipation and joy.

At around 8:30 a.m. we all set off. Babaji wore a red turban with a long tail. I kept close to him, as did David who had arrived with me and who had been given a real "war paint" early this morning at Chandan. John, like David, a doctor from America and called Dr. Dahru, and also a few Indian youths who worked in the ashram also walked with Babaji. Babaji sent all the others out in front: "You go!" He it was who always determined who walked with him and who did not.

Babaji let himself be photographed, for which he put his arm round David who, like me, had only just arrived, but not around me. He also played with Dr. Dahru, linked arms with him and seemed very close to him. To me alone he gave the cold shoulder. This could be felt most noticeably. As we went over the many, many stones and repeatedly waded through one of the arms of the river, Babaji suddenly paused, looked at me from the side, took his neckerchief and bound it purposefully round my head – he drew the knots very tight.

Suddenly, as we again were stepping through the water, he asked me: "Are you leaving tomorrow?" Shocked, I said: "No. If you agree, I would very much like to stay until the end of January or the beginning of February. Then a friend of mine will come to fetch me."

Then I pulled my little notebook out of my pocket, which held a picture of this friend. As I opened it to show it to him, his gaze fell on a photo of Marcel. He immediately asked me: "Who is that?" and took the little book into his own hands.

Whilst we continued to wander through the water he leafed through it and opened it at the picture of Swamiji: "What is his name? Do you like him?" he asked me. "Yes I like him very much. It is Swamiji Ganapati Satchidananda," whereupon Babaji asked: "Why have you not gone to him?" I answered desperately: "But YOU called me!" He shut the book, gave it back into my hands and quickly walked off with the others.

Shortly thereafter, I was walking just on his left hand side when he suddenly bent down to pick up a stone. For a second I actually saw a flame go through the middle of the stone in his hand.

"Blessing through a stone", he said in that instant, and laid it in my hand. Shocked, I stood still – but he walked quickly on into the water again, this time through very deep water, turned around and called to me, "O.K., you can stay until the end of January – as you are blessed through a stone!"

I was deeply affected by all of this and went on very slowly, letting Babaji go ahead with the others. I turned within myself. It is an understatement to say that I was affected – I was shaken to the core. Now especially, I had to take care not to become depressed.

I held the stone firmly in my hand – it was now my anchor and I tried to find peace, calmness, total calmness; not to despair, but to be peaceful, breathe, return to my own centre, breathing in – towards heaven – breathing out towards the earth. Nothing but that, thus calling to God – from the stillness within. With all my strength – call to HIM, breathe in HIM – nothing else. And in addition, I needed to be completely indifferent to the external Babaji, who had just thrown me into such confusion. So that is what I did, what I strove for even during the entire fire ceremony in Damside. And also on the way back. It was clear to me that now I would return alone.

There was a little incident in Damside: Somewhat off to the side there was a tea shop and I felt a real need to drink a cup of tea, to drink something warm. As my tea came, Babaji looked at me from a distance. I immediately developed a bad conscience about just indulging myself with tea. With the glass slopping, I ran to Babaji and offered it to him. He said: "No, I don't drink tea!" So I shared it with the others and ordered more for everyone who was near me.

The way back was beautiful. I was one of the first to go back and I crossed the river many times as it made its lively way through this long, large, loving valley, which had already grown somewhat familiar to me. I went alone and was happy to go alone. Almost all the others were behind me. Babaji said he would return with his group right at the last. After the shock on the way there, the simple thought that I had almost had to depart on the next day, I tried to recover my balance, whether Babaji paid me attention or not. His physical being, except for his eyes, was incomprehensible to me.

Now there was only one thing of importance for me, GOD: to attain him through breathing. All my longing and ardour were focussed on him. I went on in this state and became more and more centred within myself. The light and the peace of the valley filled me more and more. GOD would reveal the truth to me, since I myself could no longer comprehend anything. So I strode on valiantly, knowing only that I had to stand in my own free and independent centre, that here I had to light a fire for that which is most high, to keep the flame as alive as possible, and not to be concerned about anything else.

"Infinite God" by inhaling, "Infinite God" by exhaling, that was my mantra.

In the middle of the path, where I was just passing a stretch of raging water, there was suddenly an Indian, wearing a black woollen jacket and with a number of suitcases and bags, standing between two arms of the river. "It is a little difficult this way!" he commented, and looked at me with very alert eyes and a beaming smiling gaze – almost the look of Babaji.

I trod on and replied to him as I passed him by, turning briefly to him: "Yes, that it is!"

Strange, how he had looked at me so intensely – and I asked myself who he was and where he had come from. How had he carried all the luggage that he had standing around him through all the arms of the river? These questions occupied me for some time during the rest of the journey, particularly as I met a few Indians coming from mountain villages who all went silently past me and certainly were unable to speak English.

Very remarkable, this stranger! – In retrospect, it became clear to me that this was a messenger from Babaji in his form as Bhairav Baba.

After a while I reached the valley. Up to the right was Babaji's ashram, and below to the left his cave lay before me. His cave. It drew me powerfully!

In the morning, I had seen an American couple go in and out of it. Otherwise, I would never have dared to step into his cave uninvited. But now I did so and kneeled down at the entrance full of awe, in this cave where the Old Herakhan Baba had lived! There, a wonderful fragrance came towards me, and LIGHT – I was bathing in the LIGHT and felt being raised up. I was filled with bliss and became very still – and again there was the divine fragrance, absolutely enrapturing!

Oh my God, it was exactly the same fragrance that Babaji himself had emitted on two occasions this morning: up in the ashram, and as I followed along behind him. And now the same fragrance in the cave of the Old Herakhan Baba!

Suddenly, I heard Babaji's voice; I could hardly believe my ears. Babaji? How could he be here already? Puzzled, I came out of the cave. Indeed, there he stood looking at me. He was alone. How could he possibly be here in front of me, when, as he had said, he was walking with his party at the end of the group?

I expected him to shout at me, since I had simply entered his cave without his explicit permission. Instead Babaji asked: "Do you want tea?" I was totally taken aback – and where, here below in this cave and in this wilderness, could one get tea anyway? But then an Indian man came and brought two glasses of tea! Later it dawned on me that this was his response because I had offered him tea in Damside.

Babaji had settled himself on a small wooden box, and I sat on a stone in front of him. The tea was really wonderful; he gave his tea to one of the workers. Obviously, there was some work going on nearby. I looked at him. It was still a great puzzle to me, how this being, through whom in Germany I had had such a fundamental experience of God, could now be incarnate in the Babaji before me. As human and rotund as he now appeared, he seemed to have virtually nothing in common with that wonderful apparition.

In reflection of my ignorance, he looked at me with great round eyes.

Imploringly I asked him: "Please, help me, because I don't understand you!", since I felt that on my own I would never get a clue as to who he really was. His expression changed completely. With shining eyes, full of light and warmth, he replied without hesitation: "Yes, I will help you!"

The simple words, "Please help me!", had opened the divine gates.

Nobody knows anybody

Together we went over to the ashram, through the gentle first dusk of evening, up the many steps, when Babaji's eyes fell on a little rose cross that I wore on a chain. I caught his gaze and told him that Swamiji, whose picture I had shown him that morning, had materialized it, in that he had touched my neck. "Was he at your home?" asked Babaji. "Yes, several times," and then: "Is he known in the west?" I answered as best I could.

Then Babaji said: "Nobody knows anybody."

These words touched me deeply, and I was reminded of them later when, for example, a renowned clairvoyant was unable to recognize another spiritual leader.

"Who are you?" I asked him – and he looked at me: "Whom do you see?" "Nothing!" – this expressed the truth as close as possible to the extent of my perception at that moment.

In the meantime we had arrived at the ashram. Only a few of the people had already returned, all the rest were still on the way. We few gathered together and began singing while the others slowly arrived. Finally Babaji appeared. Only one person did not arrive: David, my roommate. Unfortunately, he had taken the key with him. Night fell and Govindi and I could not get into our room.

Finally David emerged. Excitedly, he related how he had had the most unbelievable experience of his life. I was agog and remembered how he had received this amazing painting on his forehead in the morning at Chandan, and over and above that, how on the way out Babaji had been so especially attentive to him. What had happened?

A large, long carpet, intended for the ashram, needed transport from Damside to Herakhan. David was fit and athletic and very powerfully built, and at Babaji's behest was to help a young Indian to carry it. This happened in the afternoon. The youth was thin and tall and carried the carpet as if it was nothing at all, whilst David repeatedly kept almost collapsing! The carpet had a weight of 150 kilos, and it was for him totally inexplicable how this very slender youth could take the carpet so lightly on his shoulder and carry it without the slightest sign of tiring – the entire long way. Most remarkable! Clearly, Babaji's energy had permeated this youth, or indeed had Babaji briefly taken on the form of this youth?

Monday, January 23, 1978 — My third day at the Ashram

Slowly, everything became more familiar. An early rise – walking with a torch down the many steps to the river – a cold bath – the stones there – gathering oneself together – the early meditation.

From now on, no-one was allowed to attend Babaji's Chandan unless they were called by him personally!

So for today no-one had Chandan, and I found out at my leisure where one could go to drink tea. The tea shop lay behind the ashram in the direction of the wood. It was in a small hut, and quite simply was the fireplace where the tea was prepared. There were also biscuits that one could roast in the embers. How beautiful, with a glass of hot tea in one's hand, to be able to look at the mountains on the other side of the valley and watch the awakening of the morning. Sheela, a loving and very energetic Indian woman, who obviously was often in Herakhan, got into a conversation with me. She was a convinced theosophist and since 1972 had revered Babaji as her highest master.

She told me that for many years a comet-like light had risen up each morning between the two mountains opposite. Until a short while ago everyone had been able to see it. It was no star. She further talked about "divine lights," which one could observe here, especially in the half-light of dawn and dusk. They were travelling lights which moved along in the valley and on the mountain, sometimes very fast, sometimes slowly, then in circles, and which then finally dispersed.

I realized, that indeed I had seen such a light on the mountain opposite the evening before and had been surprised by its speed, wondering how someone with a large torch could run up the mountain so fast. From the very beginning, I had felt this to be a very special place, full of mysterious life.

On Monday morning – the first really sunny, warm day in the ashram – a joyful feeling arose in me, after the pouring rain of Saturday and the sunny but chill freshness of Sunday.

After the morning Arati singing, I went into the garden where Babaji settled himself as if in paradise. David and I were told to go to Fakiranand, Babaji's "secretary," so that he could tell us new arrivals a few things and answer our questions, because Babaji seldom spoke.

Fakiranand explained much to us, and I now heard that Babaji had appeared here in 1970 in precisely the same cave as where the Old Herakhan Baba had lived! How I had marvelled at the wonderful fragrance there of the current Babaji, which had made me so intensely happy after a few minutes meditation in the cave.

The appearance of Babaji had been proclaimed long before. Now he would appear in dreams or visions to the people whom he wanted to call to himself, wherever they were living on this earth. He himself would remain in the background, also for example with respect to predictions about the fate of mankind.

These prophecies were not made by him directly, particularly in the beginning, but rather indirectly through others whom he would suddenly invite to speak publicly. He placed them in a higher state of consciousness and spoke through them. He would then confirm the spoken word, for example by laying a wreath of flowers on the speaker.

In this way announcements were made regarding the enormous changes facing the Earth, partly through war, partly through natural calamities. Thereafter a brighter era would begin, but mankind would be very much reduced in number.

Only those who were truly aligned with God would be protected. He had also said that, as of now, everyone should know what lay ahead for mankind!

In the meantime, a dark-skinned and very cultured man had come to Fakiranand. He was an ambassador from Ghana and had known Babaji for a long time: "My God, how he has changed in the last two years, totally incredible," he said. "One could hardly believe it is the same person." A deep respect was discernible in his voice, independent of how Babaji showed himself, in this form or another: "Previously so silent, always meditating, not consuming anything except milk and tea – and now totally changed, eating sweets, grown rotund, while still being the same one – this is his LILA – his game, the reason for which, and its meaning, we can maybe guess, but perhaps not understand."

Then Fakiranand read out something that a woman medium in England had related about Babaji a little earlier, after she had been shown a photo of him, without any further information. In probing within him, she was able to go so far as to suddenly exclaim in surprise: "But that is no normal flesh and blood, not a body created through birth!"

When Fakiranand wanted to read this letter to Babaji, he waved it away and said only: "Yes, she is a great soul!"

A really joyful picture awaited us when we left Fakiranand's little room and went up to the ashram garden. Babaji sat there, peace personified – painting – while Gopiji, a very fine and cultivated Indian, passed him the colours. I was delighted and went to him. He really was trying out the coloured pencils, which I had brought him. At the same time he seemed to be joking with Gopiji. Only later did I discover that the situation was often extremely serious when he was apparently making jokes; they were never just funny – they were always deep and meaningful at the same time.

"Yes, come!" he said and began to paint a picture for me. First the mountains – he always painted his mountains first, and then in layers, step by step, down into the plains. Here he let the Ganga River flow and then painted an extra lake: "This is Gopi Lake." Everywhere earth but no flowers. "I would like flowers," I requested. So he began to paint a few flowers around Gopi Lake. He had to swap the coloured pencils several times for each flower.

"How complicated is only one flower!" he murmured.

Then he turned the picture round and formed the sky, which he left free until the last. He painted blue and a yellow strip of sun and then some red in it – but everything was very delicate. "Fire in the heavens?" I asked.

"Yes, because of your temperament!" came the reply. "And the sun, where is the sun?" I wanted to know. So he painted a sun next to the biggest mountain – in red! "Is it a rising or a setting sun?"

"Rising," he answered and threw the picture into my lap – "Don't throw it away!" he murmured as I thanked him and looked at his gift. Then he painted for someone else, again with very gentle, delicate colours. I told him that he could press somewhat harder in order to obtain more powerful colours.

"No, I like it soft," he said. Now he painted magnificent mountains. "Beautiful!" I said. "No," he responded with purpose, "since Devi has gone to the Himalayas; nothing more is beautiful in this world!" and he finished his picture.

I asked him if I should oil his feet after the long foot march of the previous day.

He sniffed at the Wala oil, which I had had with me for a while and then permitted it – to my joy. Strange: his feet, with which he always went barefoot over all the many large and small stones here in the valley, looked untouched. They had none of the lines which otherwise occur from walking, nothing of the kind; just the hint of a marking in two places. And something else: in order to involve the others who had gathered around in this game, he let them pull on each of his fingers until they clicked, whilst I and then a second person worked on his feet.

So – his body now was not untouchable – he permitted everything, seemingly. As enough had been had of the good game, I asked him if I might fetch the book that I brought for him from my friend in Germany. "Yes!" – I laid it in front of him, packed carefully by Marcel in a red cloth. Before Babaji's eyes I now opened the packing, and there it lay: The book *Tantra Vidya* by Oscar Marcel Hinze with a Shri Yantra on it.

Then I showed Babaji a photo of Marcel. Babaji said immediately: "I know him – I know him! Khurpa Lama – his last incarnation. He is a very fine person!" Then he muttered something from "Pakad Singh" which meant: "mature, perfect warrior." "What is his name now?" I gestured to the book. "Oscar is his right name," he said, while he read the full name, Oscar Marcel Hinze.

Then, it just happened like this – I said that Oscar Marcel had been here in the northern region looking for him, Babaji, several years before but had not met up with him.

"But I saw him, I met him there," he countered.

And again: "He is a very fine person, a very nice man. I am very happy with this book!" For a while he held it in his hand, leafed through it, then he held it with both hands, carefully and with reverence. He was completely serious, almost solemn, as he turned to me and said: "I thank you very much indeed, that you have brought it to me!"

Then the drum sounded for the midday meal. Later, I was asked several times about the title of the book and the author, and whether it was available in English.[6]

Monday afternoon. I went down to the river, to the stones, to be alone with myself, to write, and to ponder. Who is this Babaji? He still remained a total mystery to me.

I did not understand him, but felt a great power that radiated from him.

After the singing that followed, I went up to Babaji. David and Kuschal were already standing with him and so, in their presence, I had to ask what I had wanted to ask him alone: Whether he would allow me to go to his cave more often?

"Yes, you three can go" he said, "you three and Tara Devi, you are allowed to be

there." So the other two, who had not yet discovered his cave, were included. He turned and addressed himself mainly to them: "It is a divine cave, good vibrations. You two together, you stay there overnight." And to me he said: "You can go there in the day!" Which I then did, straightaway, while it was still light.

I ran down to the cave and was again welcomed by light. This time though, without that wonderful fragrance, but light surrounded me and I entered into a deep meditation with great ease. The drumming and bell-ringing for the evening Arati, which sounded far down into the valley from the temple up above drew me out of my meditation and out of the cave.

And now a small light nearby led me to see that apparently someone lived next to the cave. It was a fine, tall, dear old lady who emerged: Tara Devi, with white hair cut in a bob, an anthroposophist and an American, who had lived with her husband for many years in Almora, India. She had met Babaji for the first time in 1972 and shortly afterwards recognized him as her divine teacher.

"He lives all those things about which Rudolf Steiner speaks," she said to me. "Through Babaji it all became a real experience for me, became reality."

So she was the fourth person whom Babaji allowed to stay down here at his cave and at present was even permitted to live here. She came to this place as often as she could, and as often as Babaji permitted. I marvelled that even though, at her age she was so delicate and fragile, she was able to live this life reduced to the utmost simplicity.

I took her by the arm and together we wandered over the many stones and steps up to the ashram to the evening Arati. Babaji repeatedly treated Tara Devi very lovingly. It was very conspicuous that, apart from Tara Devi, who was certainly around 70, most of the Westerners staying here as guests were particularly fine, beautiful and powerful people, all of them young and between 20 and 40 years old.

It was not difficult for us to feel very fond of one another immediately, and for me that was true for all the people living in the ashram, the majority of whom had only come to Herakhan for a while. And all of those here had really made a conscious decision to be here. One could feel this.

Tuesday, January 24, 1978 —
My fourth day at the Ashram

Tuesday began early with the 5 a.m. morning Chandan. Again I was deeply impressed by Babaji in his own space, the manner in which he sat there, totally alert and silent while he gave Chandan and then made offerings to the fire. So much happened while he did so. HE and HIS FIRE – this touched me deeply and anew.

Babaji planned to go to Damside once again, to a second fire ceremony for the village there. Everybody was to go except those over 60 years of age. That meant again crossing the river 20 times on the way there and 20 times on the way back, and walking over all the many stones. I was looking forward to that. This time it was not important to me to be permitted to go with Babaji and the group around him. He waved to me and said: "You go" and so I went on ahead with others. He always seemed to set off last with the small group of people whom at that moment he wanted to have around him.

It was a good chance for me to contemplate things on the way across the stones and through the clear water of the springs. Some of the time I walked with one person, then with another, but mainly I was absorbed within myself.

Babaji is totally unfathomable, if one should want to encounter him as a being in his human form. He is not such. His behaviour demonstrated this to me clearly. When I approached him as a person, he hardly reacted to me and threw me back upon myself. I understood that I should be just the one thing: Flame: keeping the inner flame alive deep in the heart, the yearning for the divine light. Nothing but that! The « Mother » of Pondicherry, my first spiritual teacher, frequently came to mind: what I had learnt through her and what is the core of Integral Yoga: Aspiration and Surrender: Longing for the Divine and total surrender to the Divine – that is what it is all about.

So the process continued in me as I took the path through the valley and the purifying water: Everything else – including the outward form of Babaji – was now of no great importance.

And the second visit to Damside was for me mainly composed of this – that I did not run after Babaji – that was pointless, but as far as I was able to, I was both centred on the infinite and outwardly alert when a question or call for help came to me. It had already occurred to me that all possible interpersonal situations arose in the ashram, be it with my room mates or others round about, and I felt that their purpose was to be small testing obstacles: Beware! Be loving, be alert, sense into what was being demanded.

Twice I had not realized this, but in all other situations I had understood the requirement, maybe thanks to the training to this effect which I had received at home in Germany. Share with others, be loving, be helpful – situations that put this to the test arose continually.

It happened similarly in Damside. Gopiji had bad feet from the walk to which she was unaccustomed, and I oiled her feet with the little oil I had left. I had already given my large bottle to Babaji. Then, as Babaji passed through the mass of people, I gave him a soap bubble game that I had adorned with freshly picked blue flowers. He blew through it once and straightaway passed it on to a woman.

Then he wanted to have a few rupees to hand out.

Tara Devi handed him her purse, but he said: "No, not yours!" I gave him mine and was pleased that he took something for the poor out of my purse. After the fire ceremony, which above all had required Babaji's presence, the call to depart was blown: "You go" he said to me and many others. As always he stayed behind with a few people – or did he remain alone this time?

I turned around. He called: "Don't look back!"

So I set off. This time I wanted to accompany Gopiji, since she had begun to relate how she had come to Babaji and how her path with him was progressing here.

As a very fine, highly cultured Indian woman, she stood not only in the ancient Indian tradition but was also familiar with the western world and the western way of thinking. She had been in Europe on many occasions. Now she told me of her first encounter with Babaji in 1975, at the house of an architect friend. At this time, Babaji was given over almost wholly to meditation, sitting erect, silent, with closed eyes, speaking hardly at all and eating almost nothing, but now and again drinking some tea.

Sheela had already told me that at first Babaji hardly ever spoke.

At that time, if he opened his eyes and looked at a person, such a fire shone from his gaze that only a few could bear looking direct into his eyes. Gopiji herself felt magically drawn to him, to this unfathomable being who acted in opposition to all Indian tradition and simply threw Prased, blessed food like fruit and sweets, among the people, and behaved in a manner totally other than normal. One day she asked him for a Guru mantra as a sign that he was prepared to accept her as a disciple. Thereupon he said to her: "Oh, my path is not a path of roses." In the beginning the path to Herakhan was much more difficult than today. There was only the cave and the small temple above it, otherwise there were just stones.

Then, one had to walk or ride from Haldwani, since the road to Damside was only built a short while ago. At that time, they also slept on the ground in the open and not on comfortable mattresses as today. I could imagine the demands that this life had made on her, a wealthy woman. And what Babaji had expected of her, as from one moment to the next he had peremptorily sent her away. This happens now too, but at the same time now there is a twinkle in his eyes. Through experience she had learnt that he was hammering at her ego, to liberate her for evermore. Her voice expressed a deep humility and respect.

I noticed that the people in the ashram remained very reserved when relating their inner experiences or telling of miracles. When I showed others the picture of my fire Swamiji, in which he stood in the midst of flames, the question was immediately posed: "But why is he showing off his powers?" Truly great people avoid doing this, since the point is not about the Siddhis, special abilities, but about enlightenment. I tried to explain Swamiji's special situation, which was then accepted.

Babaji on the other hand did not show his power and abilities. "He pretends to be the dunce all the time," said Gopiji, shaking her head: "And he always construes his miracles so that one hardly notices them, or can almost explain them through natural causes."

This statement relates to a very special experience on Kailash. "Kailash?" I asked amazed, "Where is Kailash here?" – Well it was the mountain opposite the ashram, that wonderful mountain at which I had gazed so often. So this was Kailash! There are two Mt. Kailash, I heard: one in Tibet, and this one here, at the foot of which was Babaji's cave. According to Babaji's words, this Kailash was the original one: on coming into the world Shiva had set foot on it first, and only much later moved to Kailash in Tibet.

From time to time Babaji took a group with him onto the Herakhan Kailash. Once he had wanted Gopiji to come with him as well. Since, in her feminine fullness, she was not particularly athletic, Gopiji, going up the steep path in the heat of summer, arrived at the top totally exhausted. There was no water anywhere and nobody carried any with them.

At first, Babaji rubbed a few leaves together in order to give her the juice, but of course that did not quench her thirst – she simply could not go on. Then, at the top of Kailash, where no one is normally to be found for miles around, a water bearer suddenly appeared: a figure carrying a pitcher on his shoulder. Babaji waved to him. He came, gave Gopiji water and then immediately disappeared. Gopiji never saw him again, neither in the ashram nor the village.

During the descent from Kailash, as she had a great fear of slipping in this steep terrain, Babaji simply took her by the hand and together they dashed back down at incredible speed. How all that came about remained completely inexplicable and puzzling to this day.

At my request, she also told me of her inner experiences, of visions that Babaji had given her. Once he had sent her to Satikund, the great, wonderful tree that stands alone in the middle of the southern part of the valley of Herakhan. There, she was to meditate together with a woman friend. The friend entered into a state of stillness and Gopiji had visions: The whole valley with all of its stones transformed itself, and she saw shining buildings and palaces there, made of the finest of materials, shimmering and soft, as if transparent. At the same time she was aware how she herself, in a sliding movement, was drawn to one of the shimmering buildings and disappeared inside. "This is your house where you belong!" Babaji said to her later. Oh, how well I could comprehend the truth of what Gopiji had inwardly seen. This valley with its stones had appeared to me from the very beginning to be incredibly fulfilled and in some mysterious way alive.

It was indeed no wonder that, in the inner world, the palaces of a shining city should be standing there! Gopiji herself was a rather rational and questioning person and so she said to herself, "Oh, you are a dreaming child!" She only dared to trust her vision after Babaji had confirmed everything to her.

And Gopiji further told me that she had seen Babaji as a gigantic figure of light standing on a hill in the valley. And then, from one instant to the next, he was gone from there to suddenly appear on top of the mountain. She had often made similar observations. Once, as she had inwardly prayed to him, "Show me just once where you live, where your home is!" she saw him from behind, sitting, whilst he looked towards an infinite, soft, glowing light – not white, not gold, not silver, and yet like white, gold and silver all in one. She was deeply moved: This is his kingdom.

"Platinum Land!" came into my mind and suddenly I began to realize where I was here, what this place in this world was! And He, who had appeared to me in my dream, lifted me up into his being, into this perfectly wonderful light! Mt. Kailash with Shiva was truly here, and I was in the temple of life, in his ashram.

Babaji had himself once said that every soul made his way to the Earth through these mountains and this valley, and that every soul again departed from here. This touched me deeply. Later, when I questioned Babaji about this he said: "Yes, all good souls come from here." And regarding the stones he said: "All these stones are liberated souls."

What Gopiji told me about this place reflected the inner feeling that I had had here from the beginning – everything was so alive, even though there only appeared to be stones and mountains here. Something mysterious filled these mountains and this valley, something healing and holy.

One evening at dusk, Gopiji had seen a very large light, between round and oval in shape like a huge gondola balloon, float across to Kailash from Siddheshwar. She and many others had often been able to observe lights on the mountains and in the valley, but this was the first time that she had seen such a huge light. When she asked Babaji what it was, he answered: "That was Vishnu himself, who was on a journey from Siddheshwar, his mountain, to Kailash."

In the meantime we had arrived at the ashram. Everything that Gopiji had confided, deeply touched me and I was very grateful to her for overcoming her great reserve to open something of such great importance for me. Oh, Babaji, I began to feel a deep happiness inside! Kailash was here!

And I had experienced Babaji as the Lord of my mountain, as judge who at first filled me with fear, great fear, until I broke through and was able to experience love, his love, at night in that great experience of light, which showed me who he really was. Very deep in my soul I folded my hands together and was as happy as I was grateful. I felt that I had begun to see and to understand that the portal had been opened for me, a portal to Herakhan, to Babaji, the Lord of Herakhan, and thereby a portal to Kailash.

When I met Babaji in the ashram again in the late afternoon and we were all assembled for the singing of mantras, I knew as I went towards him that I was beginning to *see*! How he gazed at me was indescribable! And this gaze elevated me. Through this gaze I was able to see the Lord of my mountain. Inside, I became flame, devotion, jubilation and great power, all at the same time. I saw that he knew this and was totally still in my bliss.

The evening came and I danced, danced, everything that was in me sang, and he danced, too – seated there he moved, looked, answered. And how he answered, how intensely his eyes penetrated me with his divine seeing!

For the first time since I had arrived, the flames were lit in order to celebrate Arati in front of Babaji. As if in a dream, I went to him and took hold of the little vessel with the fire. Some people jumped up to prevent me, since I was new in the ashram, but he, Babaji permitted it! I grasped the fire bowl and honoured Babaji with the Arati – Babaji, who began to become transparent and approachable for me:

"OM NAMAH SHIVAY – SHIVAYE NAMAH OM."

Then Babaji also took the fire vessel and together with me he guided the fire from him to me and back to him – in a horizontal oval rotating motion. I was breathless: Oh, how he looked at me. How could I describe the all-penetrating power of love and depth that I experienced in that gaze, at the same time that I was lifted up out of time in total awareness and stillness. OM namah Shivay. Then he let go of the vessel and now I moved the fire in a vertical oval rotation around him. Suddenly the thunderous sound of a bell crashed in my ear, first on my left, then on my right – SHIVA-Babaji had taken hold of a huge bell which hung behind him and, laughing, rung it in my ear while I moved the fire around him in circles. Afterwards – filled to the depths of my heart, in my blood, in my whole being, and permeated with the flaming singing of awareness, of knowing – I stepped out into the night in the face of the mountain, Kailash, whose Lord I had now recognized.

Oh Lord, grant me that I never again lose this, grant me that it remains living within me, this knowledge, this love! Oh Lord, grant me that I never again forget!

And I went down to the stones, washed myself, drank that wonderful water, felt the bright night of the stars, the stones, the mountain, the whole wide valley of Hera-khan, and through it all the gratitude, flames and stillness. I felt as if in eternity.

Nila and the stones by the river

Wednesday, January 25, 1978 — My fifth day at the Ashram

A beautiful light bright day. In the morning, I went down to the river to wash my clothes and felt a deep stillness and joy in my heart.

Equanimity in view of what I had begun to understand yesterday. Equanimity, now central, was the one base on which the inner flame could dance, my blue flame, which could only dance where there is no emotion, but stillness.

Were I to lose this firm base of stillness, the flame and I would burn up and expire. I would cease to be able to perceive, to want to perceive. With thanks I became aware that it was as if I was being held from within and that I was in a totally peaceful and open frame of mind!

How beautiful was this washing procedure at the river! How wonderful to be able to perform a simple act, which in itself could almost lead one to a devotional state, to invite God into everything that one did, always –when walking, eating, resting, talking, to allow oneself to be led by this Most High. OM namah Shivay.

The way of Ananda, the Way of Bhakti, had the flaming devotion at its core: Give God everything! Everything!

Just as I had finished my washing, Babaji came down the 108 steps – I ran to him and walked with him to the other side of the valley. "I am beginning to see you!" "Yes", he said and looked at me from the side. Then something enchanting began: While I was walking beside him, totally concentrated in stillness, devotional in my heart and turned within – his hand touched mine lightly, then again – and in order that I should not think that this had happened by accident, he took hold of my hand and squeezed it a little, then he let it go and wandered on as if nothing had happened. But then, after a while the back of his hand again touched mine, and again and then again whilst we were walking beside each other. And in order to show me that I wasn't deceiving myself, he pressed my hand very lovingly and firmly – and suddenly he had his little finger linked with mine, played with it for a while and then, quite gently, let go of my hand. Oh, he had shown me so much through this little game! Such closeness, such sweetness and such young love!

We were approaching one of the two huts and he sat down on a little stonewall close to one of the tea shops, a place where people liked to gather. Fakiranand came along his path and Tara Devi joined us. Babaji now inspected my bag with interest and took out the paints that I always carried with me and also the red book, in which I had intended to paint everything that Babaji had revealed to me that night in Germany, to give to him later. He took hold of this precise book, this empty red book with its white pages, and began to paint in it: His bare mountains, a colourful plain and then a large red flame, which was shooting out of the plain up to the left side. And above, in the sky, two clouds. The first picture! He immediately turned the page and drew the next picture: "Patal-Ganga," a large round lake from which a river flowed – the Gautam Ganga.

The words "Oh, I know," escaped me, since the word "patal" means underground.

"You don't know!" he countered briefly and continued to paint. I felt that the moment was come for me to be allowed to ask him a few things and at the same time I gave him the little piece of paper on which I had written yesterday, in the early evening after I had begun to see him: "Babaji, through your eyes I can now see the Lord of my mountain. Let me climb onto my mountain through the portal of your eyes. You are Shiva, the Lord of my mountain." Whereupon Babaji screwed up the little piece of paper, threw it behind him and said: "You have already climbed your mountain, otherwise you would not be here now!"

What should I do?

I asked Babaji what I could do – whether I should learn more about healing and naturopathic treatment. He answered: "You can do this in Poona, there is a school – or in Germany, or here. You can learn it here also!" And, most importantly, I asked whether I should myself paint and write, or whether I could do painting therapy with others, or psychology? – He answered: *"What you like most in your heart, this you should do!"*

Then I told him that Don, the friend who would come here to fetch me, had, during the flight here, twice heard a loud voice talking about Pralaya, the dissolution of the creation, and whether this had been he, Babaji. Answer: "It was his inner voice!"

Question: "So it was not your voice?" Answer: "That is the same." Later on, it was not possible to ask as many questions as on this afternoon down in the valley.

The afternoon drew to a close and the singing began. I took heart, went to the front and asked Babaji if I might be allowed to climb Kailash. He raised both hands with all his ten fingers spread wide:

"Whenever you want!" and looked at me in a very special way. He wanted to know with whom I would like to climb. "I don't know," I said, "If necessary, alone." At that he sent for Gora Devi: "She will be your guide!"

Then he asked when I wanted to do it. "If you allow, tomorrow."

"O.K." he said and then turned to all those assembled, asking who wanted to accompany us on the ascent of Kailash the following day. As no one responded, he decided that David should go with us. I was very happy and moved. In truth, tomorrow I would be able to climb Kailash, the mountain that I had carried in me for so long!

In the meantime the evening Arati had ended, but apparently Babaji had not invited anyone, in any case not me, to go to him for Chandan the next morning. Night was falling and I started to feel sad that I would have to set off for Kailash without Chandan, that very special blessing from him. Surprisingly, although it was very late, someone offered me some soup. I sat down on the lowest of the steps to the house where I slept and drank the soup. Suddenly a bright spotlight shone in my face: "Tomorrow you come for Chandan!"

Oh, Babaji, how happy I was!

Thursday, January 26, 1978 — My sixth day at the Ashram

The valley was covered by a mysterious darkness as I went down to the river at 3:30 in the morning to bathe. "Oh Babaji, please let this be a bright and beautiful day, as I want to go walking on your mountain. Please let no storm or rain come."

Because it looked as if it would. Kailash in particular was covered by dark, mighty clouds. Hardly a star was visible. But I was full of trust and expectation for the day – and indeed, around seven in the morning, just as the day came and we departed – we saw three huge fiery "fingers" coming from Mt. Kailash driving all the clouds and darkness away, until the entire sky was fully light and blue.

This exciting spectacle was preceded at five in the morning by the Chandan: I saw a few others waiting outside the little gate, which led to Babaji's small room. I was one of the last to enter the room. "Nila" – my name was called – today I was to be the first one to come to him.

There he sat, stern, shining, supernaturally awake, almost detached but still totally focussed on the person kneeling in front of him. With one hand he held my head, pushed my hair back and then drew the sign of Shiva, the three horizontal lines, on my forehead with the other hand. As well as the red dot on the centre of my forehead, he drew two additional red dots on my right and left temples and put a Mala (a *long prayer chain*) around my neck. I was so happy. How strongly I felt his blessing! Also, while he was making ritual offerings at the fire, he graced me several times with his eyes. I knew that he was transforming something in me and giving it to the fire, two or even three times.

Towards the end of the ceremony, before rising from the fire, he looked at me once more, with all HIS presence, this time full of Love and at the same time very seriously. I bowed to his fire, profoundly grateful, after he had left.

Kailash, the holy mountain

Kailash – what a mountain it is, and what a special day this was, when we climbed this mountain! The three red fiery fingers had driven away all the dark clouds, just at the moment of our departure. The entire sky was light and blue. Dear Mountain, how beautiful you are!

Below at your feet runs a clear brook, dancing steeply down from a small rise, and to the right and left of it is spread the fresh, intense green of bushes with white blossoms, and the earth covered by light blue flowers. We walked along the brook for the first one seventh of our journey. To my amazement just as we reached a little village we heard "BHOLE BABA KI" ring out (This means: Victory to the father who is simple) and Gora Devi responded enthusiastically: "JAI."

Two Indian women wanted to climb the mountain with us, so now we were seven: Gora Devi, whom Babaji had given me to be our guide, David and Manisha, another Indian from the ashram who was also familiar with the area. We went on very swiftly. Soon the two Indian women preferred to stay behind. The surroundings became more barren.

We took our first break at a huge tree. Each of us rang in sequence the bells mounted there. Their powerful resonance spread towards the valley. From far away, but still clear, we could hear singing of the morning Arati. A special magic and power were present in the valley and its surroundings. We lit incense under the tree; Babaji was present with us every step of the way.

How easy it was, ascending the mountain, full of devotion, breathing in and breathing out the OM NAMAH SHIVAY.

"The inside of the Mountain is full of gold," Babaji had once said. I always knew that somewhere in the world there was this mountain, which is full of gold.

The second third of the mountain was covered by bushes as white as snow. In no other place in the world had I seen anything so wondrous. Bushes, whose branches were covered as by the finest, whitest velvet. The edelweiss we know from our mountains is grey and rough by comparison, for the white that covered the bushes from root to tip like icing sugar was so very fine and light. Like fairy arms these bushes raise themselves from the earth, as if filled by a wonderful song that they breathe out to the air and sky from the body of the mountain, singing and dancing to it with endless gentleness. And from these white arteries grew leaves, silver on the outside and a powerful dark green within. What magic! The entire middle part of the mountain was filled with it!

My happiness increased with every step, just as did my composure. The path was quite steep and we were still hiking as fast as we could to avoid getting tired. Sometimes Gora Devi, who is small and somewhat tenderly built, cried out with all her strength "BOLE BABA KI." The rest of us then answered with a loud "JAI." Indeed, each time this felt like a shot of energy. The hotter it got, the faster I had to breathe, and the more intensively I felt the mantra breathing through me: OM NAMAH SHIVAY, with each step. Truly, Babaji himself appeared to be walking within us and with us.

We had climbed two-thirds of the mountain and we could see the last steep portion of the path. Suddenly we saw two white eagles, calmly flying wide circles in the sky. None of us had ever seen white eagles before. "Where the white eagles meet, there I am, said Christ!" recited David, who had founded a Christian Church in the USA that has white eagles as their sign. In Christian symbolism the eagle signifies the Ascension of Christ as well as the rebirth at the Christening. In addition, it is the attribute of the evangelist John.

For the Indians, as with other ancient cultures, the eagle is a sign of the Highest Deity, the Highest Sovereignty. That is the meaning I understood it to have here – on the way to the summit of Kailash, the abode of Shiva, who resides here as Mahadeva, the highest Deity, as He of whom it is said that He is in everything, but not of anything. As He, who never began and He, who always is. He, revered as the Lord of the universe, who *was* before creation came into being.

He, all pervading, omniscient and omnipresent. Our path led us to him.

We had taken staffs for a better grip on the path. Soon we arrived at the rounded summit. A little altar had been erected, made simply of stone with a trident as the sign of Shiva. There was a little fireplace and many, many bells, which we rang.

The great silence

Arrival at the top seemed to me like coming home. A powerful silence took hold of me. I moved deep inside it and felt: "Here I can be, here I mean to stay," for three days at least. Within me, I felt the breathing that carried me within this silence, which I perceived as a powerful song. I knew that this was just a tiny silence within an infinitely greater silence. Thunderous like all the oceans of the earth, being of the highest frequency whilst also absolutely still, all pervading, beyond time and space, totally alive, different and beyond what any words could ever express.

Here, where there was nothing other than stone, sky and this silence, I was touched by the realm beyond death and birth. Here was the silence that made everything resonate, and He, whom I began to see in the valley, He himself was here. He, who is white and eternal.

No, I did not want to descend again! Nothing, really nothing from the depths of my being drew me to return, to leave this place. And though I should starve, here at the portal to BEING, on its threshold, I wanted to stay and not move from the spot until the BEING had taken me up completely, through the portal of nothingness into the All. And if I should have no more water, I was certain that God himself would come to bring me some. And if it were to become cold in the night, he would warm me from within. For a moment I asked myself: and what if all possible spirits were to come when I am up here so totally alone in the night under the bare heaven? Inwardly, I saw many beings and souls floating unceasingly up the mountain. Obviously, here was their portal into the eternal. But then with a consciously deeply drawn breath I was back in the fold of the silence – the silence that was also infinitely gentle like eternity. To remain here – my longing was great.

Platinum land

Being beyond becoming
The White Land

You, my eternal home! God, You know how great is my longing to be one with You and for ever. You know how great is my sadness that I ever left this realm, to have danced down from the immensity of Your being into the restriction of becoming. To have lost You, who is the essence of my being, of all beings, in the transitoriness.

Now I come to You – my clothes are colourful – look, I am covered with wounds, wounds inflicted on me by my transience, because I believed it was possible for me to live without You – or with You only as needed, and otherwise to follow the desires and ideas of my ego or the egos of others.

You demonstrated to me ever more clearly where I was not conforming to Your will, nor to Your love, which embraces everything. And I have begun to understand, and through the wounds of many lifetimes to see You who now meets me in full power. In truth it was my soul that bade You burn everything that prevented my being in perfect oneness with You. You heard its cry. And you hastened my wavering steps. Love is absolute freedom. Is it not You who allowed me, allowed us all in Your love to go into exile, to separate from You? And who now calls us back to be ONE with You!

"Here – and not from here," I understand this task: To see the eternal in the transient, to illuminate the transient from the eternal, to free it from its impenetrable darkness. You do this, we are not able.

I must confess that it filled me with great sadness, when my companions insisted that we descend again. It was Gora Devi who strictly refused my request to let me stay up there even for one night. She said that Babaji absolutely would have had to grant the permission beforehand, which he had done extremely rarely. In general, with the people whom he brought on the Kailash, he himself guided them down after 20 minutes. We had now already stayed up here for an hour! Nothing could be done. I had to descend, even though my heart told me a hundred times that Babaji would have permitted me to stay up here for a night.

As jubilant as the ascent had been, inasmuch as the Mantra honouring God had filled me with each step I took walking uphill, so heavy, even impossible, was the descent. The OM NAMAH SHIVAY would not even enter my mind on the way down. Only with great effort did I manage to maintain my inner balance and equanimity, to be of "equal courage," or to regain it.

Just at the top, shortly before leaving the hilltop of Kailash, David suddenly stopped and called to us: "Stop, I see three figures moving towards the summit." Gora Devi and I quickly ran back up to him, but no figures were to be seen. Had David been mistaken? And if not, from whence in this solitude would three figures have come? Later, as we related our experience in the ashram, they just said: "Oh, everything is possible on Kailash."

Fortunately, the descent from Kailash progressed quickly. The path was very steep and repeatedly one of us would slip and fall down when not all our attention was given to the path. I was not in the mood for talking. Silently, my heart filled with sadness, I continued descending.

What we saw in the lowest part, right at the foot of Kailash, astounded me: Bulls, many of them, beautifully cared for, well-fed, perfectly black bulls. Until now I had never seen a black bull in India – and here, out of nowhere, appeared twenty, thirty, forty animals, that obviously had come to the drinking trough at the deliciously fresh spring that had its source at the lower part of Kailash. Never before had I seen such beautiful animals with such a silken gloss to their hair:

black, silken glossy bulls. Lord Shiva's riding animal is Nandi, the bull. Up above flew the two white eagles as the sign of deity, and down below were all these black bulls! Truly, a very lively language.

We arrived at the ashram just in time for the Afternoon Bhajan Singing. At first, I did not dare face Babaji, because I felt ashamed about my sadness during the descent. I felt that through this my spirit had been darkened and was expecting a glance, or at least that he would ignore me.

Finally after a long internal struggle, I took heart and went to him at the front. But to my surprise he looked at me very affectionately. So I asked him whether I could go tomorrow to Kailash again and stay there overnight. "Not tomorrow. Later with your friend – then you can stay there over night," he said, and to my surprise put a chain of pure fresh flowers around my neck. At the same time, he pressed the point in the middle of the forehead between my eyes. "What Did You See?" he asked, and I answered: "Nothing!" He smiled, and pressed the same point again very firmly and for a long time — "What Did You see?" Again I had to answer: "Nothing." Again he looked at me with a smile: "I showed you Shiva's Sun!" Only later I have realized, Shiva's Sun is the sun beyond the suns that shines out of the Great Nothing, the sun from which all suns emerged. It is that sun, which I experienced on Kailash.

It is the sun for which I had longed since my youth, and about which I had written poems. But in this moment I was confused. I went back to my seat, but then immediately back to the front to Babaji to return the chain of flowers for I felt totally unworthy to receive a garland. But he did not take it back. With the abundance of flowers in my hands, I ran to the temple of the Old Herakhan Baba to lay them down there, but Babaji sent a boy after me to tell me again: "This is for you! You take it home with you!" It was only later that it dawned on me that I was to bring the joy of the Lord into matter from the place of eternal presence in order to live in the here and now and bring everything into blossom here.

Then came days of great intimacy, ease and joy — for I had recognized Him. The inner gateway had opened wide, and I was full of faith, now also towards Him specifically; the gatekeepers of doubt had gone and I had now recognized Him whom I had experienced from inside, through his costume in the exterior world. And I had climbed Kailash, verily and truly!

In connection with this experience of perfect stillness on Kailash, I am reminded of one incident from my early childhood, after all the fears of the war that was about to end:

I was alone and waited for my family.

And no one came. Then I forgot my waiting; my fears were at once lifted into a sphere of perfect peace, of perfect stillness and beauty, where everything was good. The large gray stone steps. the grid on which I stood, were equally important and beautiful as the bright butterflies, the flowers and the scents in the garden that stretched up in front of me along the hill. Everything was pervaded by a sense of Oneness, it was all one. And I was part of this Oneness! I was in the light of pure being. Everything was good. Eventually, my loving mother and grandmother came. That was the first time when, as a small child of about four years, I experienced consciously the eternal Being. Now I know it was a gift from Babaji.

From today's perspective, I am also convinced that Babaji guides, inspires and protects anyone who is deeply connected to him during their entire life.

Friday, January 27, 1978 — My seventh day at the Ashram

Immediately after the morning Arati, Babaji sat down in the back part of the garden and again began to paint into my empty Red Book: He had already painted two pictures on Wednesday down in the valley. How much time seems to have passed since then! Now, using the crayons that I had brought for him, he painted a wild third picture. He started very carefully: first, with pens and pencils he very gently outlined a face with a large headdress – LORD SHIVA – followed by eight dark brown dancing flames, and then he covered the entire picture with energetic, many-coloured fiery lines and finally he drew, very powerfully and determinedly, his OM-symbol on top of it.

"I like it," I said spontaneously. "I like it, too," he said. "You are Shiva-Rasa," I remarked, as his colours raced across the page. I had wanted to say: "You are Sada Shiva – You are the Eternal Shiva," but had the words mixed up. But he replied: "No, you Shiva Rasa!" I later learned Rasa means taste, passion, joy, ecstasy. In between, he bit into an apple and gave it to me to go on eating. As another girl was watching, he bit into a second apple and gave it to her to eat.

His picture obviously depicted "Shiva, who destroys the world." "Pralaya, the dissolution of creation?" I asked. But he answered, while quietly beholding his picture: "In Germany, no war! Only nature calamities." He gave me the book and left.

In the afternoon, Babaji painted down by the cave, and I could ask him questions that were on my mind. Tara Devi would translate. Actually, translation never seemed necessary to me, but Babaji acted as if it were. The fact was that all my questions had vanished into thin air while I was sitting relaxed on the floor next to him in the sun and watched him paint. He looked at me lovingly, "Kushi Begum," Happy Queen. In fact, I was nothing but happy. For the afternoon cleansing I went with others to swim in a deep place in one of the branches of the river. It was wonderfully refreshing!

In the evening, a most beautiful Arati singing and dancing to the rhythm of the OM NAMAH SHIVAY. The next morning I tried to reach him, especially through meditation. The answer was: very intense pressure on the bridge of the nose through the whole day.

I was in a very quiet mood. Later I went to the river to do the laundry. This is a very beautiful process. After a while, Babaji came down with a group – he sent for me, as he passed the river, gave me a candy and then proceeded on his way with the group of men. When he returned, I was standing with my laundry on the stairs.

"You are Yogan," he said to me then, and went up past me. "What is 'Yogan'?" I asked one of the men in his party. The reply was that it is the feminine form of Yogi. After our lunch Babaji was sitting in the shade on the wall of the ashram. I was with him, and he discovered the water paint box in my bag. So I brought him water and for the first time he tried out the watercolours. A beautiful picture emerged. "Hintergrund," he said suddenly to my great surprise in German, pointing to himself while painting. Then he handed me the picture, although there were many others who had already gathered around him and might be wondering why he kept on giving me more and more pictures. Background, the eternal underground and background on which the creation acts out, comparable to the white canvas on which the coloured picture arises.

I continued to spend the afternoon and evening of that day in a very meditative state, quiet, turned inward, feeling the strong pressure in the middle of the forehead. Each time Babaji saw me, he smilingly let his eyes roll upward, as if to say, "Yes I see, you are going up," reflecting back to me what I was doing inwardly. At the same time this was a teaching. I realized that one who inwardly lets his eyes and mind 'go up' no longer looks at his fellow human beings from the outside.

He continues to stay focussed on the eternal, until he – after a while – with new eyes is again present down below, to participate in the transformational work here.

Sunday, January 29, 1978 —
My ninth day at the Ashram

Chandan: Today Babaji painted a long vertical red line, which continued from the roof of my nose upward to the crown, through the three horizontal yellow lines on my forehead. The meditation went well afterwards. But to my surprise, a young man who was not well asked me if he could lie down in my room, since the other room was very crowded. Although in the house where we lived, which at that time was the only house, there were a couple of rooms that still seemed to be free, Babaji put five people in the room across from mine. This, of course, greatly accelerated the learning process. This is the process of becoming a "Happy Learner" by learning to break free of one's vulnerable ego that always strives to separate itself, and to learn the appropriate lesson instead of blaming the other when one's "buttons are pressed." Instead of saying to the other: "You must change!" rather saying to yourself: "What can I change in me?"

Thus we are transformed from "square angular beings," which is what we tend to be when we begin, into something soft and open – and the freedom of oneness begins to dawn on us, which Babaji will lead us to.

It had come to pass that since the day of climbing Kailash I had been alone in the room. Surprisingly, Govindi had been asked by Babaji to leave. Originally she had made arrangements to stay for six months, but had violated Babaji's rule not to go to the fire in the shed upstairs when men were present, but was still doing it. In addition, she allowed one of the men to give her a bracelet. So she had to go; in this there was no mercy!

Similarly, Makhan Singh had to go and shortly afterwards David too. Babaji was strict. David also had set out to stay for six months and to his utter surprise was sent away after a few days. Each of them for other deep reasons. Fakiranand once confessed to me that even he as Babaji's secretary, who had left all his former life as a landlord behind for the ashram, could never be sure. For in the moment when he was not careful, not alert, had perhaps even fallen asleep, or committed other mistakes, he would have to go. When Babaji said, "You go!" – then you had to go. Prayers and supplications were of no value – unless one had a sudden insight and understood, why! That could change the situation within seconds and again make a further stay possible.

This Sunday morning I was occupied in healing the young man who lay in my room with high fever and in pain. Actually, I was wondering how one could ever become ill here, for I myself felt completely whole and well and so full of energy despite eating little and having only a short sleep. But after he told me about his experiences with Babaji in the previous days, I understood that he had lost his balance and had to be sick in order to process everything. At my request, Babaji sent him a doctor and gave me instructions for him. By the way, Babaji accepted both allopathic medicine and naturopathy – but said, the best medicine is OM NAMAH SHIVAY.

Right after lunch Babaji unexpectedly sat on the wall, ready to paint in my Red Book. As always, I watched full of attention for what would emerge. When I wanted to ask something, he responded: "Pssst!" I was expected just to watch and to be very quiet. He painted a strange figure: "Hukham Khuda" he said, "This is the Lord, giving his orders and sending his soldiers round the world!"and asked me if I had already met him, the strict GOD? This was suddenly a direct question, whereas previously he had spoken crisscross to all who were gathered around him.

An order

I paused thoughtfully and then replied: "You know better than me," but suddenly I knew it and said, "Yes!" Promptly he stated: "Yes, I have sent him to you!" and I answered, "Before I came here, at first I was very afraid." While continuing to paint: "This Lord spreads his orders in the world through his soldiers." I asked: "Tell me what are his orders for me?" Babaji: "Do not hurt anybody, praise the name of god always, do good to everybody." – Oh Babaji, I understood and felt the whole weight of your lesson !

Monday, January 30, 1978 —
My tenth day at the Ashram

Chandan – this time only for Westerners. During the morning and evening Arati, I noticed that I did not receive as much candy or fruit from Babaji as in the first days. That was probably necessary at the beginning as a means for me to learn to understand.

"Where is my book?" called Babaji, and I gave it to him. From now on he painted with watercolours.

A very impressive, dark but shiningly beautiful picture emerged: "A lake in Germany!" he said. The black sky with the white sun/moon and the cobalt blue stars above it created a night-time but very luminescent atmosphere.

Shortly after, he painted a picture on a single sheet for the American physician Dr. Dahru. Again, as before, when painting Lord Shiva, he shaped a carefully executed figure with large headdress, but this time female: "This is Mother Mary!" Later, Dahru narrated to me that Babaji had told him he would get married this year and have a child. So far, however, Dahru did not know whom he would marry.

After lunch, I hurried to be in time to help with the dishes, and was so happy that with a huge leap I jumped down the high Indian cement stairs, taking several steps at a time. Precisely at that moment Babaji walked by and shouted at me: "Tomorrow you are leaving!" Puzzled, I turned around: "Why?" "You shouldn't jump like a camel!" Loud laughter all around!

He turned to go, but I immediately followed him: "Babaji, if I don't jump like this, then I do not have to go, do I?" "OK," was the reply with a somehow serious look, which I only later understood: Be careful, do not risk hurting your body. The others were still having a good laugh about the camel.

I helped with the dishes, which was really something special: Because there was no soap, and water was very scarce and precious, the plate or the pot was first rubbed with soil and a drop of water, then rinsed with a little water, rubbed with earth again, with more water added to it. The whole thing was repeated three times and then the plate or the bowl was declared to be clean, after which of course all the earth was finally rinsed off with water.

The same process using the Earth was applied to washing one's hands. I had to think of Babaji's three commands: Truth – Simplicity – Love! Afterwards I happened to walk up the stairs right behind Babaji. He stopped and looked far into the distance: "Your friend has come!" Since Saturday, I had been expecting him. I kept looking for him, but all I could see was a girl coming through the valley.

What Babaji had said at noon came true in the evening. My friend arrived. He was already seated at the Arati when I came up from a meditation in the cave, happy and completely absorbed by it.

Because from today on, I had permission to sleep in the cave, alone. I was looking forward to that so much, to being alone in the sacred cave. When I asked Babaji for permission to stay in it, he said. "Yes, but it is just an ordinary cave!" That was probably just the necessary Zen blow that I needed.

Now that my friend had arrived, I asked Babaji if I could once again go to the Kailash, to spend the night there. He gave the reply: "Now Kailash is here!"

Tuesday, January 31, 1978 —
My eleventh day at the Ashram

Together with Dr. Dahru, who as well as Tara Devi had slept down in the temple-like room, I went upstairs. My friend Don had spent the night up above and wanted to set out immediately after the morning service in order to explore the area, while on my last day I wanted to be, if not on the summit of Kailash, at least near Babaji. And indeed, immediately after the Arati, Babaji sitting in the garden began to paint in the Red Book again: "Where is my BOOK?" The previous picture had been of a lake in Germany – a marvellous picture, dark, but very luminous and fresh. Now he painted a very living Earth, fresh greenery and a huge, rising sun, with powerful, flaming rays. I was touched very deeply by this sun, after the previous image of destruction and the picture of a dark, shining Germany. So now the rising sun, and earth. Actually, there even was a fish swimming in the lake. To my surprise, he now wanted to have white body colour. With that, towards the far left side of the picture, he painted a real house, executed very precisely and carefully, and then, next to it – a temple! He looked at me: "This is your House – and this is your little Temple!" I was speechless. Babaji sent me to fetch some fresh water.

When I returned I asked him: "And where is the house?" Indeed, I felt ready inside to go wherever Babaji would guide me. When the answer was: "In Washington," my heart sank. "Really?" Then he laughed: "No, no, in Germany!" Of course, I later thought deeply about the significance of Washington. As with everything that Babaji said, it was clearly significant on several levels.

Immediately afterwards Babaji began to paint another picture, this time on a single white sheet. I sat at an angle from him and, full of expectation, looked at the portrait that emerged. Suddenly he covered the whole face, which was carefully executed, with golden flames.

"This is Bhairav Baba (pronounced Beru Baba),[6] the Chief man of Shiva. He gives blessing also." Babaji gave me the portrait. Later I heard that Bhairav Baba is the destroyer of evil and protector of the good. With Bhairav Baba smiling lovingly on it, I realized that this had indeed been given to me as a Blessing.

"I'm Bhairav Baba.
I am the deep rich ruby red wine of human love.
The fire of love in which nothing that is not love can exist.
I burn everything

that is impure and leave only love.
I am not to be feared, because I'm only love,
Tender, sweet and kind.

But many fear my fire of love,
because they dwell in their impurities.
Only what is impure is afraid of me:
Because I'm terrible and strong
like a ravening lion
devouring the meat of poisoned tongues
and evil minds.

But for those who love
I am the sweet breath
of a scented evening,
of a rose as "she" opens her eyes to the sun,
of the soil as she sighs with her lover's moan.

I am the love beyond love.

He, who knows me, knows all. "

WORDS OF BHAIRAV BABA RECEIVED BY PETER DAWKINS, SEPTEMBER 1991,
IN *QUELL DES HEILENS (SOURCE OF HEALING)* AT LAKE CONSTANCE IN
SOUTHERN GERMANY

Babaji had promised to complete painting the Red Book. Around noon, as I walked past him, he was sitting with several others. When I questioningly pointed to the Red Book, he said: "Now, the office is closed!" But later in the afternoon at the cave, the "office" was reopened and Babaji painted the most beautiful picture: "Lord Shiva's Garden"! Here now were all the flowers that I had longed for at the beginning! Very enchanting! In the morning, when I asked Babaji regarding my departure, which seemed fixed by the booking of our return flight, he answered simply: "Well, since your return trip is already booked, you shall fly!" When I asked whether I might stay if it were not fixed, he replied "Yes!" I had had the same feeling. I felt such love, such joy – and he answered this in a soft and simple way.

Nandan Van

"Nandan Van", the painting full of blossoms, was really an expression of this love and joy. As on that first Sunday, the day of my test, when I had gone secretly to the cave and found myself surprised by Babaji, I was again sitting outside at his feet: He sat again on the small box, but this time painting, full of love, completely at peace, and I no longer was full of questions and doubts, but just surrendering to him. My whole heart and being were full of stillness and happiness. And with a look at the cave, he nodded to me: "This is your home now!" I understood and was very happy!

While Babaji painted the blossoming picture, he said, "I am energy doctor!" This was the second time that he said something directly about himself. The first word was "Hintergrund" as he pointed to himself, and now "energy doctor." In fact, I had just been wondering how it was that with so little sleep and food all these past days, I was so full of energy – except for that first day when it had been raining and I did not understand anything.

Bhairav Baba, painted by Babaji, January 1978

Transformation and promise

Babaji continued to paint. He was on the last two pages of the book: *Tibet*, a painting consisting of many coloured layers, came into being. Beautiful! But lo! What did he do? Suddenly, he dipped the brush into the red and covered the entire image from top to bottom with red spots. Suddenly I was reminded of the "apocalyptic poem" that my friend Marcel had given me to ask Babaji whether it is true. It is a poem by Uri Geller:

The RED *was coming:*
The day the wind grew YELLOW
The day the dust fell
The day opened up the skies
The day the RED *was coming*
The day the sun stood still
The day we saw the RED
The day had come, the day was now here
The day I knew the end
The day the lift had begun
The day, the RED *turned to* YELLOW
The day they laid the purple point on YELLOW
It dripped and churned, and quiet burned
The PURPLE *turned to* GREEN
The GREEN *became* WHITE *and* SILVER
But the SILVER *turned to* GOLD
And GOLD *had dripped to* RAINBOW COLOURS,
that coloured all the mist.
The mist because so heavy sunken
sank so deep above.
The colours dropped nothing, burnt again
And sown the fields
The fields had grown these colours below.
It began to sing.

What might all this mean: the countless red spots on his Tibet picture? The invasion of Tibet? Or does it have a much more encompassing meaning?

Babaji turned back to the very first page, which just like the very last page was still empty and could, so to speak, serve as the title page of the book. Babaji was now in fact painting a cover painting *Om Kareshwar – "Lord Shiva's Temple."* So he gave a title to the book and handed it to me. Now I had a whole work by him, not the book that was shown to me in my dream that contained all the events of my past lives, but a completely new one: a book that spoke of destruction and a New Beginning. A book of promise. I perceived it as a great treasure, a very encouraging book!

Finally the evening arrived, my last evening in the ashram! When Babaji came in, he dropped a bag in my lap, a bag full of film rolls! How I rejoiced! I, who had never dared to photograph him, was given so many films in my lap – "To wash them!."

Then he called me forward: "You give a speech now!" Although I had already known this inwardly since that afternoon, at first I stood there speechless. "I have no words," I said to him. "You have never even spoken to me in many words. You spoke to me through colours and I answered you in dance. You spoke to me through light, and I became a flame, a blue flame!"

Then Babaji said, smiling: "That is why I have given you the name NILA – I thought of this!" And I continued: "Yes, and one day I want to become ONE with you and be beyond all colours, there in the White Land, beyond the Gold in the Platinum Land. That I feel is your home, where you come from! I thank you so much, thank you, there are no words for all this! When I depart tomorrow, I know you are going with me, you will always go with me!"

I saw in his smiling bright gaze: "Yes, Yes, Yes," and then went back to dance with the others. To dance for him one last time. As I bowed to him, he did not pull me up as usual by the hair of my crown, but he stroked my hair infinitely gently from my head down to my neck. An indescribable bliss! I felt as if substantial light had touched me.

Late in the evening I saw him once more. He said: "Tomorrow you come to me!" This last night I was allowed to spend in the cave. Don accompanied me down there with the flashlight over the many stones. He did not understand Babaji yet and I felt his resistance. That depressed me somehow and I slipped a bit out of my centre, where I was clear and secure in the knowledge. So now it was not easy for me to reach Babaji. Instead, I felt unable to take in all the light currents that flow through this cave.

I realized I could be sitting on God's lap, but that when my consciousness was not open for it, I would not perceive it. At the same time, it became clear to me that every stone on earth is divine in every moment and is able to reveal something divine if I ensure that the light in me stays lit and that therefore the Divine can shine towards me from everything that is.

Babaji preparing to paint

"It is a divine cave" – and "It is just an ordinary cave"– in this vivid contradiction, Babaji, you have told me everything. Well, this last night I tried to pray with all the sincerity and depth that I could muster, and meditate, but could only reach a certain threshold. Somewhere in me there was a light layer of fog that veiled my free radiant devotion and happiness, and so I fell asleep.

At 2:30, after four hours sleep, I woke up in the cave and felt a clear call to meditate. But instead of rising fully from sleep, I slid back into it until 4:15.

Wednesday, February 1, 1978 — My twelfth day at the Ashram

High time to get up and quickly take a bath. Being without my orange blanket, which I had given the day before to Babaji for the ashram, I was shivering from the cold when I went up to Chandan. Nobody came except Sheela, the dear Indian friend who had known Babaji since 1972. So, for this last Chandan he had me come to him almost alone.

Again, I felt very strongly my unworthiness to be near him. Where was the beautiful flame in me through which I felt free, simple and selflessly and dearly united in love with him and all that lives? I could not attain it. But in spite of this, a part of me was still full of expectation when I came to him, as it was the last morning.

He looked at me quietly, gave me a short and cool glance and made two lines and the red dot on my forehead, nothing more. Something in me was delighted to be almost alone with him at the fire. I wanted to take the seat right opposite him and sat down right between two black stones. But then Babaji said in an indignant, sad voice, almost hurt, like a child whose building blocks had been mixed up: "This is Bhairav Baba! These are Bhairav Baba's stones. Do not touch them!" – Oh, I had hurt Bhairav Baba, whose picture he had painted for me just yesterday.

Babaji, as always, offered the food to the fire and was gone! I went back down into the cave. On this last, precious morning meeting at the fire I had not been sufficiently present in my centre. I was taken by remorse and so I wrote him: "Please – in spite of my weaknesses, please accept me!" The letter had a cleansing effect, my repentance burnt the fog within me and all that separated me from my pure inner flame. After writing the note, I put it with the red scarf, the colours and all the brushes, which I intended to leave here for him. Now I felt much better. The inner sky had cleared again.

Wednesday morning: Babaji came, and what joy, right on entering he dropped a very sweet, sunny and happy final picture in my lap. All the colours of the rainbow were present: two palms, a gentle yet strong rising sun and a singing bird in the tree, and below it a face, smiling, mysterious – was it he himself? I was overjoyed! It was the picture for the last page of his book, which was still blank. This image, the New World, he had painted all alone! It was a perfect response to the poem "The Red was coming," which I had wanted to show him from the beginning. He must have painted it just while I was burning away my weaknesses by writing the note in the cave. What joy! – What an answer of Love! Now I went to him and bowed deeply before him as a sign of my complete devotion and reverence, then laid down the colours and brushes next to him and put my slip of paper into his hand. He read it immediately and nodded, and he looked at me intensely and with love. Oh, Babaji! I was very, very happy! Dancing, I went back to my place and then what did Babaji do? Right there at his seat, he quickly set out to paint. And called me back to him. Another picture? It was a picture of the sun, a slightly tousled, joyful and large sun.

"For your friend!" he said, meaning Don who sat there seemingly closed, but had previously given his sleeping bag to the ashram by taking it to Babaji. This farewell gift from the sun, painted spontaneously, was for him!

Dancing, I said goodbye to the assembled friends because I thought we would have to depart right then, but Babaji himself rose and invited us to have breakfast with him before the trip! He had wonderful chapattis and tomatoes with honey made for us and joined us at the fire in the hut next to the kitchen. A relaxed, happy and strong atmosphere unfolded.

Nila with Babaji and his yellow hat

I sat next to him eating the delicious things with joy, when he suddenly let a candy, which he had just been sucking, stick out from his mouth while looking at me. I understood, held my hand under his chin and caught the candy as Prasad, as a divine food, and proceeded to suck it. What a sign of intimacy! How free and spontaneous he was! Then, hey presto, he even put his little yellow cap on my head, which he had been wearing the entire week, and looked at me now with the yellow cap on my head.

How many times have I been embarrassed for you, Babaji, because with this little sun hat that was much too small for you, you looked like a big child, and now you give it to me! In the following years, I discovered you simply wore whatever people gave you from their love, whether beautiful or not, whether made of silk, wool or a simple material, you wore it and then passed it on with your blessing, You kept nothing for yourself!

The farewell breakfast at the fire with him was a real festivity. Then Babaji accompanied us down. Farewell! Sheela Mataki gave me a hug on the steps.

My heart was so happy – so heavenly light. Below, two little horses were waiting for us. On one, we loaded our luggage, the other we took turns riding. Tara Devi also came to say goodbye. Again, Babaji had some pictures taken. Wearing the same blue sweater that I had worn on arriving, I climbed on the pony. How much had been opened for me in these twelve days! The heavens had opened up!

For the first time today, Babaji had wrapped himself in a beautiful pink cloth embroidered with as many flowers as on one of his recent paintings. How motherly he appeared in this cloth! Later he waved us good-bye with the cloth. Riding on my little horse through the valley, I waved, waved and waved, and for long time saw Babaji standing there wrapped in the large flower-embroidered cloth, and he too waved again and again. Oh, Herakhan valley! You, this deeply familiar and highly secret valley! You, this land between heaven and earth, valley of water and of a hundred thousand stones, through you I rode back into the world.

LORD HARIYAKHANDI – Hariyakhandi OM! I rode back together with you. What were your words on that farewell morning when I was sitting next to you at the fire and asked you: "Please give me your hand?" And you looked at me and spoke: "Not one hand – all hands!"

And this is my experience, again and again: Not one hand, you give all hands to everyone who calls for you with a pure heart!

This is the account of the twelve days of my first meeting with Babaji in Herakhan in January 1978, which on my return to Germany I immediately painted and wrote down in a big blank book, based on the entries in my diary.

This is the text – a poem of love.

Just as all the following encounters with Babaji are poems of love as well. Experiencing all the exciting moves through both light and shadow. These are narrated in the other chapters.

On the very day after I had painted and written all of these impressions of those first twelve days in the ashram, a written letter arrived from Herakhan: "Babaji sends you his blessing and wishes that you are happy!"

Smiling Babaji, surrounded
by bright colours (about 1980)

72 Encounters
with Babaji

I am you

B abaji always assumed the being and the traits of whomever he was speaking with at that moment. – I am you.

Once, in 1979, someone photographed five of us with a Polaroid camera, each separate one together with Babaji. The pictures were all taken shortly after each other. How amazing it was: on each of the pictures Babaji resembled the person he was with. On one of them Babaji had big eyes, exactly like the person he was with; on the next photo slit eyes, always looking like the particular person with whom he was engaged.

We were really touched.

How is it possible that he could assume the facial expression of each particular person in such a short time?

In the same way, during Darshan he changed his expression from one moment to the next, depending upon who came to him. For one a beaming smile, in the next second he yawned and looked away, and then very stern or very humorously playful. It changed according to the teaching that was needed by the person who came to him.

Mirror, tester and brilliant therapist

Babaji was a mirror and at the same time the infinitely wise loving teacher who, above all, led us further.

Some people coming to him were impressed by their own greatness. To such a person, for example, he might hand a staff and let him come forward to stand next to him, and say: "I have never seen anybody great like you."

After he had inflated the person's ego like a balloon, it was bound to follow that he would cause the balloon to burst by totally ignoring the person or by some other means. By this it was possible for real self-awareness to arise in the person and the soul could take over direction, which would be impossible with an inflated ego.

He treated people who had strong feelings of inferiority or of guilt and self doubt in the opposite way. For example, if they were unable to receive his love, at first he paid them no attention until they came to the limit of feeling "I am nothing" but then noticed, "But I am someone", and when the pendulum swung he gave all the love and encouragement that they could absorb.

He let one very shy girl knit a pullover for him, repeating with every stitch: "OM namah Shivay," "OM namah Shivay," "OM namah Shivay." Then he took this pullover, wore it for a short while, and as with everything offered to him in love, gave it on to someone with his blessing.

Babaji kept nothing for himself.

Although there were general rules for living in the ashram, there was no fixed pattern with Babaji. He treated everyone entirely individually. Being with him was simply indescribably lively and continually surprising. In his absolute freedom, Babaji was generous.

He once said: "Now you see the benevolent Baba who fulfils your wishes, but at some time in the future you will encounter the strict Babaji."

An Indian once said: "One day of Herakhan with Babaji is like twelve years of life." With the greatest rapidity, Babaji brought to the surface what was inside each one in Herakhan, particularly in situations when we were together. Healing can come very quickly if one understands: "Who hurts me is my doctor."

Babaji, the pure mirror and tester: though angry with the angry one, the gentle and loving experienced him always as gentle and full of love. By no means did the persons involved always recognize that Babaji was reflecting them, but rather were of the opinion that Babaji himself was angry or whatever.

To be with Babaji was like continually being on a knife's edge: One could never be sure whether one would be allowed to stay the next day. Babaji was very strict in the matter of sending people away, and it was often a case of him promptly saying "Tomorrow you go!" And always it was when one had made an error, did not understand what it was all about or was unable to absorb any more, or for other reasons which Babaji saw.

"Be polite," Babaji asked us and "love each other as you love me." That meant, respect each other, give space to the other one, for example by a question like "Is it ok for you, that I ...?"

He was very strict about the choice of people who were even allowed to come up into the ashram. On several occasions when new people arrived, he sent me down to the Chai shops in the valley with the comment: "I am only there for serious people, not for sightseeing!"

And then it was my job to make it clear to the new arrivals, such as hippies, who Babaji was and what this was all about. I made it clear to them that they might face Mundan, which meant that they would have to shave off all their hair, which most of the hippies were not exactly enthusiastic about.

On the subject of marriage

Babaji knew our Karmas, and here he led and helped us. Thus, for example, he often married people to one another. By means of the theme "marriage," he managed in the shortest time possible to bring to the surface a great deal of unconscious material in the persons involved.

On one occasion he proposed to a Westerner, who already had a girlfriend in Germany, that he should marry an Indian woman, an idea that he resisted. Everything in him struggled against this and it became clear to him that he in no way wanted to adhere to the will of Babaji. Babaji also convinced him how easy it is to care for Indian women. For weeks the young man went through a deep inner process. When he was finally ready and understood that it was a matter of real surrender and trust in Babaji, then all discussion about this marriage was at an end.

Basically, all marriages inspired by Babaji were full of explosive material – sometimes beautiful Karma and sometimes very difficult Karma.

To a young woman of about 40, who had never been married, he intimated that it was high time. She explained to me that she needed someone who would take care of her.

At that point Babaji gave her a number of little dogs to take care of. In this first act of "marriage," of binding oneself, in this case with all the dogs, she landed in my room with them.

Babaji then announced that she would be married on Shivaratri. Rich Indians came and she admitted to Babaji who of them she would like to marry. He ignored this and held her in the utmost suspense, then explained to her that her husband would be the Pujari from a holy place. The Pujari in question arrived. To her horror she saw that he had only one eye and looked extremely lowly. Her heart sank.

Babaji then called her to himself at the front. Beforehand, she had had to make Mundan in preparation for this wedding, sacrificing her long hair. As she now kneeled before him, he took a brush and painted a large OM on her bald head. Now it became clear that inwardly she should be wedded to OM namah Shivay, to merge with it.

A pretty young woman, who lived in my room for a few days, told me indignantly that so far Babaji had not looked at her even once. When she arrived, he had only looked at her bracelet and not at her, and had asked from whom she had the bracelet. It was from her friend in Germany who was very important to her.

One day she lit a cigarette in the belief that, in any case, Babaji was not bothered about her. Whack, he gave her a slap in the face. It made her realize that her whole being revolved around her friend, that she was not interested in finding God or her inner light and her self. Babaji had mirrored her own inner situation back to her.

A bright young American man, who was married in the valley by Babaji in 1976 to a young woman whom he loved very much, had returned. The relationship had broken up, to his great disappointment. He said to me: "There is only one thing that makes me really nervous, that is when Babaji starts talking about marriage again."

Babaji's finger would sweep over the people present and stop at someone: "You…" and then the finger would move on again along the row, "You marry…" and then land at one of those present: "… this one!"

Babaji's game, apparently full of humour, was profoundly deep.

Our American friend saw Babaji's finger point at him: "You marry…" and his face became pale – "Shastriji!" (see page 153). This meant: He should wed the wisdom, the love and the knowledge of Shastriji, and also much more, which only the person affected would discover for himself. One could understand his great relief.

I can recall from the early years in Herakhan a beautiful and inwardly very strong young woman, full of devotion to God. Years later she had bound herself to a partner, and I got a real shock when I saw her as she came to Babaji. There was only half of her radiant energy and depth left. At the moment this became clear to me, a candy flew across to me from Babaji, as confirmation.

This woman had clearly become deeply bound into the web of partnership and was involved with this and not, as before, freely focussed on God.

After many years I saw her again. She had got herself out of this marriage and was once again strong and clear. She was again completely composed within herself, and was possibly even more deeply and inwardly bound to God than before.

Projection marriages, even when the partner fills the sky, always call for transformation and liberation when a person wants to realize himself and God.

Through my own life I have come to understand how important it is to put God in first place, and then the partner, and when both the partners always try to live by putting God and his will first, then it will be a glowing partnership. God is love – love without conditions. What can be more beautiful than to be married with love, when soul binds itself with soul, and where primarily everything does not take place in the realm of the egos.

The marriages in Herakhan or in Chilianaula, Babaji's ashram in the mountains founded by Muniraji, are performed according to a Vedic ritual and always very festive. They take place then, as now, after the tenth fire ceremony of the spring or autumn Navaratris or after the fire ceremony on Christmas Day. Then the pair, dressed in festive costume and decorated, and bound together, for example by a sash, step together around the fire and receive the blessing of Babaji, nowadays through Muniraj.

The drummer

One day in Herakhan a huge drum arrived, some 2 meters in diameter, and when it was drummed with great energy during the morning Arati, it suddenly dawned on me, "Oh, The Drummer" – a one man play which I had written in Berlin when I was 21 years old, and which I had performed at the Academy of Visual Arts in Berlin and other locations. It was entirely inspired by Babaji.

Now it was as if the scales had fallen from my eyes and I could see that it was he who had written it through me, so I painted the words, "To you my Lord – the Drummer!" on a large piece of white paper and gave it to Babaji as a scroll.

At that time I slept in a tent on the Gufa side at the foot of Kailash, near by the place where the temples stood.

All around was wilderness. At Babaji's request I had made a heart-shaped plant bed in this wilderness with a seat in front of it for him. In the night I woke up. It was full moon. Everything shone wonderfully. When I went to his heart bed, I saw to my astonishment that something white was lying there, which had definitely not been there in the evening.

It was the scroll, which I had given to Babaji that morning up in the ashram on the other side of the river, with the inscription: "To you my Lord – the Drummer." And now I found it here on this night of the full moon in my heart bed created for Babaji!

Babaji, the drummer, he is the heartbeat of the world.

"Drummer, you drum your life
through Cities and Deserts" *(SEE APPENDIX, PAGE 122)*

My burden is light

Babaji was sitting on the little wall above his Kutiya, his small room, and I bowed deeply before him. I felt two very light touches on my back and as I righted myself again, Babaji was no longer to be seen. How was that possible?

Radhe Shyam, an American who had been standing nearby, had observed this: "Babaji climbed down over your back." And he asked: "Do you know Handel's Messiah, the aria – My burden is light?"

Horatio

One day, while Babaji was playing with a child, he said to him repeatedly "Horeshio!" He then said it to a few of us.

At first no one understood what he meant by this Horeshio until it suddenly dawned on someone: "Ah, that comes from Shakespeare. He means Horatio, the friend of Hamlet who sailed through everything as if free from destiny, whilst Hamlet, as a person wrestling with matters deep within himself, was involved in everything."

Babaji also called me to him. I was at that moment standing on a ladder painting. He looked at me very intensely and said: "You Horeshio!"– and made me aware of a special issue in my life.

Service

Slowly it dawned on me that everything was concerned with serving! Babaji had said of himself: "I have only come to serve all beings!"

So I went to Babaji, kneeled down in front of him, overcame my inner resistance and asked him: "How can I best serve you?"

He pulled a horrible grimace and asked: "Serve?" reflecting exactly what I was feeling inside at that moment. I was afraid that because of the demands of serving, I would possibly not be able to do the things that I really liked to do! Thank God that in fact the opposite was the case.

My first evening meal with Muniraj

It was February 1979. I brought Babaji one of my most important books: *The Alchemical Marriage of Christian Rosenkreutz,* and then I asked him a question which was moving me: "Was Muniraj Christian Rosenkreutz?" His answer was "Yes!" and he gave the book back to me.

On my next stay in Haldwani I greeted Muniraji in his office in Patel Chowk. He invited me to supper in his home. That was the first occasion. We ate alone as his wife was fasting at that time.

Afterwards I showed him the book of *The Alchemical Marriage of Christian Rosenkreutz* and explained to him that, to my question to Babaji, "Was Muniraj Christian Rosenkreutz?" he had said: "Yes!" I showed him the picture at the front of the book. But Muniraj shook his head negatively.

Only much later did I understand that Muniraji's shaking of his head was only directed at the picture itself. I personally had always had the feeling that Christian Rosenkreutz looked completely different, but had not had the courage to trust this inner feeling completely.

Thereafter, the knowledge of the true identity of Muniraj was again hidden from me as if by a divine veil. The time had not yet come for me to realize its importance. I knew it and I did not know it at the same time.

In front of Babaji's cave

It was February 1979. I knelt in front of Babaji at the entrance to the cave where he had appeared at the foot of Kailash. He looked at me and said: "You Parvati. You Gaura Devi. You Lord Shiva's wife."

OM namah Shivay! How should I understand this?

For God's sake, do not become self-important! At first I could only take it in by thinking that somehow the entire creation is "Lord Shiva's Wife," and that Parvati might be incarnated in different forms of expression of herself within the creation, each of which is a particle of the great Goddess.

The blessing of teamwork

We painted, several of us on this occasion, at a temple on the side of Kailash. Those whom Babaji had allocated to me were all inexperienced at painting, and I helped each one of them with a great sense of joy.

There was a wonderful atmosphere between us. We worked hand in hand on the outside of the temple. Afterwards Babaji said: "This was lovely work!"

Desire has precedence

We were in the valley and, with others, I was following Babaji. An idea came to me about a particular gift that I would like to make for Babaji.

He was walking very slowly. When we came to the stairway with 108 steps, I was in a great hurry with my good idea. At the edge of the stairway Babaji stood still and spread his arms: "Please, you go!" and let me pass by.

During my speedy climb it became clear to me what he had demonstrated to me: "Please, desire has precedence!"

Bang

It was early in 1979 that Babaji took some of us Westerners with him to Brindavan. What a beautiful experience it was, being received with respect and love everywhere along the way as Babaji's companions.

In Brindavan, Krishna's enchanting city, there was a temple with a renowned and very powerful Murti (statue) of Babaji in the form of the old Herakhan Baba. Babaji wanted everyone to spend the whole day in the great hall of the temple: singing and meditating. In addition, all the western women were to wear saris.

Now I had never before in my life worn a sari. There were enough shops with saris, but my focus was totally on something else: I was filled with a shining vision of the old Herakhan Baba, which I absolutely wanted to paint.

So I found myself a large piece of paper and while all the others went to the temple, I painted this vision in the peaceful Youth Hostel where we were staying. I spent the whole day alone and collected, in total quiet.

I wanted to bring the picture to Babaji at the evening Darshan. In order that the delicate chalks were not smudged, I arranged first for it to be framed in a small shop. Something in me could already see the picture in the hall where the singing was taking place, high up on the empty wall. In the evening I went with the framed picture to Babaji.

"Where were you?" he greeted me.

"I have been painting for you" was my reply and as I went to give the big framed painting to him, he said: "I want to give it back to you!"

That was fatal. Oh my goodness, where could I put the picture, since we were on a journey? At the same time he tugged at my silk scarf and skirt: "I don't like this – you do not follow my instructions!" Oh! I had not taken it in the least bit seriously that we should wear saris, and had given just as little attention to his order to sing for the whole day in the temple, but had even so felt myself very deeply and inwardly bound to him.

What was I to do with the picture now? As I stood there so concerned, Babaji helped me …thank God! He said: "You can give it to Mataji," a very fine elderly woman dressed in white, who was sitting right at the front. Later I heard that she was really happy with it and thought it beautiful.

Later Babaji shared out oranges at the front. I sat further back in the enormous hall full of people. Everything was working inside me. Then Babaji threw an orange through the whole room and it landed – bang – on my head. Now the tears started to flow. It was simply too much!

Christmas in Herakhan

"It is of special significance that Christmas is celebrated greatly in the Himalayas," Babaji said and added:
"There is only one religion and that is humanity. Be humane!"

Christmas 1982 in Herakhan, Babaji with Nila

It was Christmas Eve. There were night lights on each of the 108 steps. Everything was very festively decorated and the whole valley appeared to shine as well. At the foot of Kailash on the Gufa side an enormous tent had been erected. Christmas was to be celebrated there.

Everyone had already made their way there. I was still up in the ashram and kneeling in front of the temple with the Murti of the old Herakhan Baba. I was deep in prayer to the Father, thanking Him for sending himself as son down to earth. At that moment Babaji stood next to me and said very lovingly: "Nilaji." I thought that he had gone over to the Kailash side long before.

At first, just Indian songs were sung at the Christmas celebrations. I asked Muniraj, next to whom, to my joy, I sat for part of the evening, why there were no western Christmas Carols. He answered: "Christmas is for everyone," and then in the latter part of the evening there were indeed western Christmas Carols.

On the next morning, Christmas Day, a large fire ceremony took place. Babaji hung his Christmas mala round me. It was made entirely of red roses.

What love, what sweetness, what light!

Warm clothing was shared out among the villagers, and many people from the surrounding mountains, especially numerous children, partook of the great Christmas bandara, the midday meal.

A mysterious place

Once Sheela went for a walk with me out of the back of the ashram in the direction of Siddeshwar. The route was a high one, and led down to a marvellous tree in the valley.

Babaji had said "That is the Jesus tree," explained Sheela.

From here we walked down further into the valley, the area between Mt. Kailash and Mt. Siddheshwar, about which Babaji had told her that there, below the earth, very sublime yogis were living in the highest bliss. There were the most beautiful fruits, the best that the earth has to offer. They lived there in the greatest of plenty and bliss.

I was deeply moved as that is exactly what is said of the Holy Grail in *Parsifal* (a book by Wolfram von Eschenbach):

"The Grail:
The earthborn supernatural
the overflowing of the terrestrial."

A recognition in Danyan

Babaji took a number of us with him on a journey into the mountains. We first went to Danyan. When we got out of the small bus and went on foot through the beautiful pine forest, I had a clear sense of having been here before.

Arriving at the country home of Swami Fakiranand in Danyan, Babaji said to me: "You work!" I felt as if I should remain still and turn within. Everything seemed very familiar to me here.

The next day, Babaji arranged for me to be led into a particular room, a small room. In it there stood only a high bed, beautifully made up, and I sat on the ground in front of it. I immediately was aware of the presence of the Old Herakhan Baba, and I knew spontaneously that I had sat on his lap here as a small girl.

I ran to Babaji and said: "Is it true that I met you here in another life? In your previous form as the Old Herakhan Baba?" Babaji said: "You ask Swamiji."

Later, I asked the aged Swamiji and he confirmed that he knew the little girl from his childhood and said: "Her name was Devaki. And always when old Herakhan Baba came, he took her onto his lap." I asked him: "How was he with her then?" He said: "He was very sweet."

On Babaji's stage

Herakhan was also a stage on which all who came performed a role. The people changed, but the roles remained.

Fakiruli said: "Come on, let us see Babaji's theatre this evening."

On this evening we truly experienced a theatrical performance. In this, the Pujari, a little old man who served the Shiva temple in the ashram, was supposed to get married to an older and extremely dynamic Indian woman. He had no desire to get married – and she apparently did, very much so! He just wanted to take to his heels so she chased wildly after him, And Babaji at the front laughed and laughed.

Behind all the fun however, something deeper clearly seemed to be going on.

Every evening was truly a festivity, full of energy and unique every time as a result of his presence and of what happened. Always Babaji touched the heart of everyone present, each in a very different way.

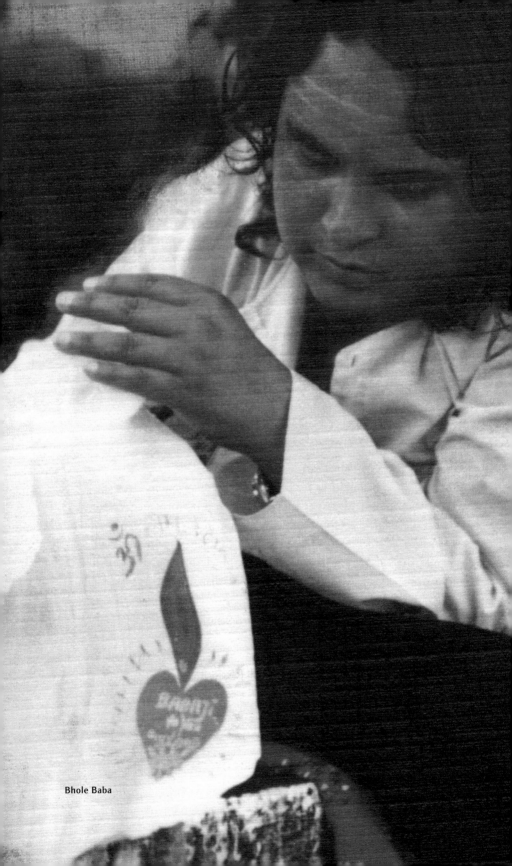

Bhole Baba

Divine lights in the valley

In those first years, 1978 and 1979 in particular, one often saw certain lights in the valley at dusk. They were either a light bluish or orange colour and sometimes they spun in spirals. It was fascinating to gaze into the valley and see these lights. In the later years, when many more people came, they were no longer visible. Later I learned that they were divine beings: the light blue ones more divine male aspects and the orange ones more aspects of the Divine Mother.

One evening, at the time of the Arati, when I went outside and looked up towards Kailash, I saw that above the entire middle part of Kailash, the heart region, there was an enormous square of light, which remained there for some 20 minutes.

Others saw it as well. We could only marvel and wonder at it. What might be happening there?

Babaji plays the violin

In February 1979, some of us were in Gora Devi's room with Babaji. Somebody had given Babaji a violin and I was full of the happy expectation that I would hear him play something beautiful.

What happened then was that while we were listening to him play, he looked at us intently and brought forth diffuse sounds from the violin as if to show us. "This is what I hear from within you! These are the vibrations that you emit. This is how it sounds."

He had used the bow more to scratch about on the violin than to play it.

What is my task?

To my question: "What is my task. What should I do?" Babaji answered: "What you really like in your heart – this you should do!" I feel that this is Babaji's answer to everyone with this question.

As for me, I wanted to help people find the way to their centre, their true self. So I began to create various workshops on self-discovery and self-development. When I went to Babaji again after successfully starting with this work, he said: "Tell me what you do!" "But you know it, you inspire it!" I said. But he wanted me to describe it.

It was precisely what he had said to me on the first day we met. To his question about what I did, I had replied: "I paint and I am in the process of developing a painting therapy for people." His answer then was: "Then you treat me!"

And it was just that which I did in the seminars and workshops through all sorts of creative exercises: to make each one aware of the divine light and being within themselves. Through painting, drawing, modelling, breathing, and by imaginative exercises and guided journeys within, to rediscover the source of joy and strength and thereby transform fear, obstacles and resistances.

Question time with Babaji

A few of the really very nice Westerners and I had many questions in our hearts. But when I for instance wanted to ask Babaji something, he was most often up and away. Clearly the purpose was to learn, to receive what in that moment he wanted to give us, and to leave behind the questioning mind.

One midday he declared: "This afternoon we will meet in front of the cave at the side of Kailash and you can ask me whatever you want."

Full of happy expectation we set off, sat on stones in a circle around Babaji, around us mostly wilderness.

Babaji said: "Now you can ask me."

Someone began to pose a question:

"What is the Kriya Yoga of today for our time?"

Babaji's answer: "OM namah Shivay. Bas. – OM namah Shivay. That's it!"

What happened then is that we were all floating in bliss, and all our questions were washed away in it.

Strange, I really could not remember a single one of the questions any more, although I had had a whole list of them. It was the same for the others.

There was simply the unbounded joy of being, and of being with him.

That was Babaji's question time.

Shiva, the merciful

On another occasion, it was at the beginning of February 1984, Babaji had unexpectedly called us up to him away from our work.

I was standing in the row and in front of me were three people waiting: One had only one leg, the other only one arm and the third only one ear. I heard Babaji say humorously: "Look at my devotees! Vishnu would never have such devotees."

Shiva, the great God, is known for the fact that in his love he receives everyone of pure heart.

The beggar

Gopiji, a very mature and beautiful Indian woman told me that one day, as she was being driven by a chauffeur in her car through Bombay, a beggar came and stood at her window when they stopped at a traffic light, and looked at her with a deep, intensive gaze.

After half an hour's journey through Bombay, she arrived at her garage. The same beggar was standing there. How could this be possible? He looked at her penetratingly. Then it began to dawn on her who it was.

Later, when she asked Babaji if he had been the beggar, he replied: "YES." Only she alone can know what Babaji's appearing as a beggar was meant to tell her.

Babaji's luggage

One day Babaji let me carry a bag for him on my head, on my thousand-petalled lotus. It was not heavy and I had no idea what was in it.

Arriving down below in the valley, in the Dhuni, the holy fireplace, he asked for his bag and started to unpack it. In it was the white sheep's wool rug, which I had just given him as a present to sit on. In addition there were numerous beautiful little velvet handkerchiefs in the brightest of colours... red, blue, green, yellow, orange, violet.

And he had the most delicious sweets and nuts as Prasad for us all in it. I understood: On the thousand-petalled lotus, there you are sitting, Babaji, on your shepherd's fleece with all the glowing colours and delicious sustenance for us all.

The white sari

For my 40th birthday Babaji sent me to the Ganges at Haridwar. Before, in 1978, a day after I had arrived, he had said to me: "Go to the Ganges at Haridwar tomorrow and bring the water back with you, without losing a drop."

On that occasion he had wanted to send an Indian with me to accompany me, but it never came to that, which I was not unhappy about as it was my first day there and my first time ever with Babaji.

This time my companion was a German who would journey back to Herakhan, while I was to travel on to Delhi to catch my return flight to Germany.

There is a lovely custom in Haridwar of letting little flower boats with a light in them sail down the Ganges. I did this on my birthday and was very happy to see that the little boat sailed for a long, long way without sinking.

It was wonderful and at the same time dangerous, to bathe in the wild, strong Ganges. One had to hold on fast to the rails submerged in the water in order not to be swept away.

In happiness and gratitude for having come to know this very special place with its strong atmosphere, I obtained a beautiful snow-white sari for Babaji. My German companion took the sari back with him to Herakhan and later told me that Babaji wound it around himself immediately and wore it in a great variety of ways for many hours so that my friend came to the conclusion: "This sari must be associated with something very special."

Many years later I read that in Haridwar, before the beginning of time, there had taken place a great sacrificial fire of King Daksha, the father of Sati.

Sati had descended from the highest realm, the eternal, in order to be married to Shiva. It was her very first incarnation on the Earth. She was a complete stranger here.

Even though King Daksha gave his daughter to be married to the God Shiva in a great festive act, he was still somehow at odds with Shiva. So he had not invited Shiva and Sati to be present at this great sacrificial fire. Sati saw all the other wonderfully attired divinities on their way there, and decided to go too.

Shiva warned her: "Don't go!" but she was not to be stopped and went anyway.

Even before she was born she had let her father King Daksha know:

"I can only stay with you on Earth for as long as you respect me."

During the great fire sacrifice, through yogic power and to the horror of everyone present, Sati dissolved her physical body in flames.

Before she departed, she turned to her father: "You did not respect me, in that you did not invite Shiva and me. Therefore I must go. But something of me will remain as a divine light in all beings."

Shiva was out of himself.

The myth tells that Shiva bore Sati's body over all the mountains for thousands of years, and another myth that he strewed her ashes in various places in India.

Sati, the completely pure, white innocence.

It is my understanding that Babaji expressed this event by means of the white sari, in that he wound the white sari, the expression of Sati, in all variations around himself, thereby expressing his love for her.

Highly indignant

I was on the Gufa side of the temple at the foot of Kailash, engaged in painting the lower part of the outside wall with finely matched colours. Having first worked at great speed, I now wanted to take somewhat more time and paint with great consideration so that every brush stroke became an OM namah Shivay.

Babaji arrived just at that moment: "You slowly paint!" And that to me, who had up until now made such rapid and intensive progress! Of course, I immediately began to paint faster.

The next morning Babaji came again, looked at the painted wall and said: "This not yet finished?" "Babaji, it is impossible!" I was highly indignant. It was an unbelievable amount of work and I had painted from morning until it had become dark.

Within an instant he was gone. I looked for him. He was sitting on a simple little bench, from where he had a wide view into the valley. He was peace personified.

Full of indignation, I stormed up to him and repeated: "That is really humanly impossible!" He had challenged me to the extreme, despite my always working very quickly indeed.

Babaji smiled lovingly at my high indignation and then explained that I should make a flowerbed in front of his little bench. "This is my seat here!"

His seat is in the heart. So it became clear to me that I would create a heart bed here for him. Round about there was only wilderness and I did my best to make the new flowerbed as beautiful as possible for Babaji.

A caramel candy

"You will get sick," Babaji informed me one day, and I was surprised: "How can that be, when I am in your grace?"

In the hot April sun I went up to Kailash again, this time with Mundan but without a covering for my head.

On my descent, halfway down Kailash, I found a large, heavy stone in the shape of a heart, which I carried down for the heart flowerbed for Babaji. As a result I was totally exhausted and so thirsty that I could have drunk the Gautam Ganga dry. A very kind Indian came and offered me a special drink of green herbs which he had prepared himself. I was very pleased, but was startled when, while drinking, I noticed how cold it was.

I felt an inner warning, "STOP! Don't drink it!" But in my thirst I emptied the glass at a single draught.

Then I felt very sick. Shortly afterwards I had a high fever, diarrhoea and terrible vomiting. In addition I had sunstroke as I had climbed up Kailash in this heat without a head covering. In no time at all I was weak and wretched. I dragged myself to Babaji: "Please heal me!"

"No!" he said with great energy. His "no" remarkably gave me strength and the insight that the entire thing had come about because I had been careless with my body.

The next morning I still could not retain anything, not even black tea. In the meantime I had become so weak that I could hardly climb a step.

Thereupon someone brought me a huge caramel candy at Babaji's behest. I had never seen such a huge candy. "He sends you this."

My mind naturally thought: "Oh, how can I eat something sweet at the moment?" but in my heart I knew that the candy from Babaji would only bring a blessing. And that is how it was:

After eating it, I was fit again very quickly and could make my return journey, since my visa was expiring.

Mikado with Muniraj

Babaji was on the roof terrace with many very official looking Indian people. Were they politicians? Babaji was busy with them.

Muniraj was there, and so, by chance, was I. It occurred to me that I had a game of Mikado with me and so I suggested to Muniraj: "Let's play Mikado together in the meantime," and so Muniraj and I began to play.

I was amazed that Muniraj only took a stick away when it lay completely free, whereas I risked everything in order to free up sticks and consequently suffered losses.

At first I thought: "This game is so boring, if one doesn't risk anything." But later it dawned on me that Muniraj was showing me how he works. He does not interfere, love bestows freedom – he lets everything unfold. He only steps in when it is necessary for the benefit of the whole, when Babaji gives him the impulse.

Babaji and children

Babaji played with children in a wonderful and enchanting way. He let them slide on him, up and down, sometimes pulling the wildest faces in the process, and then he kissed and hugged them and showed us that children really do need warmth and closeness.

There came a man, in every respect big, of great soul, large stature and enormous weight, who longed very much to be able for once to sit on Babaji's lap and to be loved by him like a child.

Early one morning, as I went up to our roof terrace, I saw Babaji lying under a blanket with this great big lovable man, fondly cuddling his head to his chest.

Individual treatment

Sheela, a highly intelligent and loving Indian woman, who always played the harmonium and sang so beautifully all morning, told us how at a particular point in her playing and singing, Babaji said: "Now you go and fire up your engine," which meant, "Now you can have a smoke."

So, for one it was ok to smoke, for others not.

Even though there were general rules, Babaji treated each person absolutely individually.

An outsider

One evening, in the middle of the evening singing, an unusual looking man entered, with wild blond curls, in thick black shoes and apparently clothed in only a black raincoat.

Whilst everyone stared with horror at his thick black shoes, which one should in any case remove immediately upon entering the ashram, Babaji shouted to him from a distance: "I like you!"

During conversation later, I realized that he was a very unconventional and lively man. He was simply an innocent and had no knowledge of ashram rules. That was o.k. for the evening, but as he wandered around the next day still in his shoes, Babaji taught him very clearly.

Babaji plays with words

Sometimes, when we asked Babaji, "May I come to Chandan tomorrow?" he would answer:

"Two-morrow!"

On another occasion:

"Three-morrow!"

Babaji played with words in an extremely creative and unique way. The messages, which were delivered in telegram style, were very pithy and multidimensional.

For example, he repeatedly said to me: "You Philippine no. 4," or "You Philippine no. 2," which apparently had to do with spiritual healing. The Vedas talk of seven different heavens, levels from which healing can be carried out.

Then smiling, he turned the "Philippine no. so and so," into a "philippaint," saying: "You Philippaint!" This was a way to express the healing that comes through painting, through my painted pictures and certainly also through paint therapy with others.

Mercy

In a dream, I encountered Babaji on the way up the mountain. Every time that I called out to Babaji he was instantly present with all his blissfulness and power.

And again in the dream my soul went to him and was given a deeply meaningful answer. On this occasion he did something extremely mysterious, it was an occult event:

We were now at the middle of a mountain made up of different layers. There was water below, an ocean full of waves. What Babaji did next, happened because I longed so much for the Divine. He opened up the layered mountain; it was the mountain of the Karma of mankind. It appeared to me to be a mountain in Jerusalem that held the Karma of the whole of mankind in the form of layers of stone or stone slabs.

He took out my layer of stone and five times, using a chalice (a cup), he extracted from it extremely strong essences of different colours. Each time he filled the chalice and then emptied it into the ocean below, I felt infinitely touched and could hardly bear it in my heart, it went so deep. I knew that he was dissolving Karma.

At the end he said: "One theme still I must leave you." And he told me what it was about.

The fire swami recognizes Babaji

Shri Ganapati Satchidananda from Mysore in southern India was again visiting us in Germany. We call him the fire swami because on particular occasions, such as Shivaratri, he places himself right in the middle of the fire and remains completely unscathed: The fire does not burn him.

Furthermore, whatever he is inspired to do at a particular moment gets materialized: holy ash (vibuthi), amulets and much more for the blessing for the people. We had experienced quite a bit of this when he was visiting us. Marcel and I had first got to know him one night in April 1975 when he appeared as a pillar of light in our room.

Now, because he was again our guest, I felt it very important to tell him about Babaji in the hope that he would understand why I had not visited him in India and why I had to go to Babaji as the Lord of my mountain.

Without saying much, I simply showed him the book called "Omkareshwar" that Babaji had painted and given me. I asked: "Swamiji, who was the painter?" He leafed through, page by page and was silent.

"Who was the painter?" I asked again – and added: "I didn't paint it!"

When he came to the last page, which carried the picture of the new world, his finger pointed to the figure in the picture, which was an expression of Babaji himself. Drawing a deep breath, he said: "Lord Shiva!"

I was happy that Babaji had revealed himself to him, and that Swamiji had immediately and completely understood. Then I showed him the book about the first twelve days with Babaji in Herakhan, which I had painted at home. Beaming, he held the book between his hands and said: "Beautiful experience – I know it all."

February 5

February 1979. I had arrived the day before, and Babaji, sitting on the wall, said to me: "Today is the initiation day of Jesus!" It was February 5.

At that time, I was greatly surprised to hear of Jesus in Herakhan in the Himalayas. Through my friend Marcel, who was able to perceive the inner levels, I knew that the earth was repeatedly permeated by pulses of light. Teilhard de Chardin and the «Mother» of the Shri Aurobindo ashram have also described this, and how over the centuries there have repeatedly been witnesses to these events. Every material object that is totally permeated by light becomes indestructible.

Through his intensive inner analysis of when this had occurred for the first time, Marcel came to the conclusion that it was at the time of Jesus.

Everyone who reaches enlightenment knows exactly when he had experienced his initial enlightenment. But it still requires years or several incarnations to become fully enlightened. And it is the same with mankind, of which we all are a part: After mankind has experienced its initial enlightenment, a long time is still required until it becomes fully enlightened.

What Marcel discovered through his long analysis and looking within, is that the initial enlightenment of mankind occurred at the moment that John the Baptist baptized Jesus in the Jordan. The waters rose up in rapture as the spirit of God descended.

The whole stands above parts, and whenever a light pulse permeates mankind, the whole of mankind, then we as its component parts, are automatically filled with more light.

Jesus represented the whole.

Thus it is my understanding that Babaji revealed that February 5, the day of the initiation of Jesus, was also the great day of the initial enlightenment of mankind.

Ascent of Kailash with Babaji

Shortly afterwards – it was on a Sunday – Babaji decided to go to Kailash and take ten or twelve of us with him. He was dressed in wonderful fire-blue silk, an ultramarine blue, the colour of Bhairav Baba.

Babaji chose the vertical path up to Kailash, not the slower way alongside the spring that I knew. It was very demanding to have to climb so steeply. Babaji explained at many places what it was:

"This is the royal queen road!"

"This is the royal horse tower!"

"This is the royal mouse path!"

It was inspiring: In my heart I understood, but not with my mind, and it was the same for the others. On this day, because of the demanding climb, I reached the limit of my strength. Then Babaji took a fruit from a tree, sucked on it and gave it to me. The fruit was bitter. Thereafter, my energy returned.

Arriving at the summit, it was clearly intended that a fire ceremony should take place, and then food, Prasad, was to be shared out.

I was extremely astounded at this. Such activity at this most holy place of profound stillness? On my first ascent, eternity had greeted me here.

Babaji did indeed carry out a fire ceremony on this Sunday up here. Afterwards, everybody was given a piece of a wonderful bread cake. Only later did I learn that a fire ceremony was performed on Kailash every Sunday to honour Bhairav Baba (pronounced: Beru Baba). Sunday is the day of the great healer and transformer, whose picture, which he himself had painted, Babaji had given me in 1978. Bhairav Baba is the main power, the right hand of Lord Shiva. He destroys evil and protects good.

Afterwards, when people began their descent, I wanted at least to feel something of the power of the stillness and to remain up there a little longer. Thus it came about that I descended together with Babaji. All the others were far ahead.

We descended the first half of the mountain together. What an intense experience! Sometimes I lost my footing. Babaji always waited for me patiently.

Then he suddenly shot off downwards like a rocket. It was breathtaking. He hardly seemed to touch the ground, whereas I continued to descend slowly and carefully. On making this descent together, Babaji had relieved me of some of the great sadness that I had felt on having to leave the summit.

The book of the transformation of OM

In 1979 I had brought Babaji two blank books, one of which was more like a writing block. "In which one should I paint for you?" he asked me.

"In the one with the leather binding." I said.

He began to paint beautiful pictures with watercolours and much gold colour in the book. Each picture on its own held a great deal of meaning. One could call it *The book of the transformation of OM*. On almost every picture he placed the OM at the top in Sanskrit and he transformed the OM very considerably:

Is this a sign that the creation will be absorbed by the creator and emerge anew?

About prophecies

When Babaji made prophecies through people who could intuitively express what he had given them with, for example through Shastriji, he was acting as a cosmic physician.

As a physician he saw the state of the world, how it was, and let it be said, he knew what would happen as a necessary consequence.

But as a physician he also gave us the medicine for healing.

Babaji let us know what would have happened if the divine mercy had not intervened, but which can only intervene when the human being calls upon the divine mercy, and when he is prepared to change himself and his life and to serve the Divine.

For example, as medicine he gave us: OM namah Shivay, the name of God, which we should repeat continually. In addition to live in truth, simplicity and love, and to perform Karma Yoga, which means to do one's best to act in love, without being attached to the outcome.

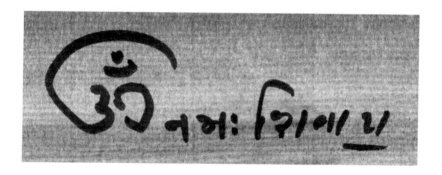

Babaji's footprints

February 1979. In the meantime a few more Westerners had arrived. We were all housed in two adjoining rooms, men and women together. Only later it became clear to us that this was the group of people who were the first ones to found centres. Incidentally, since 1980, as so many people were coming from the west, men and women were accommodated separately in additionally constructed rooms.

Babaji allowed his footprints to be made, which is an emotionally moving procedure the first time one experiences it! Kumkum, red powder, was mixed with water in a big basin and paper made ready. First Babaji put his feet in the water basin and then onto the paper, which I had laid down in front of him.

What had been portrayed was wonderful. With the first print a red blot appeared between the two feet on the paper and his heels were not completely on it, but I was so enchanted I did not see these as blemishes.

The following footprints were produced perfectly and he distributed them among us. He had asked me: "Which one do you want?" "The first one," I said, because it had touched me so spontaneously. He gave me this picture and a perfect footprint in addition.

He said: "When heaven breaks apart, and there is hell on Earth, people will run from here to there!" and pointed at the red blot which ran from one foot to the other. Then he said to me with a penetrating, fiery look: "Philippine No. 4." So I understood that people will run to the places where healing takes place.

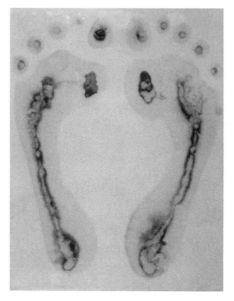

Babaji's footprint

Mundan

With two or three of us Westerners, Babaji began to snip away at our hair or beards. With me he created a flat fringe with a strange cut over the ears.

A long time later, in Brazil, I saw that the Xavante Indians have just such a hair-cut. This shaving of the head was apparently all a preparation for Mundan, which followed shortly afterwards.

With Babaji, sooner or later everyone had to go through this process. He want-ed to free us from our adherences. Saturn is in the hair, the principle of contraction and attachment. In our giving up our hair, he relieved us of much of this. At first, Babaji told each individual when he should make Mundan. Later, when large numbers came, he simply said in the warm times of the year: "Tomorrow everybody air-conditioner" which meant that tomorrow everyone should make Mundan. In many cultures it is a normal custom to shave one's own head as a means of cleansing the character. Mundan is an act of healing.

With Mundan, everyone has something of a newborn baby about them. One feels like a raw egg. I was embarrassed walking about so naked and tied a cloth round my head. Babaji came striding along the valley: "Show!" So I removed the cloth and he touched my head very gently with a staff and smiled radiantly. Not having a hat, I was soon walking again with the cloth around my head, not just because of the cold but also because I felt too unprotected.

One day Babaji came into our bedroom, sat on one of the sleeping bags, and explained to us that Mundan allows the head to generate a lot of light and that in ancient times, when there was no electricity, people practiced Mundan in order to produce light in their caves. A head covering, though, would hide this light.

"Why didn't you say that straightaway?" I asked Babaji, because if I had known this, I would not have worn the cloth the whole time. "It would have been too early!" he answered lovingly.

Mundan was very important with Babaji. If not all were able to do it – then the rule was: "One for all."

For example, Babaji told Sheela, who had already made Mundan 30 times: "You do this on behalf of other Indian ladies who cannot do this."

Painting at the temple of the Divine Mother

Babaji led us to the Kailash side of the temple, but it was no longer a total wilderness there as it had been a year ago. Now there were two temples in the process of being built. This was February 1979. One temple for the Divine Mother and directly beside it another one for the Divine Couples of Rama with Sita and Krishna with Radha.

Indian helpers had painted the enormous domes of the temple of the Divine Mother in all conceivable colours. I said: "Babaji, there shouldn't be so many colours for the Divine Mother, rather it should be completely golden." He looked at me and said: "You all golden!"

I arranged for golden powder to be sent from Delhi and, on two enormous ladders bound together and held by four Indians, I began to paint both the domes: In one hand a broad paintbrush and in the other the bucket with the powdered gold suspended in a special liquid.

At these dizzy heights I had nothing to hold on to, only the feeling of balance in my body. Whilst climbing up, I did not feel balanced at all. I was frightened. Like a shot, Joshi, one of the Indians, suddenly shouted: "How can you fear? Babaji is with you!"

Of course, Babaji was with me!

At once I lost all my fear and began to paint the outside of this very high and wide dome in a golden colour. In the process I had to keep moving the ladder a bit at a time. I knew that this was a kind of test of my courage, set by Babaji. As time progressed I felt so sure of myself that I even climbed up during strong winds. It seemed to me like a swaying dance on the ladder.

Once a storm was approaching and someone whom Babaji had sent called to me from a distance: "Babaji says: Come down immediately!"

I had almost believed I could even outbalance a storm.

Nila painting high up on the temple domes

The first fire ceremony at the foot of the Herakhan-Kailash

Babaji was on his way to the inauguration of the temple of the Divine Mother and the temple of the Divine Couples at the foot of Herakhan-Kailash.

Babaji was driven through the Gautam Ganga River in a tall jeep with a number of others who held on to the jeep through the water. When Babaji saw me he lifted me up onto the bonnet, where I felt like his radiator mascot.

I wore his wonderful sky blue silk shirt and cloth as a skirt, which he himself had worn and given to me a few days previously. For a long time it was filled with his divine fragrance.

Both of the temples were inaugurated. I saw that not far away in the wilderness a large fireplace had been dug out. A form of rice mixture lay round about on banana leaves. It looked a bit like bird food, but I was pleased: "How wonderful! Now we'll sit at the fire with Babaji and will have something to eat." I had developed a real appetite after all the effort of painting and the fasting. So I sat down at the fire happily waiting for Babaji and all the others.

Babaji came, and to my astonishment a group made up just of men assembled! Pressed closely together, they sat there but clearly not for a pleasant meal. An Indian priest came to Babaji, gave me a look that could kill and said something to him. Babaji looked at me with a very intense gaze and sent him away.

It was clear to me that something very special was happening, but what, I did not know. I then just copied what the others did. The food was not for us, but was destined for the fire and was offered to the fire by those sitting around it.

At that time I had not myself experienced such a large fire ceremony and only knew Babaji's Havan, his daily fire ceremony in the darkness before the first light of dawn.

When everything had ended, Tara Devi, the wonderful old lady who was an anthroposophist from America and who had been with Babaji since 1972, rushed up to me: "You must be indescribably pure for Babaji to have allowed that. From ancient times it is forbidden for a young woman to make offerings to the fire. Babaji will now have all the Gods against him!"

I was deeply shocked!

Shortly thereafter, Babaji was walking beside me and was gentle and loving. In his hand he had a thick round package, which he gave to me.

To feel his love, his peace and his warmth was very calming for me, and also to know that he had given me a gift.

Later I saw that there was Chandan in the package, a wonderful fragrant yellow powder, which I then used for many years in the little temple, which I built six months later in our garden at home.

Fire ceremony at the foot of Mt. Kailash, Herakhan (1979)

The response of the Gods

On the evening of the same day I went once again to the fireplace at the foot of Kailash. There was wilderness all around. I bowed deeply and thanked God that I had been allowed to participate. Then I went through the valley up to the ashram. Arriving up above I suddenly noticed that I had a big wound on my left leg, which developed a growing white rim as I watched.

Shocked, I ran to Babaji: "Look! – look at it!" He replied: "Yes, I see."

Because it dawned on me why I had got it, I requested: "Draw everything out of me that is not yet completely pure."

"Okay" he said.

Shortly after I flew back to Germany, as my three month visa had expired. In Germany a doctor wanted to treat the wound with strong allopathic drugs or transfer me to a clinic, as she found the matter uncanny. I was not in favour of this at all, and instead found an alternative practitioner who did her best but without success.

In the meantime the wound had spread. Finally I drove to Dina Rees, a clairvoyant and very lively woman, who was also a professor of medicine. Her diagnosis was: "That was the Asiatic mosquito. Its bite causes death in a week, but the Lord had held his protecting hand over you."

But now she had no advice as to how the wound could be healed.

Inwardly I implored Babaji: "Help me!"

And in a dream he said: "Injections."

Shortly afterwards I heard of a doctor in our village who worked with electro acupuncture and who had apparently worked wonders with his injections. I went to him without delay: He tested Similium together with everything that I was lacking, and thanks to his many homeopathic injections I was finally healed.

OM namah Shivay!

Babaji takes everything upon himself

When I returned in 1980, Babaji was away on a journey. While waiting for him, as easily happens with the change of climate, I got a cold, but I went down into the valley to meet him on his return.

A large number of Westerners were gathered above, all waiting for him, and all inspired by Gabriele Wosien's first book about Babaji, which had been published in the intervening period.

Before, only the people whom Babaji had called in a dream or vision, or who had been told directly about him by a friend had come there.

In the meantime, in Germany, I had built a little temple in our garden, just as he had painted it. Babaji came riding through the valley and, apart from a small belly, he was slim. He had come from Bombay where he had apparently gathered with some very good devotees.

Having arrived up in the ashram, and after spending two hours with the many new Westerners, he had become round and heavy. Incredible!

All of us who came to him brought our own issues and problems with us, which were an expression of the issues and problems of the world. Babaji absorbed all of this, bore these burdens and transformed them all within his body.

A pictorial teaching

A friend who had come to Herakhan because of what I had told him, seemed unhappy. He was a fine, very nice person and I asked myself:

"What has got into him?"

In the rest break at midday Babaji told me to bring him down to him. Babaji was settled in a flat stone area in the garden and was supporting his face in his hands. He took a match and, whilst observing the friend, began to poke around in his left ear.

Then he took the matchstick out, had a look at it to see what he had fished out, and then, looking at the friend, laid the match aside, took another match with his other hand and, again watching the friend, started poking around in his right ear.

Once again he looked intently at the friend and at what he had fished out of his ear. He laid the match aside and said: "Now you can go!"

I was speechless.

Only later, when I heard from this friend about the lies some people in Delhi had told him about Babaji, did I suddenly understand what it was that Babaji had shown him. He had come to Herakhan with his ears full of dirt.

I am your help

Once again I was allowed to go walking in the valley with Babaji. When my shoulder bag fell to the ground, the entire contents spilled out: comb, soap, handkerchiefs, a split purse, coloured crayons, notebook. Everything lay spread across the stones on the ground.

I was very embarrassed and wanted to clear everything up as fast as possible. But then Babaji bent down and helped me: "I am your help!"

OM namah Shivay!

Honeycombs

Fakiruli and I were quartered together in the same room. In the morning, after she had had a very exciting night of dreams, she intended to give me a severe lecture: "Do you fear God? You have such a stern view of God within you. You always have to be perfect! God is love!" And she continued to talk in this way.

When, directly afterwards, I went to Babaji who was sitting up in the ashram in the garden on his stone seat and bowed down to him, he gave me a honeycomb which somebody had just brought to him. I sat down near to him and it took me quite a time before I had eaten it.

Then he waved me to him again: "Come," and gave me another big honeycomb!

"My goodness, how can I manage that?" I asked myself. "You eat!" and so I nibbled at the second honeycomb and it took even longer to get it inside me. It tasted really very good. I had hardly finished the second one when he waved again and gave me a third one!

If it had not been clear to me before, then now it was absolutely clear: that God is love, full of sweetness and so rich in love that we can hardly absorb it all!

After the third honeycomb I was close to bursting.

Everything was unforgettably clear. How could he possibly have made it clearer to me?

Babaji as friend (about 1981)

Mundan, 20 days of silence and a thermos flask

When in the spring of 1980, I came to Herakhan for the third time to stay for three months, Babaji very soon let me make Mundan. I was not to speak with anyone for 20 days, but to remain silent! Only to him I was allowed to speak. I should only eat and drink what was given to me, apart from the waters of the Gautam Ganga. I could drink as much of that as I wanted.

It was often fairly cold, and unfortunately no-one had got the idea of giving me some hot tea – and I had enjoyed drinking hot drinks all my life.

Again, I was painting the temples at the foot of Kailash, this time on the temples' rear wall. It was cold and I felt alone.

So one morning I decided to buy a thermos bottle and get it filled with wonderful hot chai. Carrying it under my poncho, I went over to the Kailash side. And who was sitting there in front of his cave? Babaji!

He waved me to him and I bowed down in front of him. But he looked silently at me with really sad eyes. I knew why.

"I love your colour!"

It was spring 1980. As well as the temples of the Divine Mother and the Divine Couples, Rama with Sita and Krishna with Radha, two new temples had been completed adjoining them at the foot of Kailash: the temple for Lord Dattatreya, the embodiment of the Oneness of Brahma, Vishnu and Shiva, and for Guru Goraknath, a previous manifestation of Babaji.

I wanted to start painting the inside of the temple of Lord Dattatreya straightaway to express great devotion, because I knew that, according to Babaji, Muniraj is an incarnation of Lord Dattatreya.

But another person, an Indian man, also wanted to paint this temple at all costs. Unfortunately, we were totally at odds regarding the colour scheme. What could be done? It did not help for me to explain that I am a painter, because he countered that he was an artist.

At that time I had no idea that it was this same Indian man who had carved the statue of the old Herakhan Baba which Babaji had let a woman friend bring to me in Germany in the summer of 1978, saying: "It should stand where many people can see it." It now stood in my little temple.

Unfortunately, the Indian man and I could not reach an agreement, whereupon my great indignation manifested in a high fever.

At the midday break I was able to see my annoyance as the cause of my fever and I decided step back and give in to the will of the other, and instead to paint the temple for Guru Goraknath. Thank God , because there I had a free hand!

Still highly feverish, I climbed up a long ladder, wanting most of all to paint the high dome of Baba Goraknath in the blue of outer space, unaware that it was not customary to paint the inside of the temple domes right up to the top.

At the top the domes are very narrow, and I stood there in a high fever, inhaling the intense fumes of paint and turpentine. I pushed away the idea that all these fumes could make me fall unconscious. I was deeply convinced that I was doing just the right thing.

After I had painted the inside of the dome blue from bottom to top, I too was totally blue, and: The fever had vanished!

When, that evening, I was trying to clean all blue colour off me at the river,

Babaji came across the river on a small board. – "I love your colour!" he called to me.

On the same evening, after Arati, he let sandals, padukas, be handed over to me: "These are Baba Goraknath's sandals!" They were really beautiful, richly carved padukas made of wood, of the kind that we still today decorate and honour at home during a paduka puja.

Naturally, it was clear to me that it was Babaji himself who at that time was Baba Goraknath on Earth.

The whole time I was painting, I thought: Oh, Guru Goraknath is such a sublime divine teacher, is it possible I have ever seen him?" Through my friend Marcel I knew that Guru Goraknath accepted only the most highly evolved disciples. Marcel had been with him, Babaji had confirmed that, but what of me?

With the gift of the sandals he had given me the answer. What grace!

Tipsy with laughter

It was incredible how Babaji always appeared where something special was happening, where a teaching was needed.

Once, during the midday break, I went to the tea shop and met Fakiruli there who was very unhappy with herself and the world and complaining loudly: "Je me sens comme un chien. – I feel like a dog." I really had to laugh at how she was shouting with deep conviction and honesty but seeming so funny at the same time.

She went on complaining, ranting and raving. And the more she huffed and puffed, the more I had to laugh. Finally the wind went out of her sails and she became infected by my laughter. We became happier and happier and could not stop laughing: it developed into a real intoxication!

In this condition I set off to the ashram. And who was waiting at the exit to the ashram? Babaji! Tall, white and innocent!

I could not think of anything other than to fall at his feet.

But because of all the laughing, I was totally exhausted and empty, I had no idea how I could get to my feet again. I glanced up and saw Babaji's long arm hanging loosely down. So I took his hand and began to pull myself up on his arm.

Incredible! He, who otherwise gives blessings and who evokes our deepest respect, allowed me simply to pull myself up on his arm. At that moment it was the most natural thing in the world.

Finally I was standing right next to him, eye to eye and he looked at me with childlike innocence, reflecting my condition.

Intoxicating laughter, beyond good and bad.

Omnipresent

One morning, very contrary to my normal habit and also the general rules of Karma yoga, I lay down on my bed in broad daylight. I had experienced so much that required internal reflection. Overwhelmed by it all, I needed tranquillity and simply shut my eyes.

And who was standing by my bed at the very moment I opened my eyes? Babaji – looking at me gently and calmly, nothing else. This made a deep impression on me!

He sees everything, he knows everything, he is omnipresent.

For a moment, a bad conscience arose for having simply lain down, rather than doing Karma yoga. But this melted away like snow in the sun of his love.

A husband explodes with rage

Once Babaji linked arms very lovingly with an elderly woman and led her up the slope. He even tweaked her arm.

I was walking behind with her husband, a Spaniard.

Babaji flirted with her, calling her Jewel, whilst her much younger husband foamed with rage and almost exploded with jealousy!

As he was much younger than his wife, it had always been he who had flirted with the women. Now Babaji played out the situation in reverse in front of his eyes.

Healing

Babaji returned from one of his brief journeys just as I arrived back in Herakhan from Germany. Because of overtiredness and the change of climate, I had a fever and a rather sore throat. It was then around midday and warm. Dressed in light clothing, I ran down with the others to greet Babaji.

I was allowed to accompany Babaji, and with a few others and full of joy I went beside him past the temples. But I could feel my cold. Just at the moment that I was thinking to myself: "I had better go back up in order to cure my cold and finally take some rest," Babaji said: "You water all Gufaside!"

Instead of inwardly protesting, I simply gave myself over to the task as I carried the water, bucket by bucket, from the river, up the small hill and watered the fresh-ly planted trees and plants. The mantra that vibrated in me during this time was:

"I am in you. I am in you. I am in you" – for hours on end.

An Indian came along to help me but made it clear: "I am not helping you for your sake, but because of Babaji!"

Suddenly I noticed that the sun was setting, that I was sopping wet from carrying the water buckets up and down, that it had become cold and: That I was completely well again!

No trace of a fever or sore throat, whereas I normally get a sore throat just from having wet feet. So I ran to Babaji and kneeled down in front of him – wordlessly.

Many times I shook my head from side to side in disbelief and could not grasp it, whilst Babaji nodded his head just as many times.

Open discussion

We were in a small group of Westerners travelling with Babaji. A young woman kept assuming the role of policewoman, commanding and correcting all of us. It was a nuisance for everyone, but no-one said anything to her.

As I liked her a lot, I suggested that she sit with me for a moment in the big open tent while the others took a break, and I described the situation to her and how it affected the others. She was totally surprised because she was completely unaware of this. On the contrary, she was really convinced that she was doing her duty. Now she was simply grateful for what I had told her.

At that moment Babaji appeared high up on the balcony and looked lovingly down on the two of us: "I like fights!" whereby he expressed his wish that we should speak openly with one another. Babaji said this to us on numerous occasions.

He wanted us to deal honestly with one another, so that light and truth might reign between us and we tell each other everything directly, and not speak or think badly of others behind their backs.

Marry Shastriji

On that same day in the morning I had seen Shastriji bring Babaji a beautiful green head covering of the finest silk and set it on his head.

I was very touched by the simplicity, naturalness and humility with which Shastriji did this.

And I thought: "I would like to be like that."

Babaji promptly said to me: "You marry Shastriji!"

Shivaratri 1983

Babaji had told some of us Westerners, myself included, that we could accompany him to Bombay. Before departing from Herakhan, he suddenly asked me: "You go to Calcutta?" Naturally I was astonished and said: "No, I am coming with you to Bombay."

Four of us travelled by train and therefore had to take as little luggage as possible. Although I could not imagine that Babaji would have time to paint on a journey, I asked him before our departure from Herakhan, just to be on the safe side: "Should I take colours and a painting pad with me? Do you want to paint during the journey?"

The answer was: "Yes!"

The festivities in Bombay took place on the coast in a multi-storey building with eight floors, which was mainly inhabited by Babaji devotees. We had been told we would be housed on the seventh floor. When we arrived, we were received in a friendly manner, but also told that the seventh floor was for "the top staff only," for Muniraj for instance, and they would have to find out where we were to be accommodated, probably it would be below in the courtyard.

And so it was. We landed in one of the small tents, which had been put up in the courtyard. The huge tent for Shivaratri had also been put up there.

There was only one water tap for all the people camping in the courtyard. One of our women friends clearly found this difficult. For her, the situation and circumstances were impossible. She immediately fell ill and soon afterwards had to drive home. The other three of us accepted the situation. I recalled Babaji's comment about Calcutta, and it was now clear to me what he had meant by it: these circumstances that we were now undergoing. It had been his gentle warning about what was awaiting us.

In any case, the moment that Babaji appeared everything felt good.

Babaji was accommodated on the uppermost floor, the eighth, and there we met with him. It happened that some wonderful singing, and also, for the first time, an "OM namah Shivay" was recorded then.

The recording was played to Babaji and unfortunately, it was not perfect, parts were missing. Babaji said: "Play it again!" And on the second playing, it was perfect! He had cured the recording!

Shivaratri is Lord Shiva's birthday.
Of him, who was never born,
Of him, who, coming from the eternal
Is without father, without mother,
Of him, who is eternal.
Thus it is the celebration of the eternal being of Shiva.
Of him, who has no beginning, of him, who eternally is.

We Westerners who travelled with Babaji were allowed, together with a number of Indians, to visit him at 3 a.m. on the Shivaratri night. My breath stood still. Babaji sat there, unmoving in Samadhi. We looked at him from the side. Clothed only in a loincloth he sat there with his many curls and an expression of infinite innocence and purity.

Each of us was permitted to pour a little milk on his feet. I was so overwhelmed that I also poured milk on his knees. His appearance penetrated deep into my heart, indelibly so.

Later, early, at half past four in the morning, we got Chandan from Babaji, and then the masses started to come streaming to him. In a beautiful shop, I had obtained a very special sweet as a gift for him. It was large, thick, wonderful and round. And while I was standing in the queue, I was continually thinking: "It is like you!"

When I reached Babaji, he pulled a terrible face – as he often did before something very beautiful occurred. "What is this?" I answered simply: "It is sweet." He put his hand on it and said: "You eat!" And I received the entire wonderful substance back as a gift.

He emanated such deep love that I had to cry. I withdrew behind one of the furthest pillars of the great tent and would have dearly liked to be invisible. His love made me cry more and more, and his appearance in the early morning gripped me utterly and totally: this innocence, this purity, his beauty.

After a while Sheela came as a messenger from Babaji, to bring me a life thread from him. I, who was so gripped by his love that I wanted to be invisible by everybody, felt overcome that he should send somebody to search for me amongst these innumerable people and find me in the remotest corner.

After a while Sheela appeared again. She now knew where I had hidden myself and she said: "Babaji calls you, you should come to him." So I went forward just as I was, flushed from crying, to where he was surrounded by all the distinguished, wealthy Indians, and bowed. He said: "Bring me my colours!"

I must fetch him the painting pad and colours in the middle of the Shivaratri! Babaji made a sign on the pad, which, as I was kneeling in front of him, I could not see, and he spoke to someone at the same time. Then he turned to me, who wanted nothing else than to be invisible: "Okay, now you can go!" The pad with the picture he gave to somebody else.

Around midday, after the great celebration with all its singing and observances, an Indian came and returned the pad with the picture to me and said: "Babaji gives you this picture" – and in Hindi he wrote on it what Babaji had said about it.

Babaji had painted an inverted Trishul (trident) that streamed out downwards, thereby giving me his blessing for the book, which then I did not even know that I should write.

Directly after Shivaratri, the three of us were relocated from the tent into an extremely comfortable room on the first floor.

In the following few days, Babaji took us Westerners with him to meet many of his Indian disciples. A meeting at the home of a special Indian devotee and his wife was very impressive. He was a famous Indian film director and actor. A lovely man with a very loving wife.

Through Babaji, there then occurred the initiation of Kali, one of his disciples, who became Shani, Saturn. The hostess inwardly saw how smoke flew out of Babaji's nose, ears and mouth and was drawn into Kali. "Now he is Shani," Babaji said and gave him a black Trishul.

The journey continued on to Vapi with an inspirational train ride through the Indian countryside. In Vapi, a beautiful ashram in the countryside, Babaji gave us all Bang, a delicious energizing drink, whereupon everyone got very high, each in his own way. One of us three women friends giggled and laughed the whole time, another saw her own thoughts in three-dimensional forms and I went into deep meditation.

No more separation

In Germany, I heard about a European who had been with Babaji for six months and cried continually. When I returned to Herakhan and saw who this man was, namely someone whom I knew well from earlier meetings, I was amazed and asked: "Why are you crying so much all the time while you are with Babaji?"

His answer was: "The separation!"

He meant that he had been separated from Babaji for so long that it caused him to cry continuously!

As Bhole Baba, Babaji became for all of us like the father who is as simple as a child. But for this friend he was like a thousand mothers!

Unconditional love

A pleasant young man from a good Indian family, who had borne much suffering, most of it self-inflicted, had become an alcoholic. He greatly respected Babaji whom he had got to know through Babaji's visits to his family.

One day Babaji let him participate in a longer pilgrimage into the mountains towards Badrinath. They were a large group. The young man was very concerned about how he would survive these days without the whiskey of which he was so much in need. To his great surprise, relief and gratitude, Babaji had actually brought along a bottle of whiskey for him, and also a black wool blanket for protection so that he should be at peace.

The young man told me that he would never forget what Babaji had done! He was overcome by this unconditional love, which knew how things were for him and did not demand the impossible of him. Babaji picked up everyone at the point where he or she was, not where he or she should be.

Be happy

At strategic moments, Babaji would ask one or another of us: "Are you happy?" Often the response was simply a beaming "Yes!" and one was in a deep resonance of delight with him.

On other occasions, by the question: "Are you happy?" Babaji brought out everything about which one was unhappy. Mainly this had to do with personal expectations, annoyances, fears or frustrations, our shadow-material.

In the shortest space of time Babaji brought out so much from within us, and at the same time gave us the strength to deal with it, so that it could be healed and transformed.

Hiraman's story

Once I brought Babaji a book by an author of the Self-Realization Fellowship, founded by Yogananda. The author was a person whom I had told about Babaji's present incarnation and shown him photos. However, this person could not recognize the identity of Yogananda's Babaji in the present Babaji. I gave Babaji his book and begged him: "Please let this author realize that you and Yogananda's Babaji are identical!" Babaji gave me the book back, and it was with the book in my hand that I met Hiraman, a friend from America.

Hiraman had blond curly hair, bright blue eyes, and when he came up to Babaji, he gave him a sort of flag with the inscription: "Love is sun energy!" – and that was exactly how Hiraman was in himself!

Hiraman saw the book with the picture of Babaji in my hand and said: "Babaji appeared to me in Hawaii looking exactly like that!" The picture on the book was of Yogananda's Babaji.

And he told me his story:

Babaji first appeared to him in a vision wearing a Himalayan cap (Topi). Hiraman did not know who he was. He knew only one thing, that this was his master. So he set off in search of him and in 1977 he travelled to the Khumba Mela in India. He hoped to find his master there, because all the great masters and teachers made a practice of going there.

He vowed to himself: "I will neither eat nor drink until I have found him." Now the fourth day had come after making the vow, and he still had not found him!

Hiraman looked through every opening, into every tent, and finally he beheld a photo of the precise being who had appeared to him!

It was the picture of the old Herakhan Baba with a Tibetan cap. Hiraman entered the tent and saw the present Babaji sitting there. He recognized immediately from the vibration that this Babaji was identical with the apparition of the old Herakhan Baba!

OM namah Shivay!

Benign Babaji (about 1983)

So Babaji first appeared to him as the old Herakhan Baba.

Then, as Hiraman, at Babaji's command, was building a temple for him in the wilderness of Big Island – initially without resources and with this direction from Babaji: "You may only come back again when you have completed the temple" – Babaji appeared to him in the form reproduced on Yogananda's book cover.

Hiraman said: "That was a wonderful apparition!" That was the second appearance of Babaji before Hiraman.

And the third time Babaji appeared to him as Bhole Baba, in the form that we now know him, with all his warmth, power and love.

Hiraman is a person whom Babaji has blessed with these three forms of apparition of himself.

Tibetan story

In 1982, by chance, Marcel and I met the Tibetan Lama Ayang Rinpoche, who taught Phowa. I was immediately very touched. Phowa is an exercise, which one should practice during one's life in order to rise to the highest level of consciousness at the moment of death, a practice that is also described in the Tibetan Book of Death.

Here, this was all embraced in living practice. In me, there was a sense of deep recognition. I felt that I knew all this well from another life.

Because Babaji had painted a large picture of Tibet in the first book that he had given me, I invited the Lama to visit us in Daisendorf in Germany, not then knowing that a completely different Tibet was awaiting me.

The Lama was very moved by the energy of the place and wanted to erect Stupas everywhere in our garden, which I most certainly did not want. "Buddha, Christ and Babaji, they are all one!" he said.

Later Marcel and I invited him to hold a nine day Phowa-retreat for friends in our house. I thought that some of them, if they were to experience the divine presence over their heads through this exercise, could recognize Babaji, since Babaji had previously raised me up into the eternal to himself, through the thousand-petalled lotus above my head.

In order to practice this Phowa exercise, one had to repeat a particular Tibetan mantra many times over.

I wrote to Babaji about the Phowa and the exercises. He replied: "You can do that, but then don't come back to Herakhan."

But in the meantime the Lama had already been invited! When, shortly afterwards, I told Babaji about this in a second letter, there came two letters in reply at the same time, though sent at different times.

I opened the first letter from Babaji, written in Gora Devi's hand. In it was written: "Because you got involved in this Tibetan story, you never come back to Herakhan again! You never write to me again!" I was deeply shocked.

Then I opened the second letter which had been sent five days later, but which arrived on exactly the same day. It had been written by a friend whom I had inspired to go to Babaji. This friend had asked Babaji: "I have written a letter to send to Nila, do you have a message for her?" The friend then described how Babaji, sitting on his little wall, began to shine like the sun and then began to sing. His sung message to me was: "You have become one with the Buddha, with God!"

God be thanked that both letters arrived at the same time! The message became clear to me: "You have already attained enlightenment, you have climbed the mountain. And now you want to do the same exercise again, which I have already taught you! What I want to show you now is that the teaching here in Herakhan, for this time, is of another sort. Here we are not concerned with how one successfully leaves one's body at death in order to attain the highest, but with serving, serving in the here and now, with Karma Yoga! Serving creation, serving your fellow men, nature, everything. With the continuous repetition of the name of God in your heart."– OM namah Shivay. The penny had dropped.

But now I was in the fatal situation of neither being allowed to go to him any more, nor to write to him.

I became very active in telling people about Babaji and his message for our time. I set up Monday evenings with meditations, Arati, and narration about him and spiritual themes, a practice which still continues today. I did what I could. And I begged for mercy!

Some two months later I received an unexpected letter, a postcard from Muniraj: "You can come to Herakhan for Christmas!"

Now I dared to write a letter to Gora Devi in India and asked for Babaji's confirmation of Muniraj's invitation.

Babaji's comment was: "Jay Hanumane Lala."

What I understood was: "Victory to dear Hanuman! Victory to those who serve!" Hanuman is the servant of God, who, through his love for him, can move mountains.

That meant "Yes!" and so, with a great feeling of relief in my heart, I flew to India in December.

A sequel to the Tibetan story

After the dazzling Christmas there was a sequel to my Tibet story. On January 24, 1983 I asked Babaji if I might perform the evening Arati for him. It was on this day in 1978 in Herakhan that I had recognized, for once and for all, that He is the Divine Being.

He replied: "No! You can do Arati for Buddha only!"

"Oh," I thought, "now he's stirring up the whole Tibet story again."

Then Babaji said: "You go home!" and I countered: "I'm going to Kailash!"

"No! Home!" whereupon I responded: "Kailash is my home. If not the external, then the inner Kailash." Whereupon Babaji said: "Yes!"

I went to an ancient Devi place high up on a hill outside the ashram, from which one had a wonderful view of Kailash.

There I spent several hours and secretly prepared for the evening Arati, even at the risk of his saying "No." In the evening, however, he gave his permission and even helped me with it. It was a large festive Arati, after which he gave one of his first longer talks. His talk was about the Law of the New World, which he called Law No. 44.

Babaji's talk No. 44 on January 24, 1983

"Whenever Arati is performed here in Herakhan by the national of a particular state, all the men and women of that country have to participate. This applies to the Swiss, French, Italians, Americans etc.

This is a new universal law, laid down in Herakhan Vishwa Mahadam. This law is of universal character. It applies not for just one country, but for the whole world. The new law for the kingdom that embraces everything will have its source in Herakhan.

»Dharma 44«, Law 44, is the name of this commandment. Everyone can be punished for not adhering to this law. Each one of you has to obey this law, as it applies worldwide. The whole world will be *one* Kingdom, there will be *one* King and there will be *one* Law ruling the entire world. The old laws and decrees have lost their validity today, because the ministries of justice are corrupt. The new law will be like a morphine injection with immediate results.

Do not take the law into your own hands. Rather let yourselves be guided by the law. I repeat, do not control the law in that you take it into your own hands!

Shirdi Maulana makes all this known to you. You should know about Shirdi Maulana. He lived in India during the time of Mohammedan dominance. He moves about the world in his spiritual body and helps people in ways that are invisible. He is with us now and speaks through Shri Mahaprabhji. Babaji says that "I" and "my" thinking has spread a veil around the heart of men. Humans have become selfish and egoistic. How can peace rule when the human spirit is filled with such thoughts? Who is of such high mindedness as to be able to commit himself to serving mankind and loving his neighbour? Men have sunk so low that they are ready to kill others out of egoistic motives.

Every single one of you has to help to get rid of the corrupt laws and to place true right in its stead."

Babaji's fragrance

Once again, I went for a walk through the valley with Babaji with his umbrella in the hand. At the end of a long morning together he emitted his divine fragrance! He had a pen in his hand and was playing with its top, saying over and again: "– opening – closing – opening – closing!" In so doing the fragrance arose, disappeared – over and again, this extremely wonderful fragrance, Babaji's fragrance.

Whereupon I asked him: "Babaji, why not opening the whole time?" But he put the top back on the pen and with that, the matter was closed for this day!

The impact of OM Namah Shivay–
An inner journey from 70 to 108

Babaji guided me in a deep meditation. With my eyes closed, I sat bolt upright and experienced how my hands performed very precise mudras, which activated energy throughout my entire body, and at the same time, this set free deep knowledge within me.

With my breathing consciousness I went through the middle of my forehead up to the crown chakra and experienced, on the way, that there exist within exits to various divine worlds in the form of numbers.

Moving up my forehead consciously, I intensively experienced the Christ energy. The portals to these magnificent realms expressed themselves as the numbers from 70 to 90. The crown chakra had the number 100 as the portal to the infinite. There were also yet higher levels that amazingly were not reached by rising yet higher, but by voluntarily descending again. But this time the way was not via the forehead, but down the back of the head. As easy as I had found it to ascend through the forehead, so, inversely, I found it strenuous to descend through the back of the head.

From one level it led to the next, through the portals from 101, 102 to 103, to 104. Each time it required an inner stepping back, a kind of ability to renounce that enabled entry into the next level. This inner path led from the back of the head down to the base of the skull. It needed my complete inner strength of conscious mudras in order to move further down. I reached level 107 only with the greatest of effort. I was then at the end of my strength and asked: How do I get to 108?

Then I saw the mantra OM NAMAH SHIVAY spread over the world like the finest icing sugar from the highest to the lowest level, and saw also that everyone who repeated the name of God with devotion, for instance in the form OM NAMAH SHIVAY, is immediately in the highest level. That means that every ordinary person who ploughs the earth lovingly in the name of God is already in the Supreme.

What a teaching!

How deep must God's love be that he makes it so simple. In this way it was shown to me that the highest divine region cannot be reached by one's own efforts but only through the repetition of God's name.

OM NAMAH SHIVAY. I surrender to you, oh Lord.

When two or three gather in my name

It was in 1979. At the lower part, the foot of the Kailash, there was intensive digging of earth and stone in order to build further temples – all by hand, merely with a shovel and a wheelbarrow. It was an enormous mission, only possible with divine grace.

A wheelbarrow full of earth and stone was in the way when I walked by with Babaji and an elder lady. He told me to move it towards the slope.

With fresh energy I grabbed the wheelbarrow but did not succeed in moving it even a single millimeter further – that heavy it was! Hereupon Babaji asked the small older lady to help me. To my surprise the two of us were suddenly able to move the wheelbarrow with ease. It was very impressive!

"When two or three work together in my name," impossible things can truly happen.

A teaching about February 5

It was February 5, the day of Jesus' initiation, as revealed to me by Babaji in February 1979. On the morning of this special day, together with a few others, I was meant to beautify the garden around the Dhuni, the holy fireplace.

I was in the process of weeding the beds, conscious in my heart of the meaning of this day, when Babaji gave me a blow on my back: "This is not allowed." What did he mean by this today?

I understood: "For me, there are no weeds. I work with all, with every person, with every being."

As so often, Babaji used the outward situation to reveal something within. I felt that in another context it would surely have been good to remove the weeds.

With Babaji one always had to be alert, alive and flexible and to understand intuitively.

Massaging Babaji's feet

Again and again, Babaji let me massage his feet. I always felt that oiling and massaging his feet was a great gift. He only permitted it for as long as I was in the right state of consciousness. When a personal feeling of some kind or another arose, I had to stop immediately.

Sometimes I got the impression that I was massaging the continents of the Earth. Deep things happened thereby. A holy, and often a very wonderful, process.

Watchman of his Kingdom

It was 1983. In the evening, Babaji told me: "Tomorrow I paint for you!," very unusual since he used to paint spontaneously, without any announcement. And I always had to be prepared and ready with the colours in my bag.

The next morning, however, I was told that I should be the watchman of his kingdom.

This was a new Lila (game) that Babaji had created: Whoever was chosen for this duty had to climb onto the roof above the exit of the ashram and, holding a staff and facing the forest, watch over whoever came in.

At first, I thought: "What a pity. Babaji had told me he would paint for me today, and now I have to be watchman!", but duty always comes first, this was clear.

So I stood for hours with the staff on the roof in the sun. I had a small painting book in my bag and had just started to draw something spontaneously while engrossed in thinking of the castle of the Grail.

Around midday, food was brought up to me, but as I wanted to greet Babaji briefly, I arranged for someone to take my place. As always at midday, Babaji was settled on his little wall above his Kutiya, his little room. From a long way off he called out to me: "Where have you been? I told you, I would paint for you!"

Undaunted, I went to him and said: "You made me watchman of your kingdom. Look, I have painted something for you," and showed him the little sketch. At this, he was radiant and said: "I painted that! This is a door to heaven!"

This picture has become the sign for the centre *Quell des Heilens* (*Source of Healing*), the joyful place that Babaji, through us, has created by Lake Constance.

Throughout the construction of the place, he gave us the feeling that it was we who joyfully discovered and carried out everything by ourselves, but it was he who inspired and did everything through us.

When painting

While Babaji was painting and I was sitting directly beside him, he always gave me the feeling that it was as if we were painting together. A feeling as if we were colleagues. It was simply wonderful.

Once I had made a small sketch of the circle of the Grail and, contrary to my normal manner, had expressed it very figuratively. I brought it to Babaji and he said straightaway: "I don't like it!" Then he wanted the sketch pad, and set to work.

In great sweeps, he painted a beautiful picture with just a few brush strokes, thereby reaffirming my original free way of painting.

On another occasion, he had taken a long time, going into great detail, using a very large pad and differentiated techniques, to paint a picture with a large golden mountain, I was to take it to my room along with two other large pictures by him. I was convinced that they were intended for someone else since he had already painted two entire books for me. I took the picture with the golden mountain back to him and said: "Babaji, don't you want to continue painting it? To me it doesn't look finished." To that he answered: "No! This is finished," and gave me all three pictures.

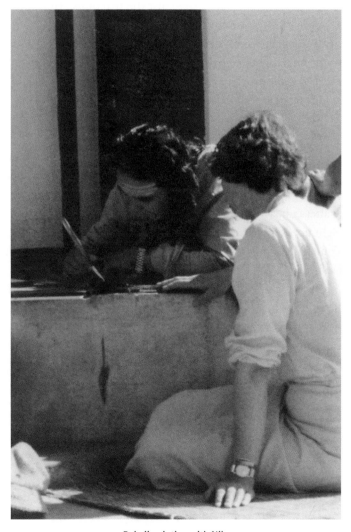

Babaji painting with Nila

117

Babaji's second painted book
and its continuation

In 1979, Babaji had half painted a wonderful book that contained the transformation of OM.

In 1980, I brought the book back to Babaji and asked whether he wanted to continue painting it. He took the book and went with me onto the roof terrace, telling me to sit in the corner of the terrace. He himself stayed in the middle, sitting on a small stone wall. There were just the two of us. This time I was not allowed to see what he was painting. He was busy with the book for some 20 minutes. Of course, I looked from a distance to see what he was doing and saw that he leafed forward and back through the book, and then dwelled somewhat longer on some pages. So Babaji was very busily involved with the book. Finally I observed him take a thick felt pen and draw something.

Then he waved me over to him and gave the book to me: "This is finished now!"

Of what he had done, the only thing that could be recognized was that he had placed a bold "OM namah Shivay" on the last picture he had painted the year before. It was a green and very exploded picture that suggested how the earth might look after radioactive contamination. In the OM symbol, the front line was extended right up, as if the creation were being led back to the creator.

The second half of the book, through which he had leafed so intently, appeared to me still to be blank.

Many years later a friend who went through Babaji's pictures and the blank pages with radio aesthetic measurements discovered that Babaji had painted the apparently empty pages in the etheric.

I mentioned this to Shastriji and he explained: "Those are pictures that Babaji will paint through you."

This truth happens over and over again – very happily.

Once, not long ago, I had a picture that was to go to an exhibition and I wanted to remove some touches of colour that were very thick, although they looked very beautiful. I hoped that in that way it would dry more quickly.

At precisely that moment Babaji's presence could be felt with great intensity, and I heard him say within me: "What are you doing, taking away the energy of my painting?!" I was shocked, naturally, and immediately stopped removing the thick colour.

I had understood. I will definitely never do that again.

Bhole Baba on a journey

Shastriji told me that he very often slept near Babaji in his Kutiya, his little room, which he had closed up from the outside every night by Man Singh. That meant that Shastriji was unable to go to the toilet and so had to make other arrangements.

What Shastriji then experienced was that many times Bhole Baba was gone in the night, together with his body, and that he was always back in time, before Man Singh opened the door again in the early morning.

A Heart Arati

February 5 had come round again, the day of Jesus' initiation, about which Babaji had spoken to me in 1979. This day of the baptism of Jesus in the Jordan was the great day, on which, through Him, the Holy Ghost descended onto the Earth, and filled the Earth with light. Thereby occurred the initial enlightenment of the Earth, and at the same time that of mankind.

It was February 5, 1983 when I asked Babaji whether I might make Arati before him. His answer was: "Yes, together with Hargovind," who was standing beside me at that moment.

Hargovind left the entire preparation to me. In the afternoon, I picked flowers for a beautiful blossom mala and prepared a large Prasad bowl for everyone. Instead of the usual scarf, I had brought with me a new snow white sari for Babaji, and for the celebration of this special day I made a crown from stiff paper with Indian gold bands for him, whom I understood to be the father. Then I cut a heart out of cardboard, painted it white in the middle with rainbow colours all round it and fixed flowers around it too, until there arose a blooming sun's heart. In order to be able to hang it round Babaji's neck, I fixed it on to a sandalwood mala (prayer chain).

I was so feverishly busy that at the end I had no time left to tie the blossom mala as I had planned and as is customarily required for an Arati. The evening bells were already ringing. I quickly made four little bouquets out of the available flowers and simply laid the remaining flowers together in a bowl with all the other treasures for the evening prayers.

Babaji sat there bolt upright as I started to wind the white Sari around him and attempted to hang the blooming heart on him. But it would not go over his head. The chain was too short. And so the blooming sun's heart remained suspended at the top of Babaji's head, his 1000-petalled lotus, whilst the mala hung down to the right and left side of his head and framed his face. But where should I put the crown? The spot on Babaji's head was occupied. Babaji said: "Give it to Hargovind."

Babaji in festive attire during Arati

I put scent on Babaji's hands and feet, and of the four bouquets, I spontaneously placed two between his toes and two in his hands, as he was sitting upright in the perfect position for this. The bowl with all the rest of the blossoms I simply placed in his lap. Babaji went along with this totally. Since he no longer had a free hand to take fruits and sweets from the Prasad plate that was offered, I gently placed some of these in his mouth.

He sat there fully like a Murti.

There followed a blessed Arati in front of a radiant Babaji, who glowed like a sun. And all of those present were allowed to come up to him and circle the flame in front of him.

At the end, he took the blooming heart from his head and laid it on mine. Before I could react, it had slipped down and now hung over my heart. Happy, I then shared the Prasad among everyone.

Afterwards two Indian priests came up to me and asked me: "Was that a Bengali Arati?" I shook my head, laughing. I realized that they could not imagine that all this was not written down anywhere, but had come about spontaneously from love, and was responded to by Babaji, just as spontaneously, in love.

Appendix

The Drummer

Drummer, you drum your life
Through towns and through deserts,
Drummer, you drum your dying
through this way of the world.
Drummer, what will set you free
From the endless beat of the drum?

The drum's message –
Sealed
How can the seal be opened?

In the turning circle he who flies turns into him who flees.
Sun-sleeper was I, knowing nothing
about a message, a drum, which exists.
Sun-sleeper, there I saw
Stones are sleeping the light
Flowers are scenting the light
Birds are singing the light
People smile it.

But then I saw the world –
I saw something else: is that supposed to be life?
The moving from small joys to greater
From small suffering to greater
Now this friend, now that enemy
Or watching – or idea – or desire –

And one has work which
Fills a certain number of hours of the day,
And one says to oneself as if to comfort oneself:
That which is important – the other – later then…
World sealed with shadows – hard to live
With people to whom a shadowy light
Appears as real and the Whole

— yes,

...I went along the lamplit streets of men
Through houses of lamps and streets and the appearance of men
through, always through –
Houses and streets of thoughts, the appearance of thoughts
And through the appearance of thoughts on through
where is there an end, where? –
there I see pictures coming towards me
and out of their midst there comes a messenger –
fear jumps up in the room, blows holes into the room.
Pictures, all these pictures –
Is this all me?

ME? –

Message of the Drum,
That is when I heard the call for the first time.

Sun-sleeper once upon a time? Awoke I am, a shadow dancer now.

There are masks here, many masks,
I must dance, live, die,
One mask after another:

Through – and – off.

How many masks do I have still to die,
until finally what is true can live through me?
There, look at the vagabond:

Vagabond
Here you are in red, searching for the blue
There, you have the blue, searching for the red –

Prisoner, you are in black, searching the white.
Flyer, you have white, searching for the black,
All this the vagabond
– Vagabond –

And through everything he seeks the Gold.

Message of the drum
through everything, the Gold –

Why this message,
Sealed so deep in the sign, in the image?

I asked fall of the flyer and the lust to trumpet
Asked lust of the dreamer's need and the must of masks
Asked the masks: WHY? And heard:

…what did I hear, what did they tell me?

Drummer, all ways I hear the drummer only
Drummer, he drums his life through town and through deserts
Drummer, he drums his dying through my way,
through your way, through our way of the world.

… yes, the rhythm, how you wander
Strangely far is the love that is leading you –
And your march goes through the pictures,
Through the signs, long, how long the path –

But I believe in purity
And expect the mirrored place of my star

*

In the turning circle he who flees turns into he who flies

*

And then it happens,
That finally all the pictures, all the signs
have been overcome –
freed
from pictures – signs – and masks

you are able to die.

It is then that you have gained your face
That the sealed light is set free
It is then that the drum's message it lives.
Released is the drummer from the endless beating of the drum

*

WRITTEN AT 21 YEARS OF AGE IN BERLIN,
AS A PLAY FOR ONE PERSON
BY NILA (RENATA CADDY)
INSPIRED BY BABAJI
(ABRIDGED)

Lord Shiva drinks the cup of poison

Babaji's Mahasamadhi 1984

"Please, Babaji, when you go, call me and let me be with you then!" At that time I thought that he would go into the woods somewhere, as it has been told of the Buddha, and then, from the gross to the subtle, he would dissolve one layer after another.

I wanted so much to be with him then.

In response to my question, Babaji raised his hand, moved it slightly, as if to say. "What are you thinking of?" – but he said nothing.

When I asked him in March 1983 at the end of my stay in Herakhan: "When may I come again?" he said: "You can come in January." When January 1984 came around and I wanted to book my flight, I heard from various people that Babaji was travelling for six weeks and "He doesn't want anyone to come to him during this time."

I wrote to Herakhan immediately, asking whether this was indeed so, and as a reply from Babaji heard "You come in March!" I read "March;" this word opened up a yawning emptiness in front of me! He had said "January" to me. Why did I have to ask again! I called up friends in India in order to find out when exactly Babaji would set off.

The answer was "On January 20."

I became aware of an inner alarm bell ringing – very clearly – to go to him straightaway. The next possible flight was on January 17, 1984.

My friend Gisela, who had long ago planned to travel to India in January, because she had no other alternative as far as time was concerned, flew with me.

From the airport in Delhi we immediately took a taxi to Haldwani and from there we went straight on by jeep to Damside, and then on foot to Herakhan, crossing the Gautama Ganga river many times.

We arrived at Babaji's on January 18 around 3 p.m. He received us sitting on his little wall. Without words, Babaji radiated such a profound vibration of love that we were close to tears.

Right then, I was allowed to massage and oil his feet. He asked "Which is Heart Oil?" – "Rose oil," I replied. After that I was allowed to massage his feet every day. It was so intense!

Babaji departed, not on January 20 as we had heard from Delhi, but only on January 21, and was travelling not for six weeks, but seven days, with a few men to accompany him. Every moment spent with him was of such depth that words could not express. How he kept on giving! What he revealed from within…

Again and again, I experienced him as pure being which permeated everything – and not only that but also as the deep loving divine Self, which, full of mercy, took our burdens from us, on all levels, if we were prepared to surrender everything to him.

On the evening before he set off, I said to him: "Babaji, you take too much upon yourself!"

I had simply seen this.

In the morning before his departure he announced that during his absence three of his disciples should sit in front of his door and meditate for 24 hours –continuously. I was one of these. – I really felt the love that led him to say this.

After Babaji returned, each day was again richer, deeper and more precious than the one before. He gave and gave – he almost gave us more than we could absorb – certainly more than I could take in.

On February 5, 1984, I asked Babaji to be allowed to make Arati in front of him. Of all the Aratis this was the most beautiful. I saw him as pure shining being, as incarnated eternity, as the innermost of everything that is, which carries everything, releasing and freeing that which is ready to be freed.

At the same time the knowledge and the experience was renewed and deepened that Babaji, with his mercy, is also the Lord of the Grail and of the transformation of matter, which means the penetration of matter with light.

On February 9, a talk was given by a very fine elderly Indian, a disciple of Mahendra Maharaj, who had just arrived. In it he expressed with shining clarity that Babaji is the incarnation of highest divine mercy, pure love of the highest order, and that he is the eternal being in everything.

He expressed exactly what I knew in my soul.

Babaji then requested of him that he embrace some of us, one after the other. First the men whom Babaji had initiated as yogis, then he called me to the front followed by two other women. The elderly Indian embraced each one of us.

Through the embrace, his wisdom seemed to be transferred to us, or served to confirm our own inner knowing.

The next evening, February 10, the wise elderly Indian, whose name was Makhan Singh Baba, gave another talk at Babaji's behest. This time he spoke about the divine incarnations and their Kalas, i.e. the aspects of power that they bring with them.

Rama came with 12 Kalas, Krishna at first with 8 but then received a further 8 through the grace of Herakhan Baba, thus he had 16 Kalas. Rama and Krishna were incarnations of Vishnu. As Mahendra Baba, he came with 108 Kalas, and now as Herakhan Baba, Babaji had come with 1008 Kalas.

I must admit that at first I was astonished at the immense difference between 12 and 1008, from Rama with 12 aspects of power and Babaji now with 1008 aspects of power. That meant that he had come with all his power.

Next morning, February 11, sitting in a chair on his terrace, Babaji gave Darshan while he had a fever. The first to arrive he received singing lightly. Babaji wore a black pullover, and, as on all the following days, I was allowed to sit near him, together with a few other yogis.

I still had some unanswered questions about the talk the Indian had given the evening before. The whole thing moved me deeply.

Then Babaji began to pull bits of fluff from his black pullover, and as I began to collect the bits of fluff that had dropped on the floor, he said to me: "This outside!" It was clear to me what the bits of fluff symbolized. In this case they were the expression of my questioning, my doubts concerning the previous evening's talk, of which he thereby relieved me completely.

As always, each day it was exciting and illuminating to experience how Babaji responded to people who were standing waiting in the queue to come in front of him. Since I was sitting on the ground next to him, I could observe very closely the condition of each of those who came to him, and how Babaji responded.

One he blessed, another he ignored, looked away or even yawned; at the next one he beamed, gave him something, or simply looked at him full of compassion. From one second to the next his expression changed, often very subtly. There was a constant, living, deep Darshan – I am you and I guide you – even now while having a high fever.

I asked Babaji about my return flight which I had booked for February 17, whether I might stay for Shivaratri, or even longer. To which he replied, "Tomorrow you go to Delhi and change the ticket!" and then, "After Shivaratri you can go!" He stretched out his feet – and whereas every day previously I had been allowed to massage his feet, mostly when all the others had left, today this was not so.

I saw his feet, stretched out in the white socks and all of a sudden "The white feet of eternity" shot through me.

During Darshan a young man had brought him a book about Hiroshima. Babaji looked through the book very attentively. Another had given Babaji two oranges wrapped in a map of the world. He also looked at this map for a long time, and became sad as he did so. Then he asked for a minute's silence for Andropov, the president of Russia, who had passed away.

In the afternoon the weather turned very strange. There was frequent thunder without rain and there was something ominous in the air.

Babaji was ill and he did not come to the Kirtan Hall for evening Darshan. In my experience that had never happened before. However, his light presence could be felt intensely. It was said that something was wrong with his lungs, like pneumonia, and he had a high fever.

I immediately had the thought, "He is taking the polluted air of the future upon himself!"

I inwardly asked, "What can we do for you?" The idea came to me to perform a puja for the healing of the air. I simply invented a puja at the river below.

Next morning I was supposed to go to Delhi. It was unthinkable for me to sleep with Babaji being so ill that he was unable to come to Darshan. So, after evening Arati, when it had become quiet in the ashram, I began to dance for him in a prayer for healing, outside on the space leading down to his Kutiya.

I had often heard others say "Babaji always helps us, but what are we able to do for him? Isn't the only thing you can say, 'Lord heal thyself'?"

The rule that Christ gave us occurred to me: "When two or three are gathered in my name…", and so I prayed for Babaji, that the love which is there between the human and the divine being should heal him.

The incredible occurred: His fragrance came, the fragrance that was otherwise a gift from him for only a few seconds, but now this divine fragrance remained for hours! At the spot, up on the terrace, where the OM is painted on the little wall that goes around his Kutiya, the fragrance stood like a living presence. For hours and hours and hours. What an answer, what grace!

So I danced blissfully throughout the night, in the presence of his divine fragrance and in prayer for the healing of him. In the morning I was convinced that Babaji would be much better and I waited at his little gate.

In response to my question "How is Babaji?", one of the men who came out of his Kutiya said "No better! Babaji says: Outside pain, inside good."

Oh… and I had thought he was certainly healed after this wonderful night. So it occurred to me to bring him Tiger Balm to rub on his chest, and a fresh white scarf washed in the Gautama Ganga and dried in the wind to warm him, with the prayer that it might help him.

Shortly afterwards Babaji did appear on his terrace for Darshan. I was the first to run down and fall flat on the ground in front of him, deeply emotional. Babaji was completely veiled; one could only see his eyes and his nose. It seemed to me that he was wrapped in precisely this same white scarf.

To everyone who came he raised his hand in blessing, and I saw, as I had never seen before, the blessing flowing through his hand from far away. As if from a great distance he blessed each and every one of us. He was very serious and silent, touching all of us deeply.

Finally Babaji said quietly and gently to me and to a woman sitting next to me: "Jao!" – "Go!" This was at the end of Darshan, when most of the others had left. I bowed deeply, not knowing that this was my last Darshan with Babaji in this human form. As I stood up, I saw that precisely at that moment, down below in the valley, a truck was coming in which I was to travel. This time I took the truck in order to get to Haldwani as quickly as possible, and then on to Delhi and back again.

In Haldwani, I met Muniraj briefly who surprised me by saying, "When you come back, you can also take the night bus." I had no idea that there was a night bus. Then he added: "When you arrive, you can come to my house!"

In Delhi next day, February 13, I was able, with God's help, to change the date of my return flight at the travel agency without any problem. I stayed with the Lal family. The old lady, Vimla Lal, whom I liked very much, asked me to stay and see her new-born grandchild. This I did, but then I felt an extreme urgency to hurry back.

I took the night bus, which meant I appeared in front of Muniraj's house at about 2 or 3 a.m., grateful that I was able to go there at this hour. His sons told me that Babaji had called Muniraj to go to him immediately!

This caused my inner alarm bells to ring again and I wanted to set off for Herakhan immediately: "Please, please arrange some kind of means for me to go to Damside now!"

His sons explained to me: "Nobody will drive you in the night! Over this rough road!" I insisted.

Finally they found an uncle who was prepared to drive me at daybreak, but not before. Having arrived in Damside, everyone tried to stop me going on straightaway: "Wait. Later there will be a truck." But I was already on my way through the river, completely on my own, into the dawn.

I arrived in Herakhan shortly after 8 a.m. It was Tuesday, February 14, 1984. Just at that moment Muniraj came up the stairs out of Babaji's room. In reply to my anxious question: "How is Babaji?" Muniraj replied: "Heart pain!" – I fetched the heart drops immediately and gave them to Muniraj for Babaji, – and anxiously waited upstairs.

Then I heard that in the meantime Babaji had gone through the worst of the pain. On February 12, he had said to Gora Devi: "My heart is broken, wounded by a thousand knives, my body has thousands of wounds and there is nobody to heal me. Why, oh why? The moon, the sun and the stars are all within me and I carry the entire load of the Universe."

He let Kharku, one of his yogis,[7] hold a Shri Yantra to his heart for an hour, whilst Babaji sang love songs from Mira, which Gora Devi translated whilst he also touched the disciple's heart. What love!

On February 13, Babaji was worse. I heard that – supported by two yogis – he had walked shakily step by step to the Sheesh Mahal, a large room built for him close to his small Kutiya. His face was grey, he could scarcely breathe.

On another occasion, when one of the yogis who was accompanying him inwardly posed the question: "How can you be Lord of the Universe and be so weak?" Babaji straightened up and proceeded to walk with ease, looking radiant as if to demonstrate: – Of course I can do this, but that isn't going to transform the suffering – and then he went back into the pain, was ill, gasping for breath, was unsteady, had to be supported.

Seated in Sheesh Mahal, Babaji again looked for a long time through the book about Hiroshima, and said quietly: "I have taken too many diseases upon myself, now I have to dissolve them all."

On this February 13, at around midday, Babaji gave a short public Darshan; it was to be the last one. Babaji had been treated for pneumonia and when he was asked to take the medicine, he laughed, took it, but said that he could not get any air. One moment he was in great pain, the next cheerful, still giving teachings. No-one had any idea of what was about to happen.

In his great pain, time and again he got up from his bed. On one occasion, he stepped into the middle of the five or six yogis who were with him and had them all lay their hands on him from all sides. In this way he made himself the centre of a wheel, and they the spokes. He had them repeat this three times.

Babaji's words came to my mind, which he had said about six months earlier to a few who were very close to him. When one of the women cried and appealed to him imploringly, "Oh Baba, Oh Baba…", he interrupted her:

"No Baba, no Baba, only Adesh, only the law!"

"I never cry, because nothing of this world touches me any more.
Whoever goes and comes, is born or dies.
I have no attachment whatever to any of these things.

My heart has dried up and has turned to stone.
Every drop has left the ocean.
But who asks about my pain?"

On February 14, I stood by the small wall up above and looked in anxious expectation to where six or seven yogis were waiting outside Babaji's Kutiya. Inside with Babaji were Muniraj, Gohari, the young temple priest and Ramesh Batt.

Then the news came from below: "Babaji has stopped breathing, but his hands and feet are still warm." A little later it was said that his hands and feet were now also cold. One of the yogis, who was a doctor, added: "Clinically, one has to say, he is dead."

Nobody could or would believe it. At this precise moment I felt a powerful ray of light on my forehead. That was at around half past nine in the morning.

We all thought that he was in Samadhi and would return… It was a long wait. Finally I also went down and saw how Babaji was lying there on his bed in his little Kutiya. His face looked as though he had been through a mighty storm, as if he had fought a great fight. Tremendous.

On his bedcover there were marks…

There was an absolute stillness around him. Outside, nature too seemed to be holding its breath, not a bird sang. For hours. On the terrace directly above his Kutiya, at the spot where two nights before his wonderful fragrance had touched me, there was now a kind of suction, an emptiness, and there was the smell of wet chalk.

When the yogis initiated by Babaji, who had been waiting below, came up and one of them sobbed, I embraced him firmly and heard myself saying, "This is not allowed!" I was so filled with Babaji's power of joy and light, and not in the least with pain.

Babaji had always, and especially in these last few days, let me experience his being, his eternity, so deeply; this had led me far beyond the physical body to a new awareness: "I am the centre in everything that is, I am the light which penetrates all matter, radiating way, way beyond…" So now I was so immersed in the freedom and the power of the light, that there was no place for sadness.

It stayed that way for a long time.

Babaji, who with every breath had taken the topics, the problems and the pain of the world upon himself, and, full of mercy and in extreme humility, had transformed everything – regardless of what people thought or said – he had suffered to the very end, and he was at the same time eternally free.

"Are you crying because without his physical presence, you feel abandoned? Surely, you know that Babaji is absolutely faithful and true; he will continue to guide you, from within."

"Or are you crying, perhaps, because you saw his suffering, but didn't dare let yourself truly feel your compassion for him, and so could not ask the Perceval question: 'Why are you suffering? What is the matter? What can I do for you?'

On the evening of this February 14, 1984, St. Valentine's day, which is celebrated in the Western world as the day of love and friendship, Muniraj sent the message out into world that Babaji had left his human form.

Babaji had given Muniraj – Shri Maha Muniraj – the responsibility for everything. He had always said: "Muniraj's work will begin when I, Baba, go."

Babaji had given us everything there was to give. What more did we want?

Whilst Babaji's human form was still lying down below in his little Kutiya, a vigil was held during the night, singing "OM namah Shivay."

Muniraj was below with him and also, in turns, were some of those who lived in the ashram, such as Gohari, Man Singh, Gaura Devi, OM Shanti and Swamiji. There was only space for a very few in the small room.

Early in the morning Babaji's human form was laid on a bed covered with blocks of ice and blankets and placed on his terrace under his Pipal tree. Whereas on the previous day Babaji's face had looked wild, his appearance now became, from moment to moment, ever more tender, ever more beautiful.

At around 9 a.m. the first Indian devotees from outside arrived, Babaji's close disciples: Sheela came first from Bombay, Deviji and her husband Lakshmi, Gopiji and others – beautiful people.

Around midday Shastriji, who had had a long journey from Rajgarh, also arrived – Babaji's beloved Shastriji – together with Dr. Rao and many disciples.

More and more people came, so, so many...

We few Westerners, together with the Indian devotees, now kept watch over him, whose form lay outside under his tree, for the whole of this second day.

How young and beautiful Babaji's physical form now looked, lying there in complete innocence.

I stood by his body for hours and took him deep into my heart. Even though at that moment it was not comprehensible or clear to me, I felt that something very deep was happening to Babaji's body (see page 182 – Day 2).

In the evening the sky, which had remained misty during the daytime, became clear. The air was as soft as silk, filled with divine love.

That evening, as Pujari and I went down the stairs of the ashram, we glanced up at the heavens: there was the bright full moon, surrounded by an immense wide circle as if formed out of the finest diamonds. – Truly, a sign from God!

Full of awe, we paused. Never before and never since have I seen anything like it. It was utterly and totally overwhelming!

During this second night, which was gentle, warm and so full of love and sweetness, many people kept watch by Babaji's human form which he had left. Throughout the whole night, no doubt like many others, I slept very little or hardly at all. There were enormous energies present…

On February 16, very early, everyone was again assembled around his body. We sang…

Babaji's face was absolutely beautiful, inwardly glowing – like a Murti. He had been revered as such. Now his body was decorated with an abundance of flowers and malas.

He, the eternal one, who had danced into this world, the Maha Maya (the Great Illusion), with all its themes, who in his love had taken all our burdens upon himself, who had played his 'lilas' (divine games in human form) with us in order to free us, he had completely absorbed the quality of transience into his human form and transformed it in order to lead this Murti, his human form, through death and then to give it to Mother Earth.

It is significant that this time Babaji did not dissolve his human form into light as previously; but that he went with this form through death and gave it to the Earth, in this special time of mankind and world history.

"I adore You, guardian,
of the South-Eastern quarter,
ruler of the universe,
eternal bliss personified,
omnipotent, all-pervading Brahman,
manifested in the form of the Vedas.
I worship You, Shiva, oh Lord,
shining in the light of what was
before creation came into being,
devoid of material attributes,
undifferentiated, desireless,
all-pervading consciousness,
clad with nothing but ether,
element of purest light.
I bow to You, supreme Lord,

transcendent, trans-cosmic,
source of all that is created
beyond speech, beyond understanding
and sense-perception,
terrible, yet gracious,
seed of the mystic syllable AUM,
ruler of Mt. Kailasha and devourer
even of the cosmic time:
essence of all virtue.
I adore You, Shankara,
all-merciful, Lord of the Universe,
unfathomable, yet loved by all…"

VERSES BY TULSIDAS, IN PRAISE OF SHIVA

The countenance of love – Lord Shiva in human form

We saw the still countenance of Love – Lord Shiva in human form.

In the meantime, the governor of Uttar Pradesh, who is a great admirer of Babaji, had also arrived along with countless others.

Beside the Kirtan hall a large deep hole had been dug lined with precious silk cloths. Babaji's human form was carried by seven of his yogis from its place below the Pipal tree to the burial place which had been dug for him, and was gently lowered into the earth with the head to the south, looking towards Mt. Kailash in the north.

That was on Thursday, the 16th of February 1984, the day of the full moon in Aquarius, between 11 a.m. and 12 noon; it was a beautiful sunny day.

Babaji's face was so tender and beautiful.

He was surrounded by flowers, Malas soaked in perfume, with all the required ritual objects, like a bucket of water, a blanket, cotton scarves, food, spices, incense, money, silk and an ocean of flowers. I could see all this very clearly because I was standing up above with 2 or 3 others on a very small patch of ground at the edge of the Kirtan hall – his grave was directly below.

The surging crowd pressed forward to the grave. Muniraj, Shastriji and Governor Singh performed for us all the last Arati in front of Babaji's human form.

Afterwards, incense, kilos of rice, dried fruits and coconuts were laid around his body. Then came salt placed on top of him, salt and more salt – 500kg of salt. It touched our hearts when the first offering of salt fell upon his face.

And finally, earth covered the human form of Babaji. It was all so deeply moving that one could hardly take it in.

To my amazement, most of the countless numbers of people disappeared again just as fast as they had come.

In the next few days Babaji's presence and inner guidance could be felt incredibly strongly. Everyone experienced this in a different way. For me it came especially through his divine fragrance. Whenever I was in the vibration of love, the heart's oneness with someone, there arose his totally delightful fragrance.

During the next days we were sitting there where his precious body lay under the earth, in deep gratitude for his profound sacrifice and the infinite gifts he had given to us.

Babaji's human form, which we had laid here in the earth of Herakhan, is the same form as that in which Babaji had appeared at the beginning of the 19th century on top of the Herakhan Kailash out of a ball of light, as a radiant being of 20 to 25 years of age.

This appearance in human form of the Divine Being was then recognized by Yogananda as Mahavatar Babaji, later as Baba Herakhan, whom many knew and also deeply revered because of his healings and raising of the dead. In August 1922, he dematerialized before the eyes of several disciples at the place where the Kali and Gauri rivers meet; after that, he still appeared to individuals.

In June 1970, Babaji appeared in his cave at the foot of Mt. Kailash in the same form, but younger and somewhat altered. – "It is always the same body," Shastriji said – and since that time Babaji had been among us.

His human form changed tremendously in consequence of all that he then took upon himself and then transformed.

It is of truly great importance that Babaji let this materialized human form, through which he had done so much, go through death so that it could be given to the Earth, the earth of Herakhan, and did not dematerialize it into light as all his devotees had expected. Obviously, the Earth needed this substance. This is a great and extremely precious gift for her!

Even though this time Babaji allowed his physical human form to pass through death, "He himself has not gone! He can appear at any time and in any form" Muniraj always emphasizes.

Babaji is the eternal being. He is always there, omnipresent. He guides everyone, and helps everyone who calls him from the heart.

In order to thank him a little bit for his sacrifice, which he fulfilled in this form, I arranged for a velvet cloth to be sewn in the ashram in the form of a 12-petalled lotus. In the centre of the velvet cloth I shaped a large OM out of a thick Rudraksha mala, which I sewed onto the cloth. I laid this dark red cloth on the fresh earth, below which we had placed his human form.

It remained there for a long time.

A year later when I returned, OM Shanti, an Indian woman who lived in the ashram, gave the cloth back to me with the words: "I have looked after it for you." This cloth later accompanied me to Tibet, to Mt. Kailash there, and it is this cloth we use every Friday for a particular meditation. A marble temple has now been built over the place where his body lay in the earth.

Babaji is also the King of the Grail,
who, in this form took not only the suffering
of the land and the Earth on himself,
but something much greater.
"Not only the Earth is in danger, the entire Universe is in danger," he said
repeatedly. (see "Revelations concerning Babaji's Mahasamadhi," page 177).

Babaji's sign

Once, he let his sign be set upon a large white flag: A cross and on it the OM. It is a powerful combination:

The OM fixed on the cross, and at the same time the OM that liberates the cross.

Three days after Babaji's body had been placed in the earth, there were wild storms, thunder and lightning with torrential rain, hail too – the elements were out of control. The Gautam Ganga river was so swollen that for days we could not leave Herakhan, neither through the valley nor over the mountains.

At night time it was extremely dark, almost eerie…

Traditionally, the wake should last 12 nights, up in the Kirtan hall or below in the Dhuni, where the holy fire is located close to the river. Babaji had lovingly formed the eight-sided fireplace of the Dhuni with his own hands for the fire of the Divine Mother. She is honoured there with the fire every morning and every evening.

"Everyone can find liberation there" – Babaji had given the Dhuni this blessing. Now it felt so good to be within the intimacy of the Dhuni, and to feel Babaji's presence, freedom and peace within the living flames. – He and the Devi, the Divine Mother, are one.

Through the heart's profound reverence the divine light becomes visible.

Babaji's sign: OM in the cross

Divine Mother as Herakhandeshwari Ma

Babaji's words in February 1984

Love all mankind!
Help all living beings!
Be happy, be polite!
Be a source of inexhaustible joy!
Recognize God and the good in every face!
No saint is without a past,
No sinner without a future.
Speak well of everyone!
If you can't find praise for someone,
Then let him go out of your life!
Be original! Be inventive!
Be brave! Take courage! – time and again.
Don't imitate others! Be strong! Be upright!
Don't lean yourself on others as crutches!
Think with your own head!
BE YOURSELF!
All the perfection and virtue of God are hidden within you – reveal them!
Wisdom is also already in you – give it to the world!
Let God's grace make you free!
Let your life be that of a rose,
Silently she speaks the language of fragrance.

In retrospect

As surprising and sudden as this surrender of his body was for all of us, there had been various indications that Babaji would leave his body and when it would happen. This had either not been understood or was only recognized later.

- In 1971, Shri Nantin Baba, a renowned saint from the north of India, had openly announced that Babaji was a manifestation of Shiva, and that he would leave after a few years, when he would have completed his special mission, in order to return again as a young boy.
- In February 1973 this was confirmed by Shri Gangotri Baba, with the additional indication that it seemed as if Babaji would leave the Earth in seven or eight years, unless a special disciple came, for whose sake he would stay for a few years more.
- Ram Singh from Okaldunga had announced in 1970 that Babaji would depart in 1984.
- In 1980, Babaji told an Indian, Hem Chand Bhatt, that he would leave Herakhan in 1984. Asked when he would return, Babaji replied that he would return if someone would call him as much as Mahendra Maharaj did.
- In August 1983, Babaji told Ram Dass, one of his yogis: "In 6 months I will be in Samadhi." Ram Dass was puzzled about what exactly Babaji meant, but he did not get the idea that Babaji would leave his body.
- At about that time, Babaji led Man Singh, who served him the whole time, to the place near the Kirtan hall and said to him: "You will dig out the grave for me here," whereupon Man Singh began to cry.
- Gora Devi, Babaji's first female disciple from the West, met Babaji in February 1972. He told her then that she would be with him for 12 years. This period was completed in February 1984 and she asked herself what was going to happen.
- On February 9, 1984, Makhan Singh Baba, a temple priest from Babaji's ashram in Madhuban, came at Babaji's request. Upon his arrival Babaji informed him that he would leave his body in the morning of February 14, but that he should not talk about it with anybody.

What Babaji teaches us,
in his own words

"I only like Zeroland," – the land of nothingness –, I once heard Babaji say this and I was touched deeply: Zeroland – the eternal being, the kingdom of Lord Shiva, beyond duality, that at the same time penetrates, embraces and supports all that is.

Asked: "Who are you?," Babaji gave several answers:

"I am nobody and nothing. This body is only here to serve all beings.
My name is Mahaprabhuji, the great Lord."

"I am like fire. Don't stay too far away, because then you would not feel the warmth. But don't come too close, so that you don't get burnt. Learn the right distance."

"I am everywhere."
"I am in your every breath."
"I am the mirror in which you can see yourself."
"I am Bhole Baba, the father, who is simple."
"I have come to help you, to guide you. Place your burden at my feet.
I will carry your burden."

"I have come to lead you to the awareness of oneness beyond duality, to dispel the disunity caused by confessions of faith, religions and castes.
There is only one humanity, be human!
Seek to experience in your awareness that we are all one.
I want to show you a freedom beyond your perceptions, where the lion and the goat are drinking together from the same spring."

Babaji standing (1972)

"Seek harmony in everything that you do. I am harmony.
If you are in peace, so am I.
If you are troubled, so am I.
If you are happy, so am I.
Be happy!
I am you.
Have faith, everything depends on faith.
Always carry the name of God in yourself."

"The quickest way to realize God is the continuous repetition of his name.
By the repetition of the names of God (the Mantras) the human mind is
cleansed.
This is the only remedy for the sickness of the mind.
If your mind and heart are not pure, how can God live there?
The water to cleanse your heart is the name of God.
Everyone should repeat God's name, everywhere in the world."

In particular, Babaji taught the repetition of the Mantra:

OM NAMAH SHIVAY!

"I bow down in front of God" –
or: "I take refuge in God" – "I surrender to you Lord!"
or, freely translated: "God, I love you."

Babaji said:
    "OM namah Shivay is the great original mantra,
    it is one with the primal sound of the creation.
    The power of OM namah Shivay is infinite,
    it is stronger than all the atomic bombs of the world."
    "Teach everyone the invocation of God's name,
    everywhere in the world."

Babaji came in order to re-establish the Sanatana Dharma, the universal divine
law that has existed since the beginning of time.

No-one can say when it began. It is so spontaneous and natural. Just as it is the
Dharma, the being or the nature of fire, to burn, and the Dharma, the being, the
nature of water to flow and of the air to blow – in just the same way, it is the nature
of the Dharma, the being of the soul, to become one with the Divine Spirit.

Spiritual practices through which this Oneness is reached express themselves
completely naturally out of the soul's spontaneous need, this longing of mankind,
and can be found in all religions.

Babaji encouraged carrying out these basic natural practices:
• The worship of God,
• The repetition of God's divine names.
• The remembrance of God, the constant awareness of the Divine Spirit.

And he emphasized: *"True religion is to serve mankind."*

The Sanatana Dharma is like an ocean out of which the various religions have sprung like rivers. Babaji said:

"To live in TRUTH, SIMPLICITY and LOVE,
is the highest duty of man.
Since all religions lead to God,
follow the religion of your heart.
Service to mankind is service to God, is worship of God.
Love and serve others as you love and serve me.
I myself have come to help all beings, to serve all beings.
Everyone should see himself/herself as a humble servant
of other people, of the earth, of the world."

Babaji's work, which began in 1970, has not only resulted in the establishment of many temples and ashrams in India and the West. He himself has also initiated a large number of welfare projects, which have made available medicine, education, clothing, food and shelter for the poor in India, and also the means to help themselves.

He has also initiated hospitals, veterinary clinics and free mobile health treatments in remote regions. Babaji taught that through the practice of Karma-Yoga, which is the dedication of all actions to God and the non-attachment to the fruits of action, a person purifies and protects himself.

"Find out your duties in this world and fulfil them with love, thereby
devoting everything to God."

"Working is service of God!"
"Try to do more than you believe to be possible.
Be prepared to do any kind of work.
While you are working, have always God's name in yourself.
Work until your last breath.
A lazy man is a dead man.
Work, and become light!"

"In this time at the end of the Kali Yuga the gateways to heaven are only
open for Karma Yogis. The way of action will lead you into freedom."

*"Act with courage! Yoga, the way of union with God demands courage.
To be disappointed or to lose courage is not Yoga!"*

*"All living beings, including animals, flowers and stones, have been given
a form by God, in order to fulfil a duty in this world. My body, too, is
here only in order to fulfil a duty: to serve all human beings, all living
things.
When human beings enter this world, they forget their duties and they
fall in attachment to the illusions of the material world, they fall into "I"
and "mine" und thus they forget God."*

*"I have come to give, only to give, but who is able to receive what I really
have to give?"*

It was also Babaji's wish to re-establish the awareness of the original meaning of
the Yagna, the fire ceremony, which, according to the Vedas, is the most powerful
means for the harmonizing of cosmic energy in order to balance all levels of life.
The Yagna is of great importance. Babaji has brought it back into life again.

Babaji himself performed a Havan (Yagna), a short fire ceremony, every day
before dawn, and on many special occasions, like Christmas, Navaratri, etc. he
celebrated big Yagnas together with many people.

*"I do not want thousands and millions of followers.
One perfect being is enough to change the world.
Rama, Krishna, Christ – were not many.
Each of them was only one, but they changed the world.
Buddha was only one, too, and he changed the world.
I am telling you these things so that you won't think that the number is
important.
One spark of light is enough to illuminate the world."*

*"I want to wake up mankind.
I want to show the way to peace and happiness.
This is only possible when the bad elements are removed.
Mankind is enslaved by his lower nature.
I have come to lead man onto a higher way.
The higher self must be developed in man,
thereby his lower self will dissolve and his heart will be transformed.*

Be human!"
"Today, not only humanity is in danger, but all the beings of the universe.
I cannot just take care of mankind, the entire creation is to be saved…
How is this possible? (long pause)
It is almost impossible. The calamities approaching the earth cannot be
avoided. No time can be compared with this time. The revolution will
not even last minutes, it will be over in seconds. The countries which
have produced these destructive weapons should not believe that they are
safe…"

In the last time before he gave up his body, Babaji often called us "my children."
To one disciple he said:

"My son, now is the time to keep the spine straight. The time has come to
move forward, for your good, for the world, for the good of all, it is neces-
sary to keep the spine straight. Because the time has come."

"A great revolution is coming, such as it has never been between heaven
and earth. It will happen everywhere at the same moment, very soon, it
will sweep like a scythe from one end of the earth to the other. It will be
total. Where there is water, there will be land. Where there are moun-
tains, there will be valleys. Those who are sleeping will die while sleeping,
Those standing will die while standing.
I will burn fire and water together and I will be in the middle of fire and
water. I will remain there whatever happens."

"Universal peace is my main goal and only purpose.
A new kingdom is coming.
Only a little time remains until you will see the New World."

Shri Muniraj Maharaj

Babaji handed his responsibility during his physical absence to Shri Muniraj. He said: "Muniraj is an incarnation of Lord Dattatreya" – that is the oneness of Brahma, Vishnu and Shiva – a highly exalted being. Muniraj has come to serve the world and all living beings with great love. He has descended deep down into this life in order to demonstrate that one can lead a divinely fulfilled life even as a family man – the father of nine children – and as a business man. Many years ago Babaji had encouraged everyone to bow not just before him, but also before Muniraji.

Babaji also made it clear that Muniraj is the guru of the people of the West. My pen always first comes to rest when I want to write about Shri Muniraj, his being and his works. The world is full of stage holy men. Shri Muniraj is the exact opposite.

His being, as deep as it is hidden, as great as it is simple, is full of compassion and of natural humility. Like water which is neither sweet nor salty, but pure.

Depth has to be experienced, one cannot speak about this. When one wants to truly encounter a being like Muniraj who reaches into the heart of the Earth and to the Highest, one has to go deep within oneself, to listen and to receive.

To the superficial gaze he remains hidden. One might experience that he is very loving with small children, that various dogs surround him happily, that his look is of wonderful human warmth, very clear and radiant – sometimes stern as well. A dignity surrounds him. He is completely poised and an ocean of stillness. In his presence, stillness vibrates and light becomes tangible in the silence of his love.

Babaji once said: "When Muniraj smiles, then all worlds smile. Shri Muniraj is of world encompassing consciousness and actions."

Once Babaji spoke of Kakbushundi, a highly enlightened being who lives in the form of a crow on a hill in the Himalayas: "He will survive all pralayas (dissolving of creations) as he wishes absolutely nothing for himself. The same applies for Christian Rosenkreutz and with certainty also for Shri Muniraj.

Shri Muniraj, a great protector on so many levels, is always there to help all those who ask it of him. He sees everything, guides and inspires from within and acts in oneness with Babaji. In himself completely free, he partakes deeply in the suffering of the whole.

Shri Muniraj with Chandan (1984)

In the autumn of 1984, in Chilianaula, something beautiful came to pass.Kharku Anand, a very dear friend, on his birthday went to Muniraj in order to bow to him. When he looked up again, instead of Muniraj he saw Babaji sitting there. – Overwhelmed and completely at a loss he ran out of the room. When he returned after some time to talk to Muniraj about the event, the latter only commented: "Sometimes Babaji does these things."

This event shows how deeply Muniraji lives in total surrender to Babaji and how perfectly Babaji works through Muniraj.

Muniraj is there for all people of the west and the east who turn to him. He has travelled to the west on many occasions, inspiring and supporting the various spiritual centres there and the people who have called to him.

The Navaratris, the nine-day celebration in honour of the Divine Mother in prayer for the healing of all beings, are celebrated under his guidance in spring in Herakhan and in autumn in Chilianaula (in the ashram built by Muniraj for Babaji). Celebrations of enormous power, which are attended each year by hundreds of people from India and many other countries of the world.

Here is a personal example of Muniraj's work: In September 2008, I was driving alongside Lake Constance. It was raining and while I was driving, I had fallen asleep, crossed over to the oncoming lane, had mown down several of the posts marking the edge of the road and then experienced, as if in a dream, how a sovereign and very calm energy steered my car and brought it back onto the right side of the road. It was then that I recovered myself and stopped the car, still dazed. Amazingly, I was filled with a great sense of calm.

Shri Muniraj and Shastriji with Peter Caddy at Findhorn (1988)

A young woman, who had apparently been driving behind me, brought her car to a stop in front of me and came to my window. "You fell asleep, didn't you? You've lost your bumper and your number plate. You must have had a shock, stay sitting there, I'll fetch everything for you." She ran back in the rain and collected everything up. She seemed like an angel to me. OM namah Shivay!

Later I discovered that I had mown down eight wooden posts, which I reported to the appropriate authority, but the good man said: "They were in any case due for replacement" – and, "It is seldom that someone is so honest. You don't have to pay anything."

First I asked myself if it had been Babaji who had steered my car – but as I brought to mind that sovereign calm, I realized that it had been Muniraj. When I called him three days later to ask him about it, his answer was: "Yes!"

OM namah Shivay!

How wonderful, that right in the moment of danger, he was there and acted. I am so grateful to him for his manifold actions, also on inner levels!

Shri Vishwa Acharya Vishnu Datt Mishra: Shastriji

Our golden Shastriji, with his depth of heart, full of such great love and warmth, is the great seer and, as Babaji said, "the holy poet and world teacher through all time." Babaji also said that he wrote most of the great epics of the east and the west through the ages. He is an ocean of wisdom and likewise a wonderful protector and healer, now active in the inner world.

In 2003, 97 years of age, he left his physical body. He too was a family man with eight children, a widely known scholar and author of 65 books, one of which had 1000 pages and presents the works of Babaji through time (as of this date, only in Hindi). In addition, he was a renowned Ayurvedic doctor.

As far as possible, Shastriji was with Babaji. Usually, Babaji invited him to sleep by him in his small Kutiya.

He was Babaji's voice. As Babaji himself rarely spoke at any length in public, Shastriji held the talks, inspired by him, and recited the mantras at all his fire ceremonies – including on journeys.

Shastriji told us about our past and our future. "I see everything, but only very little passes my lips," he once said to me. But what was "little" for him was a great deal for us!

After Babaji's Mahasamadhi, Muniraj usually took Shastriji with him to the west, together with a number of devotees. It was also such a great pleasure to accommodate Shastriji in our home. We – my husband Peter and I – took Muniraji and Shastriji and the whole crew to Findhorn as well, in June 1988. Findhorn is the international spiritual community in the north of Scotland, which Peter had co-founded in 1962 and which is home today to about five hundred people live.

It was also a great pleasure to visit Shastriji in his country house in Rajgarh, which was always an extremely inspiring, richly deep time.

Although Shastriji was very spontaneous and lively, and of a great natural humility, how can we know the depth of his work behind the scenes?

Here is a little story: Whilst at Shastriji's house and shortly before departing for Germany, I suddenly became very ill. Vomiting, diarrhoea, very high fever.

I had totally upset my body by eating some of the Indian sweets, which I had brought for everybody from the little town for the full moon celebration.

"Oh Shastriji, I have to go to Delhi early in the morning to catch my flight to Germany. How can I possibly travel? I feel extremely weak."

"This is very bad," he said, sitting at the foot of my bed and looking very concerned. Suddenly he made some movements with his hands in my direction, it all happened very quickly – and the spirit of life returned to me.

In the shortest possible time I was fit again, and able to travel next morning.

"I usually don't do these things", he commented when I then profoundly thanked him.

Shri Shastriji reading Holy Scriptures

Om Namah Shivay

2. A Garden of Heaven Comes into Being

The little temple and its transformation

Nandan Van / Garden of Heaven, painted by Babaji
in the book *Om Kareshwar* (1978)

Once upon a time there was a temple. It had been there for hundreds of years. At some point in time it moved from being visible back to being invisible, and had its effect from there.

Following a picture of Lake Constance, Babaji painted a picture of our house with a little temple in his first painted book. There followed a picture of "Lord Shiva's Garden," a garden full of blooms with a large OM written above it, a picture of "Tibet" and at the end, "The New World." The whole book, which had other pictures on the first few pages, he called "OM Kareshwar," "Lord Shiva's Temple" or "The seat of the Lord whose name is OM."

When, through a friend, in the summer of 1978, Babaji sent me a small carved wooden Murti, a statue of the old Herakhan Baba, together with the message that it should be placed where many people could see it, I began to ask myself anew what was meant by the little temple that he had painted.

Below and in front of our house there is a large wild garden. When my friend Marcel, who is very clairvoyant, sat at the writing desk on the second day after we had moved in and looked out of the window, he said: "Now then, what have we got here? It's as if Heaven is penetrating vertically into the Earth here. Not as usual, Heaven above and Earth below. The energy of Heaven is penetrating into the Earth like an acupuncture needle and that, moreover, directly in front of us in the garden."

Even during moving in, we had noticed an extraordinarily high vibration here, which very quickly brought to the surface everything in us – now that we were four, not only two people – which was not of the light.

In the meantime, in February 1979, I had again been in Herakhan and it had become clear to me that I would build a little temple, inspired by Babaji. To my question: "Of wood or stone?" he answered, to my surprise at that time: "Of wood!" Only later did I understand why.

On August 17, 1979, the little temple, which was very simple, was inaugurated by a Philippine healer. It was so delightful to see the little temple in the wild garden. The daily service of Arati, a ceremony of light and meditation, had the effect on the temple that it increasingly began to glow; it grew and became ever more lovely, beautiful and rich. Every day I used the wonderfully fragrant yellow Chandan powder here, which Babaji had given to me in a round parcel right after the first fire ceremony by Kailash. It was clearly meant for the little temple, which at that time did not yet exist.

The temple was given a walkway around it, a Trishul on its extended roof and much more. I painted signs for all the elements on its walls: earth, water, fire, air and the ether. I had dedicated it to the divine flame which is in all there is, and painted for it a picture of a magnificent golden flame, behind which stood Babaji, tall and sublime.

Jesus had found his expression in the temple, and also elements of all the spiritual movements that were dear to me. When I had a spiritual sign or symbol not drawn in its rightful place, I noticed that until I found the right location, I did not find peace for days. Thus I received the impression that this little temple also had its counterpart in the inner world.

In the middle of the garden a fireplace was created which we set deep into the earth, as I had seen it done in India. To start with I carried out a fire ceremony once a year, always on August 17, the birthday of the temple.

All my friends loved the little temple with its coloured glass windows, its golden painted floor, its OM sign in the golden ground, its flaming heart symbol on the ceiling and – with Babaji's intensive presence.

In 1981, Muniraj came to Europe for the first time, and also visited our home. As I stood with him on the balcony and he looked into the garden, I said to him: "Look Muniraj, there is the little temple." He responded: "It is not a little temple, it is a great temple here!"

We celebrated each of the temple's birthdays with many friends, often with children as well. It was always a unique celebration. The temple became more and more beautiful: It was made of pure love.

In 1980, when I gave Babaji a painted photo album I had made of my little temple, he took it, held it to his right and then his left cheek and to his heart, then again left and right to his cheeks, full of love and tenderness. It was enchanting. How could he express his love for the little temple more clearly?

Years later, after Babaji's Mahasamadhi, the wife of the architect who had built the enormous temple of the Chilianaula Ashram on Muniraji's orders for Babaji, told me that when Babaji came to visit them in Delhi he frequently said: "Please, bring me my favourite book!" His "favourite book" was that lovingly painted small photo album of the little temple. I felt deeply touched that, even after the death of his body, he showed me his love for the little temple in this way!

After 12 and a half years, as I placed a dancing Shiva statue in the walkway around the temple, I said to Babaji inwardly: "The little temple is now complete. It is perfectly beautiful. I have nothing more to add to it."

And Shiva danced!

Precisely four days later the temple ascended to the heavens in flames. Peter Caddy, my husband who had married me in 1987, charged into my room at 1 a.m.: "Your temple is burning!" The fire brigade was already there in the garden. Naturally I was totally shocked, even though the scene presenting itself to me then was very beautiful. I saw a large blue flame like a huge S or a C repeatedly dance up through the other flames and I knew everything to be under divine control.

That same night, deeply moved, Peter and I rang up our friend Peter Dawkins, who commented: "That was a fire ceremony on a big scale!"

On the next morning it could be seen that indeed only the temple had been on fire and the trees and everything around were as good as unscathed. The Herakhan Baba Murti had transformed into a lingam, a symbol of Shiva. Very touching! All the holy yantras or symbols were still whole whereas the massive bells had melted.

The comment of a clairvoyant friend about this was: "Your temple was a saint and those are his relics."

The energy of incredible joy filled the garden. This stood in intense contrast to the part of me that was understandably deeply shaken, sad and completely puzzled: Why? How could this happen?

I had myself been the last one in the temple and, as every night, had left a few tea candles burning. This all happened on the Monday night from February 24 to 25, 1992, one of Babaji's holy nights.[8]

Peter, my husband, who had no further thoughts of temples in his mind, laid out a rose bed there immediately. The trishul, which had been on the top of the roof of the temple, has remained untouched, and we placed it in the middle of the rose bed. A large fire-blue glass sphere, which was close by, was totally undamaged, whereas the stick on which it had been standing was charred black.

Over the years the whole garden had developed into a temple, mainly since I lived there with Peter. In 1988, before Peter began to tame the wild garden, he had asked his friend Peter Dawkins, who was involved with the science of temples, how this great romantic garden with its wonderful vibrations was to be formed according to God's will.

In his inner vision of the garden, Peter Dawkins saw all the energy centres which expressed a perfect Tree of Life, in the image of man as described in the Kabbalah. According to Peter Dawkin's research, this is also the guiding principle of all cathedrals and temples. Now we realized that the great temple, of which Muniraji had spoken in 1981, comprised the entire garden. The little temple had been the anchor for the great temple.

We then buried the yantras, which had gone through the fire and remained undamaged, at all the important spots, deep in the earth, so that the energy of the little temple permeated the entire garden. We also spread its holy ashes across the whole garden.

Babaji gave me a vision in which I saw the little temple glowing blue in the inner world and visited by many spirit beings.

None of this helped to soothe my pain, my non-comprehension. The question deep in my heart remained: Why did it happen? After all, the temple had been made of pure love.

Shortly afterwards, as I was in Herakhan for the spring Navaratri, all the sadness welled up again and inwardly I asked Babaji with all my heart, with all that I was, for an answer. The explanation came:

Even before the temple had been built, it was destined to depart again.

The reason was this: Babaji had allowed that I, as a young woman, had made offerings that first fire ceremony at Mt. Kailash. At the time Tara Devi had said to me that all the Gods were now against Babaji and demanded my life (see "The first fire ceremony at the foot of the Herakhan Kailash", page 97).

But Babaji had said: "You may not take her life, but you can have the temple which she will build." The time for this had come 12½ years later.

I asked Muniraj if this was the truth. He answered: "It is true." At that I was relieved and thankful. I had dedicated the temple to the flame, which then bore it up to heaven.

A little later, when Peter Dawkins visited us for the first time after the incident of the temple and meditated in the garden, he perceived something new: "Your temple has become a star!" He was very moved and said that I should ask an astronomer whether a new star had been discovered. I took that silently into my heart, however, and in gratitude left it at that.

After the little temple had gone up in flames into the heavens, all our attention became focussed upon the great inner temple, which extended over the entire garden.

The garden revealed it was a small cosmos in itself. It unfolded and, like a living being, revealed the locations of its various energy regions.

We discovered that it had a head region in the north where the little temple had stood, a heart region in the middle where the fireplace is located and a lower region around the place where there is a fountain. Right down below at the base area lies a large stone.

Always listening to the voice within, we now worked towards the completion of the great temple which, stretching from north to south, expressed itself perfectly in the whole garden through the tree of life with its chakras and its double cross.

Exactly nine years later there was again a fire in the garden. It was on the same Monday night in February 2001, only this time on February 26. Together with some others, I was preparing a puja in the meditation room in our house. As I was about to begin, I stopped suddenly and said: "I have to take the flame into the garden now, please carry on here." A friend, Rudolf, said: "I'll come with you."

The garden was covered in deep snow. Going past the place of Mars in the middle of the heart region towards the fireplace, I was surprised to see that the little light from the place of Mars was not radiating in direct lines, as it usually does, but rather appeared to form curls in the shape of roses. With my back to the place of Mars, I looked towards the flame that we had brought into the middle. Suddenly Rudolf, who was standing opposite me, shouted: "A fire!" Following his gaze I turned around and saw how a tall blue column of fire, maybe one and a half meters high, arose out of the night light in its small holder on the place of Mars.

Nila with Shri Muniraj and Shri Shastriji at a fire ceremony at her centre
Quell des Heilens – Source of Healing (1985)

A pure sky blue fire. We stepped closer. I calmed Rudolf: "Look, how beautiful!" It was truly breathtakingly beautiful, sublime and holy. We stood there, silent in amazement. After a while the fire fell back, very slowly, gently. Moved, we related this event to our friends.

Very early the next morning a friend of mine went into the garden and saw no sign of soot in the snow at the place of Mars. Everything was clean and untouched. When I told Shastriji on the phone about the blue fire, he said: "Now the name of your place is 'Sublime Healing Centre.'"

After this holy fire, various divine beings indicated their locations in the garden very clearly. For instance, between the places of Mars and Mercury, a special energy suddenly became very noticeable to me and to others. Who was announcing himself? To my surprise, I suddenly knew: This is Buddha.

When I told Shastriji of this – at that time I rang up Shastriji more often than Muniraj in order to get his advice and confirmation on each important detail of the garden – he said: "This place for Buddha between Mars and Mercury is of great significance" and I remembered that according to Rudolf Steiner the appearance of Buddha fell precisely at the end of the Mars period[9] and the beginning of the Mercury period of Mankind.

The presence of Jesus in the garden could be felt from the beginning, but now his place was clear; it is specifically on the opposite side of Babaji's stone seat. The same happened a while later with Krishna and Radha and with Rama and Sita. They showed us their places, all within the roundel of the heart. Full of joy, we created a special place for each with a fine oval stone on the ground, surrounding it with beautiful decorative flowers and bushes, and put a holder for a night light in front of it.

Then in the water roundel under a tree, the lower female area of the garden, a very remarkable energy could suddenly be sensed. I asked myself who this could be? There was already a place in the garden for angels, for the angels of protection and healing and for the four angels of the four cardinal directions. The Divine Mother as the World Mother had her enchanting place at the water roundel, and as Mother Maria she had already lived for a long time in the roundel of the heart.

This enormous energy under the huge tree, who could it be? I put a beautiful light there and thought: "Perhaps this spot is intended for the ancestors?" At the very moment that I wanted to invite them with incense sticks, Kali[10] unexpectedly stood there in front of me! OM namah Shivay!

Shortly after this, in two places on the opposite side of the water roundel, a special energy became manifest: first Saraswati,[11] then Lakshmi.[12] Again, I checked this with Shastriji. "Yes," he confirmed everything.

Thus the light and the energy of the "blue fire" enabled the descent of the various forms of expression of the One Divine Being. Since then, we greet and honour them every day. All of this happened after the entire garden was expressing the great temple through the fully unfolded tree of life.

Thus a "Garden of Heaven," called Nandan Van, brought itself into being on Earth, deeply connected to the heart of Europe. It is a garden which serves the immortal aspect in creation, and which in a deep way nourishes and heals. The name of the centre as a whole is *Quell des Heilens (Source of Healing)*.

We celebrate, among other things, the eight solar festivals of the year with fire ceremonies, a powerful means to balance and heal the elements in us and in nature, and much more. Many people come to participate and enjoy. Here are a few words which Shri Muniraj said about this Garden on March 8, 2011:

Quell des Heilens / Source of Healing
Nandan Van

"This Garden is created by Babaji's Grace.
It is a universal Place.
It is a Garden of Creation.
It is like the Heart in the Heart of Europe."

3. *Further Appearances of Babaji and Revelations*

Peter & Renata Caddy

With Peter on the way to Herakhan: Babaji's appearance

Peter and I went through the valley to Herakhan, repeatedly crossing the Gautam Ganga river. This was the first time for Peter. We knew that we would be married at Christmas with Muniraji's blessing at the foot of the Kailash in Herakhan.

We stood in front of a particularly deep river crossing and Peter was busy tying the laces of his tennis shoes tightly while I waited. Suddenly I saw three women balancing tall baskets full of grass on their heads, wading through the river. They went past us close by.

Walking directly behind them was a most beautiful figure with a sky blue head covering of the finest silk. He had the same sky blue silk draped around his hips. He wore a Brahmin thread diagonally across his bare upper body and was holding a long staff in his hand. His face was radiantly beautiful, with shining golden brown eyes. His gaze, encompassing us both simultaneously, went right through us and into the distance. He went past close to us. That was on Sunday, November 29, 1987.

My first thought was: "Is that the messenger of a king?"

In the following days and nights, this apparition would not leave us in peace. We both found ourselves thinking of it again and again, and the feeling deepened in me that this was Babaji, welcoming us both into his valley and giving us his blessing for our life together.

We asked Muniraj: "Who was that?"

His answer: "That was Babaji in the form of Bhairav Baba."

Exactly the same answer came from Shastriji when I visited him with Peter. From the very beginning Shastriji felt great respect, friendship and deep love for Peter. Seeing all his lives and actions on earth, he once said to me: "Peter is a very mysterious being."

Encounters with Hanuman

When we visited Shastriji again in his beautiful, simple home full of light, surrounded by greenery, in Rajgarh, where he lived with his family, he inspired us to drive with others in a small bus to a place of Hanuman in the jungle.

It was September 28, 1988. In the bus, on the way through very remote regions with wild animals, I saw a really beautifully shaped young man speedily approaching us, very alive, full of energy, tall, with wide shoulders, joyful curly brown hair, shining eyes and a Brahmin thread around his bare upper body.

Where did this beautiful young person come from in this lonely wilderness?

He walked along the side of the bus and directly past my window, travelling in the opposite direction to us.

A deeply familiar being.

Later, when I asked Shastriji: "Who was this?" he replied: "It was Hanuman."

On another pilgrimage, Peter and I were travelling in the mountains to Badrinath, but first we wanted to visit Dronaghiri, a holy place of the Divine Mother. On the way there I suddenly saw a young woman clothed in a fiery orange, coming along the path at a brisk pace. She had short, dark blond curls standing out from her head, very un-Indian looking, and was dressed in a loose orange dress and orange top.

I was very surprised by her appearance.

Later, when I again asked Shastriji about this, his answer was, "That was the female Hanuman, a gift from the Divine Mother."

This happened on Sunday, October 9, 1988.

A messenger from Babaji

When in 1989, together with my husband Peter, Peter Dawkins and two English women friends, we were on our way through the valley to Herakhan, a heron came flying towards us. From a long way off we saw how this great bird came towards us, gliding close to the surface of the Gautam Ganga river, and then went majestically past us.

We were all very moved: A messenger, sent by Babaji? I had never seen anything like this here before, and Peter Dawkins said that the heron is a symbol of the Grail King. The King of the Grail is the being in whose body the suffering of the land, the suffering of the world is expressed, and known in the west as King Amfortas, who is freed from his suffering by Perceval's compassionate question.

On one of the following days, as we began our ascent to Kailash, the heron again came flying towards us. It glided down from above, passing closely over a waterfall that arises from Kailash, thus greeting us. What a language!

Truly, a messenger from Babaji!

Nila in the river

The mystery of Herakhan Kailash – A vision (October 26, 2004)

A view into the far future

After the Navaratri in Chilianaula, I was shown a vision in which the inner mystery of Herakhan Kailash was revealed:

I see a thick layer of ore lying all around the Herakhan-Kailash. An eye appears, an all seeing eye, on the top of the holy mountain.

It looks down vertically, forming a shaft of light through the mountain. At the same time it looks to all sides, in all directions.

And – it looks upwards into eternity.

It is the "Primeval Eye."

In the mountain much that had previously been sounding, singing and shining has become silent.

In the Tibetan Kailash there is perfect life. All majesty, all hierarchies are gathered there around the eternally glowing flame, always burning in its centre.

Babaji directs everything from there, while the Herakhan Kailash, surrounded by its thick layer of ore – I see the number 110 – is very still inside.

Deep within the mountain, in the hidden heart of the Herakhan Kailash, I now perceive a pink substance, which is extremely delicate, glowing and in motion. A sacred alchemy is at work here – highly awe-inspiring.

Within the deep red heart of the mountain, there is a new life in the process of being born, all pink, breathing, made out of pure joy, most precious, sweet like a pink baby!

New life: The New World will arise from this.

Babaji made this possible; he provided the substance for it. He took the darkness, the suffering, and the problems of the world upon himself.

He carried it all, transformed it within his human form and thus created the five elements anew. Then he gave his body to Mother Earth, the earth of Herakhan: It was his divine sacrifice and his powerful work which made this New Birth possible.

The deep red heart is surrounded and protected by the finest platinum substance which fills the whole mountain from within, right up to the thick layer of ore covering the outside of the whole mountain.

Both mountains, the Herakhan Kailash – the original Kailash – and the Tibetan Kailash, are deeply connected. They work together.

In the Tibetan Kailash: the eternal flame of life, and in Lake Manasarovar, the Tree of Life.

And in the Herakhan Kailash: the New Life, the New World in the process of birth, this extremely tender substance, so fine, so sweet, so precious, like a holy sacrament in the breathing heartbeat of life.

All of this is surrounded and totally protected by the deep red heart of the Divine Mother.

Herakhan Kailash

Like the two halves of a heart, Shiva and Shakti, dancing together, they form the New Life. Light waves radiate in all directions, a living sun comes into being – the sun of the New Life.

Pink transforms to gold.

The Gautam Ganga, flowing underground for so long and thereby touching the Eternal Being, is essential to this process, as is the platinum which fills the entire mountain. The massive covering of ore that surrounds the mountain is an expression of the old creation and has to be cleansed.

The all-seeing eye appears again at the top of the mountain. Babaji says: "What you now see, you see through this eye."

I see much blue, Madonna blue.

It covers the ore completely with its power of gentleness and peace. The ore cracks and stirs – the blue silences the ore from outside.

From within, the ore is touched by the platinum, the highest substance.

After the blue, the white will appear.

Inside the mountain: The breathing New Life.

When the white covers over the blue, the birth will happen. That which is inside will be outside: A radiant sun being – it will be born everywhere at the same moment.

One cannot grasp this with the mind.

The Light has provided for Everything at the Tibetan Kailash and Lake Manasarovar.

When the white lays itself over the blue, the turning point is reached and both Kailash mountains will join together for the birth of this living, breathing, new substance which will be born everywhere on Earth at the same time.

I see an enormous wing – in Akashic blue – coming from the Tibetan Kailash to the Herakhan Kailash.

This powerful wing contains many wings within itself.

Within this tremendous wing there is fire, a mighty fire causing explosions. This Akasha-blue wing with its fire appears to break open the ore completely, and only then will the Madonna blue cloak of the Divine Mother be laid over the ore, and only then will the ore come to rest. The ore had been unredeemed, it still needed this fire…

It is very clear that this wing of deep cosmic blue, full of fire, comes from the Tibetan Kailash and from Lake Manasarovar, from the eternal Babaji who guides everything from there. –

The fire does not last long. Then the blue follows, and then the white, and thereafter a delicate green filled with light – the New Life flowing in all directions...

After the enormous wing bursts open the ore of the Old World, there now appear beautiful, light blue, silvery star beings.

They all stream out from the blue cloak of the Divine Mother. Truly, the Divine Mother is and causes everything.

Then the turning point is reached and the Golden Being will be there, born in everyone – shining, radiant...

Now I see much red, a deep and powerful red. Dragons in orange red come and fight with one another and have fun in consuming one another. The human consciousness awakes in the deep red and in its dignity.

All true human beings kneel and pray, shoulder to shoulder, very close to one another – they become one single deep prayer.

This causes the dragon fight to dissolve into mist.

A fine delicate yellow comes down from above.

Below, on the Earth in deep red, the people are all in prayer for divine mercy.

This connects them all with the Herakhan Kailash and its birth process.

The turning point is there.

Black comes to the people in deep red.

The black seems like physical death – but all those in prayer are firmly connected to the birth of the New.

They are hardly aware of passing through death in order to become new beings.

Babaji has already taken death upon himself.

He has shown us that death is the gateway to transformation.

For those who pray the shadow is short.

But for others it may seem as if it is the end.

Glowing pink permeates all there is, most delicate love surrounds the Earth. Life blossoming in all colours and a wonderful fragrance fills everything.

Human beings now have finer bodies.

Everyone moves freely on the Earth.

God is with us, we are in Him. Babaji is there.

Revelations regarding Babaji's Mahasamadhi

21 years later

Day 1

On the anniversary of Babaji's Mahasamadhi, I was again very deeply connected within my heart with what had happened at that time in Herakhan. In 2005, the anniversary of the Mahasamadhi was on February 12th, because in India that very special day, February 14, 1984, is calculated anew each year according to the moon calendar.

Since the early morning a great inner coldness had begun to spread through me, particularly in my heart region. I was overcome by shivering and all my efforts to get warm were unavailing. I remained cold and shivering for hours. It seemed to me to be endless.

"Why?" I asked.

The words "Blood is dripping from the clouds" came to me. I was alarmed, went into stillness and had the following vision:

On the Earth's surface I see openings from which fountains spring, pale blue water, pure and light – and other openings from which it just bubbles up. Below there is something heavy, dark and yellowish, which does not emerge.

I see black ships in the sky, something dark is happening above as if the ocean were overhead. Then enormous arches appear like fiery rainbows in various colours. Everything seems to be connected to Babaji and the fact that this time he gave his physical body to the Earth.

From the right, a leaden silvery army comes marching towards the middle. Each one is like the other, small in size, all equal, not touching the ground, they are from another realm. Who might they be?

From the left, tall figures with enormous spears enter the picture. Are they angels of Satan? – My heart is fearful. – They attack the leaden silver army with their spears.

Geschenk der Freiheit / Gift of Freedom,
painted by Nila with Babaji in 2008

Now I see golden, almost transparent knights. Men from God: above, below, right, left and in the middle, they come from all directions.

The divine energy is with them.

They take part in what is happening.

Now something dark violet, almost black, thunders powerfully down, vertically from above. Immense spheres are breaking up the earth: the heavy dark yellow of which the earth could not rid itself.

The violet spheres from above have broken open the Earth in the form of a funnel. The funnel – like a crater – extends deep into the Earth.

The Earth is open now, it can breathe – a liberating breath – relief for the Earth, but pain for its creatures.

Now, the Earth is no longer round.

Colours become visible in the opened Earth.

The layers are red-orange, yellow, light green and, right in the depths, deep dark blue.

From the deep dark blue, a white figure now rises.

The Goddess arises from the depths.

The white now rises.

The violet bombs were from the Lord of the Creation.

The white figure frees itself out of the depths in the crater.

Song fills the opened layers of the Earth, as – like a pearl – the Goddess raises her head out of the deep dark blue of the depths. She rises up.

This singing is like sunshine.

She is the queen of the world and the soul of the Earth.

Now she stands high above the Earth, now broken open, extending her arms wide as if she was protecting everything. – Love is there.

The Lord himself made possible the rise of the Goddess. The elements were rejoicing as she rose up. There is a praising of the divine power.

From down below she rises up.

She stands sovereign over everything, a great, beneficent presence – and from her arms there flows a veil enveloping the entire Earth. A blessed sleep sinks over the Earth.

Also, it is as if a new Earth is simultaneously being born at the spot of the impact hole.

The Goddess rises up and the singing, which is born of deep adoration, is like the sun, is sunlight.

A singing of thanksgiving and the joy of the shining colours, of the elements, for her, the Queen, who is the Mistress of this Earth.

This veneration, this love, is indestructible.

The spot opening in the Earth vibrates, it is highly alive – but not the other parts of the Earth.

The flowing white veil of the Goddess comes loose – a shift takes place.

The entry point, the funnel, reaches down into the innermost of the Earth and encompasses one seventh of it.

It is as if there, at the funnel of the entry point, a new planetary substance has formed and as if, through the singing that is like the sun, a New Earth is beginning to separate itself there.

A sun-like Earth is being lifted out of the funnel.

The Goddess has draped the white veil around the Earth, her gift. The old Earth closes up again, heals within the white cloth.

The new is born. The New World is shining.

The Goddess herself is translucent gold – She stands there now full of light without her veil.

The old Earth is covered in white by her veil. Devi herself has tied it together, Gently knotted at the entry point, So that the old Earth be at peace.

The point from which the Goddess emerged forms a very special spot. It is as if, through the funnel, the old Earth has been given a healing substance, a substance for rest, which it needs. –

The old Earth may sleep.

The new planet shines from within. The New Earth is shining, like the sun.

At the moment that it separated out from the old Earth, medicine immediately flowed in for the old Earth, a milky white substance, which permeated it.

Through this substance the old Earth forms itself anew.

She needs a long time.

She has now a pause, a time to rest.

The substance is a substance of grace.

Devi had been as if imprisoned in the deepest waters.
   God has freed her.
   She is the soul of the Earth.
   The Divine Mother has given herself into the depths.

Devi has risen up from the deep blue space in the core.
   The elements, the colours shine, all beings sing.
   Singing, which is like the Sun.

The New World will be filled with praise...
   Pink, rose, gold – these are the colours of the New Earth,
   delicate and fine,
   a planet of love and reverence.

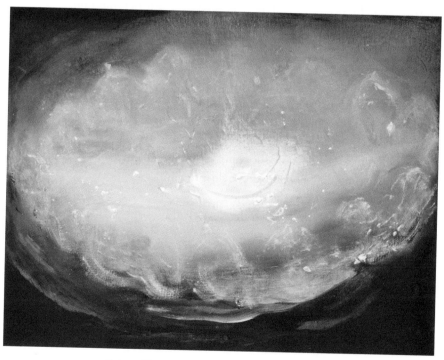

Heimat / Home, painted by Nila (with Babaji) in 2006

Day 2

A day after Babaji had left his physical body, it was laid outside his Kutiya on blocks of ice beneath his holy tree.

Now, 21 years later, on February 22, 2005, I was given an inner vision of what happened at that time when, with others, I stood watch over his body, deeply moved.

White birds came, snow white heavenly doves.

They moved their wings very quickly and covered Babaji's body completely.

In doing this, they took out all the jewels and precious stones which had formed in his body.

Now a larger bird appeared, a young eagle, light grey, a very special being.

He sat on Babaji's head, thus protecting it.

While the white doves, now very still and each dove sitting next to the other, covered Babaji's body completely, the young eagle removed the jewel of Babaji's third eye from his head and swallowed it. All for the sake of protection.

I saw many of the opposing powers waiting to take all this for themselves. But the eagle and the white doves protected everything.

Suddenly the eagle gave a sign. At that moment, all the white doves and the eagle rose up and flew off with all the treasures to Kailash.

The portal of Kailash opened and was immediately closed again, and sealed shut. Now, after the treasures had been safely brought to Kailash, a wonderful being came and enveloped Babaji's body.

It was the great Goddess and she completely covered it in her blue cloth, so that the opposing forces could no longer get close to him.

In Kailash there was great celebration.

The precious substances which the doves had brought were not only for the Earth but also for various stars. I saw some of the jewels ascend to the stars.

The universe was being ordered anew.

When Babaji's body was put in the Earth, Mother Earth immediately absorbed its substance.

Babaji's body brought light and colours to the Earth. They shone.

They were bells, the colours sounded in the Earth.

They brought love, they sang.

They set in motion a gentle deep melting process.

The Earth needs time to integrate all this.

Babaji came in his physical form to carry out the alchemy, the birth of the new, and then to give this substance to the Earth.

A great being, dark, almost black shows itself.

Is it Death?

Something new has happened – an opening which did not exist before has emerged in death.

This occurred as Babaji allowed his physical human form to pass through death.

When one does not look at death, but looks through the opening, one can see the stars.

Great souls could always see this, but now it is attainable for everyone.

Day 3

21 years later – a vision given to me in "Nandan Van," our "Garden of Heaven," on February 23, 2005:

Inwardly, I saw the Divine Mother in the garden, sitting on her stone seat in Ananda colours. Behind her stood Lord Shiva.

She held the Body of Bhole Baba in her arms, like a shell, a form.

Then both she and Lord Shiva were sitting together on her seat holding Bhole Baba's body.

A child was born from Babaji's form – a boy of 4 to 5 years of age.

He sat upright, alone on the stone seat, with dark curly hair – most beautiful, full of strength, radiant, giving blessings…

Babaji's incarnation for the New World!

Nandan Van

A deeply secret realm in the Herakhan Valley
between Mt. Kailash and Mt. Siddeshwar

I was again walking through that deeply secret realm between Mt. Kailash, Lord Shiva's mountain, and Mt. Siddeshwar, Lord Vishnu's mountain, which Sheela had shown to me in 1979, and about which Babaji had said that there, below the earth, live very sublime yogis in etheric bodies and in a state of extreme happiness. There was abundance of the most beautiful fruits, the most precious that the earth has to offer.

During my visits to Herakhan I often returned to this realm, full of devotion, but I only saw stones and more stones – beautiful stones, as everywhere in the Herakhan valley.

This time I found one of the places where the Gautam Ganga, which has its source in Lake Manasarovar and flows for a long time underground, finally emerges close to the Herakhan Kailash. Highly delighted, the next day I led my friend Gisela to this spot. We bathed in the delicious water.

While we then walked across this mysterious piece of the earth between Kailash and Siddheshwar, I told Gisela what Babaji had said about this lovely place. When we arrived at the Jesus tree, this area revealed itself, and a vision was given to me. This happened in April 2005 during the spring Navaratri:

I see a wonderful kingdom, a holy place; it appears to be a place of everlasting life. A place which is both oval and round. Two levels of ovals seem to penetrate each other and vibrate through one another. In this way, a fully alive circle is continually being created anew, with a vibration of undying life.

I perceive that "Nandan Van" is the name of this wonderful kingdom.

A place surrounded by 12 gateways. Six precious jewelled gateways alternating with six green gateways.

The green gateways look simple. In the centre of each green gateway shines a flame, the flame of life that never dies. Perfectly beautiful.

The other six gateways that, full of precious stones, surround this place, were arranged in the following order:

To the northeast is the blue gateway, the gateway of faith, adorned with lapis lazuli and other precious blue stones.

The green gateway looks to the east, the gateway of peace.

The golden-yellow gateway of the sun looks to the southeast, the gateway of the redemption through the sun.

The ruby red gateway, the gateway of love, looks to the south.

The amethyst gateway looking to the west is the gateway of knowledge, where knowledge and action are in complete harmony.

Pointing towards Kailash in the north the white gateway can be seen, the Zero Land gateway, full of diamonds and crystals.

Through these precious gateways love, knowledge, power and healing are radiated out into the world.

One cannot enter by these gateways, one can only enter this place through Babaji. One has to be called from within.

Glückliche Neue Welt / Happy New World, painted by Nila (with Babaji)

In the middle of the holy place is the bread. It lies on a Chintamani stone. A stone that looks like a living nothingness. It is an extremely precious stone, through which all wishes can be fulfilled.

In a circle around the holy bread – the bread of life – sit 12 shining white children who watch over it.

Behind the children of light there are 12 fountains. And behind the fountains there is a circle of flames.

This bread is eternally nourishing.

One who eats of this bread over and over again will not die. This bread is an expression of the Holy Grail.

This bread is like the Holy Grail, about which it is said in the Perceval book: "Whoever sees the Grail, will not die for a week." The Grail renders immortal those who look at it again and again.

In Nandan Van in the Herakhan Valley, the bread is the Grail; the bread makes immortal those who eat of it again and again.

And the bread does not diminish, remaining always the same.

"Take fullness from fullness, fullness remains."

This bread is charged with life, it nourishes all beings from the source of being.

Through the presence of this bread there will always be food on Earth.

In the centre above the bread of life shines light, a magnificent light, the divine presence, by which a dome of light is continually being formed anew over the whole.

Many enlightened beings are living here. They are mostly human beings who have gone through evolution.

Animals are present as well, shining from within, just like the people and nature and everything else that is here.

The green is totally fresh, like life itself. The trees and the shrubs here never lose their leaves.

In all things, all beings, plants, animals, human beings, there is the light of life that radiates out of itself.

At this spot, heaven is reaching down into the depths. An unbelievable power, a white light flows up from the depths. It is a spot that extends equally far into the depths as into the heights.

On high there radiates gold. Everything is filled and permeated with Babaji's presence, with the living divine presence.

Thus is "Nandan Van," the place of the living bread, the place of the bread of life, between Mt. Kailash and Mt. Siddheshwar – a place from which deep healing flows out for the world – and the cosmos.

4. *The Three Tibet Pilgrimages in 2000, 2004 and 2006*

Tibet I –
The first pilgrimage to Tibet
in 2000

Messengers from Kailash

The inner call to go to Mt. Kailash (6,714 m) in Tibet came at the end of the autumn Navaratri in 1999 in Chilianaula in India.

I was just looking at the first set of photos for a book about Tibet and Kailash, put together by Gianpaolo Barberis, a very gifted artist. – As I looked at these pictures I was deeply moved. I suddenly knew that many of the pictures that I paint in oil are inspired by Kailash.

Then I perceived very clearly the inner call: "Now come yourself."

"How can I dare to do that?" – I went with this question to Muniraji. Physically I am not trained. I had climbed the Herakhan Kailash many times, but otherwise I had no mountain experience at all.

"Yes, you can go!," said Muniraji with a radiant smile. His radiant yes, Shastriji's absolute inner support and above all, my love and my trust in God bore me along through everything that surfaced before the journey, and then throughout the entire pilgrimage itself, which was so deeply blessed.

My trust was tested to the core: I received a sting in the throat from a poisoned mosquito and until a week before my flight half of my throat was flame red up to the ear!

I prayed intensively and asked Babaji and his reply was: "When I call you, do you believe that I would let you down?" "No, definitely not."

And so I relaxed in his love.

A doctor who was a friend gave me antibiotics, that I otherwise never take, and indeed, from the moment when the trekking began, I was well. Thanks to divine grace, this remained so throughout the entire pilgrimage.

I travelled with a group from Findhorn. We were twelve people from the West, more or less physically trained, who all had faith in God and had all learnt to be flexible in unexpected situations, and who brought a great deal of openness for each other.

We did not have a doctor with us. We were healers for each other when one or the other had a problem. Each of us came back well at the end, blessed with deep and unforgettable experiences.

Our journey began with a flight from London to Kathmandu (1,300 m above sea level) and from there on another plane to Nepal Gunj. Then a very small plane, which was only able to fly in good weather conditions, took us to Simikoth (2,900 m).

Our trek began there on June 4 and from that moment on we spent 24 nights in tents. In Nepal we marched about eight hours a day.

The route led us up and down over the mountains and through the valleys of Nepal, so that slowly but surely we were able to acclimatize ourselves to the height.

A team of Sherpas accompanied us, mountain guides who knew the route. They looked after us most helpfully, pitching the tents, cooking the meals and much more: a really very kind team.

Our tents, kit bags and luggage were carried by small horses in Nepal and by yaks at the Kailash. Tenji, our head Sherpa, who reminded us all of a little Buddha, was full of love, strength and humour and led us very well and safely.

Because of unexpected heavy rainfalls, which lasted for one and a half days, we became soaked through and were forced to make a stop. Fortunately we found an empty house of the Nepal Trust with an oven in it. The Nepal Trust was established by the Findhorn Foundation. Most of the group slept in the house, whereas two others and I slept outside in tents.

Thunder could be heard the whole night long, but there was no lightning to be seen, and I asked myself, "How can that be?"

The next day we heard that there had been mighty landslides everywhere, right through to Tibet.– And it continued to rain.

We sang and prayed and tried to remain in good spirits and hoped that all our wet material that we had laid out around the oven would dry.

Finally the rain ceased, but because of the landslides we had to find completely new routes for our trek. In part, these new paths were extremely dangerous, especially for the little horses carrying our luggage. An unexpectedly perilous trek for both man and animal. The higher we went, the more some of us suffered from the symptoms of altitude sickness. But due to our love and trust in God and our medicines, we were able to overcome these difficulties.

In one emergency case, a "Gamma bag" which we had with us solved the problem. (A "Gamma bag" is an inflatable decompression chamber, which simulates the descent.)

We all arrived in Tibet (4,500 m) safely and in good time on June 10, after we had got well through the Chinese customs in Sher and then in Purang.

Because of the landslides no jeeps were able to come and pick us up, and so we went on foot into Tibet.

What a blessing to experience, with all our senses, how truly beautiful this land is, how charming and gentle the movements of its hills, how powerful and fine the colours of its rocks and stones! There is hardly any green. Only the sky and the earth, as on the first day of creation. Pure and still, but certainly not a place where it is easy to live!

But wherever there was a little water, there was immediately greenery.

For example, we saw a large beautiful rose bush simply growing out between the stones.

After several hours of walking through this wonderful landscape, three Land Cruisers came to drive us through the highlands of West Tibet.

How majestic and still is this vastness, this stillness – it is breathtaking!

Kailash came into view in the distance. It raised itself above the plain like a crystal, very gentle and fine.

We all got out of our cars, bowed and greeted Him full of joy.

Mt. Kailash has for ages been honoured and experienced as the seat of the highest Divine Being, however one wants to call it: For the Tibetans it is Buddha, for Hindus Lord Shiva, or simply the Father.

A powerful majesty and a feelably deep blessing emanates from Him. The holy mountain is circumambulated respectfully, not climbed. To those who had tried to conquer him long ago, he sent storms and ice, so that they had to flee. It is said that no one would ever risk again trying to climb him.

After a while, hills of infinite gentleness, grace and beauty showed themselves to our right, lifting up my heart. These were the foothills of Gurla Mandhata, I was told. Then Raksastal, the lake of the moon, came into view to our left. It is also called the Lake of Demons.

This lake greeted us with its fascinating turquoise colour and the dynamic change of sparkling light and shadow. Deeply moved, we all got out. Four of us, myself included, jumped spontaneously down the slope and walked along the shore. The temptation was there to touch the waters, but a quiet "Stop" from within held me back. I preferred instead to first touch the waters of Lake Manasarovar.

Mt. Kailash seen from the South-west

Tenji told us that there are many Brahmins who, out of fear of the demons, would not even look at this lake.

"But that means that the demons won't be transformed," I thought quietly to myself.

Mt. Kailash's southern face, which has a clear cross in it, looks over Raksastal. The lake, as lonely as beautiful, has a craggy shore and has something of the shape of a crescent moon. There is no life in it, Tenji told us, and there was no longer a single Gompa (monastery) by it.

Shortly after Raksastal, the other lake, Lake Manasarovar, appeared to our right. It is called "The mind of Brahma" or "The Lake of the Sun." A wonderful lake, full of love, wide and completely round. One can feel at home here straightaway. It is full of life, fish, ducks, birds, and it is always changing its colour, from deep blue to sky blue, silver, pink or rose-gold.

There are seven Gompas by this heavenly lake.

To the south of Lake Manasarovar, the mountain Gurla Mandhata (7680 m) with its wonderful dreamlike silhouette rises up over the lake like a sleeping beauty. It is regarded as the mountain of the Divine Mother, the female counterpart of Kailash.

According to a prophecy, the time is near when this mountain will become as sacred as Kailash.

The legend also says that only when water again flows from the somewhat higher lying Lake Manasarovar (4,500 m) to Raksastal, will Tibet be happy, and so will be the entire world.

Spontaneously, I performed a simple fire ceremony in front of Lake Manasarovar, in prayer for protection and blessing for all of us during our circumambulation of Kailash.

At my request, Tenji had given me a little metallic bowl from the kitchen tent, in which I lit a small fire using the pads of cotton wool soaked in purified butter which I had brought with me. He had also given me some rice for the sacrifice, but everything else, such as the offering of flowers and fruits, I did inwardly whilst reciting the mantras.

I also had with me the cloth of red velvet in the form of a twelve-petalled lotus with the OM sign in it, which in February 1984 I had made for Babaji's Mahasamadhi and which had lain for a long time on the earth over his body.

I spread this cloth out here, as at all the special places on our pilgrimage, so that in this way Babaji himself would touch and bless all these spots.

After the fire it was wonderful to bathe in the holy waters of the lake. It is said that bathing in Lake Manasarovar releases one from all negative karma.

On June 15, our kora, or pakrikama, began, the circumambulation of the Holy Mountain.

We had left as much of our luggage as possible behind in Darchen, a small hamlet at the foot of Kailash, and set off on our journey with very little luggage, which was carried by yaks.

To start with, we all prayed in a circle for blessings on our kora.

And then, as many times before, a friend, in this case it was Craig, the leader of the group from Findhorn, said to me: "You go ahead."

The inner joy seemed to lend me wings, so that I could walk quickly and with ease, without altitude problems.

It was not difficult to see where this 1000-year-old track of the kora ran. A few Tibetans were already walking along it and I followed them, not knowing that my friends in our group were still involved in going around a holy stone mantra wall at some distance away.

Then something wonderful happened: I saw a child coming gracefully down the hill, full of energy and verve, and radiant like the sun. He had his right hand raised in blessing. The boy was about 10 years of age and looked Tibetan, had short dark hair and was beautifully dressed in a snow-white silk shirt, perfectly ironed, and a deep dark red skirt. Pure joy radiated from every cell of his body as he descended the hill.

A Tibetan woman who was walking in front of me was completely enchanted by the boy. She expressed her pleasure out aloud, and he said something to her. Then he came up to me and said something in Tibetan:

"Tashi Delek!" ("I greet you" or "happy day.")

His radiance was so moving that I spontaneously touched his hand; for just a moment our hands met in perfect joy. This took place on Thursday, June 15, 2000.

A messenger from Kailash!

He moved on, and I continued upwards on my kora.

Later, towards the end of the kora around Kailash, it dawned on me who this child was. This boy who was so full of the power of the sun and of joy, and who had opened up an inner door within me to Kailash.

The day after this wonderful encounter, on June 16, the day of the full moon, the Tibetans celebrated Sagadava, the celebration of Buddha's birthday.

According to western esoteric tradition, this is the time when Buddha and Christ meet to bless the world.

The Tibetans came from every direction to Tarboche, 4,700 m to the south west side of Kailash, to celebrate by the raising of a gigantic pole with thousands of new prayer flags on it. The Tibetan belief is that when the wind reads these prayers, they will be fulfilled.

The Tibetan nomads were so erect and strong, men and women alike, and how loving and caring were the children to their parents!

We camped very close to Kailash, directly in front of the south west face, with a rock in front of it that looked like Nandi, Lord Shiva's bull. I felt the closeness of Kailash very moving.

It was overwhelming to experience the majesty, clarity and beauty of the Holy Mountain in the light of the full moon, which lit the whole mountain. On June 17, the route led us through the cathedral-like western valley along Kailash, with fantastic awe-inspiring rock formations which truly seemed to me to be the seats of the Gods. Finally, it led us up to the northern face of Kailash.

The breathtakingly beautiful northern face, certainly the most powerful face of Kailash, felt to me like one huge diamond! It rose steeply up to its gently curved icy white dome!

Mt. Kailash seen from the North (in 2000)

We were all deeply impressed, even though at first Kailash was half hidden by clouds. Our tents were set up at the highest point where it was possible for us to camp as a group beneath the northern face.

"Are we allowed to camp so close to the seat of the highest deity?" I asked myself. "Please, dear Lord of the Mountain, allow it! It makes us so happy to be so close to you!"

I was so filled with love for the mountain, so drawn by the majesty and beauty of his northern face that, with a beating heart, I went further up towards his dome. Alone. I repeatedly stopped climbing and asked: "May I go on?"

I had come to an arrangement with the being of the mountain that, as long as he continued to lift his clouds, I would be allowed to continue my ascent.

After each few steps I again asked for permission to go up further, and the mountain did indeed continue to raise his clouds higher and higher.

The air was charged with a high vibration.

After I had ascended to a frozen snowfield with a few glacial streams, I realized that the lower part of his dome, which at first had appeared to be so near, was in fact still some distance away.

Then the mountain stopped raising his veil of clouds and it was clear to me that I should go back down. I got back to our tent just in time, before evening fell.

I left my tent open during this night. I did not feel the cold, but only my love for the mountain. I spoke to him, opened my heart completely to him and prayed to Babaji and to the entire brotherhood and sisterhood of light...

And then the answer came. An overwhelming answer. It was almost more than I, as a human being, could bear. In the middle of my forehead there arose an indescribable pressure. It was as if I were exposed to the hardest stone in the world, for a long time... Finally the pressure eased, and then there was just pure light there.

The essence of all the mysteries appeared to be sealed within his northern face. I felt it to be the third eye of the Holy Mountain and that through my love I had come into harmony with his vibration.

The following day, June 18, before sunrise, Kailash stood there in white, in almost transparent shining beauty under a crystal clear sky. Just to see him like that made us feel to be born anew.

In the glory of the rising sun he then turned totally golden. A golden jewel in the heavens! What a blessing for all of us, for all the pilgrims who had come in order to make the kora at this time of the full moon.

The path led on up to the Dolma La pass (5,600 m). It was a steep climb. At this height, every step up the mountain demands a great effort from the body and especially from the heart and lungs.

We saw one person who had made the entire circuit of Kailash with prostrations. That is, lying down at full length, standing up again, taking a pace, and again lying down. Thus he went around the mountain indescribably slowly, exposed to every kind of weather.

As he did this, his smiling loving expression and his great shining eyes were totally amazing. This very beautiful person who performed this sacrifice did it certainly not just for himself, but for the benefit of the whole. – Who could he have been?

At first the path led up through the Shiva Tsal, a hill graveyard of stones, where the pilgrims traditionally leave something of themselves, a few drops of blood, hair or clothing... and then the path went on steeply upwards.

Finally we reached the Dolma La pass, the highest point of the Kora, marked by a huge boulder with hundreds of prayer flags, to which we added our own. Dolma, or Tara, is the Goddess of compassion, of mercy. There, together with my Findhorn friends, I performed a light ceremony, with a deeply felt greeting to the Divine Mother. At Dolma La there was the feeling of celebration all around us.

Then began the steep descent towards Gauri Kund, an enchanting oval green lake, called "The Lake of Mercy."

It is one of the highest lakes in the world (5,550 m). It moved me deep in my soul to see this lake. Then we went further on down to the eastern side of Kailash which seemed much less severe and dramatic than his western side.

On the following day we arrived at a Gompa connected to Milarepa, the singing yogi poet of Tibet.

We trekked over the most amazing stone tracks with rock walls in all colours. From there, marvellous views opened up to Raksastal and to Lake Manasarovar, the sibling lakes, which lay like two precious jewels in radiant beauty below in the plain.

Finally we arrived in Darchen, the small village to the south of Kailash, from whence we had set off. Here our group's ways parted until the end of the whole pilgrimage.

Eight of us travelled with Land Cruisers to Lhasa, whilst only four of us, one of them myself, returned via the entire route by which we had just come.

At first, we spent two days by Lake Manasarovar.

There I performed an inner fire ceremony of thanksgiving.

We again bathed in the holy waters of this wonderful lake, where the skies can be transformed from one moment to the next by sudden thunderstorms, from colours of angelic pink and silvery-gold to dramatic darkness, white, violet, blue and yellow. And then again, back to a wide blue peace, as if nothing had happened before.

Since setting foot in Tibet, I had quite simply felt one with its earth, its gently swinging hills and mountains. It filled me with deep joy. But now, on our return route, as the day approached when we would have to leave Tibet, I became sad.

How deep was this sadness! I simply had to cry and could not stop crying…

To leave Tibet, with its jewels of Lake Manasarovar and Mt. Kailash, was so difficult for me that I began to comprehend how difficult it must have been for our souls when they left paradise.

In the afternoon of this June 21, our last day in Tibet, we camped in a valley not far from the Nepalese border.

When my friends decided to walk to the nearby village in order to learn a bit more about Tibetan life, as until now we had only got to know the open and free nature of Tibet, I went with them in the hope that I could overcome my sadness.

The great monastery there, parts of which had been destroyed, was being restored, using all possible efforts.

Together we drank butter tea with a very fine western man, Nic, who inwardly seemed to me like a brother.

Later, when I was in my tent again, a little girl came to me. She took my hand and we went out together. Hand in hand, we walked through the evening and again she led me back to the monastery and from there to Nic, who lived outside it. To get to his place, one had to pass through a big courtyard in which a large group of guests were sitting, including a white haired man. Nic was busy preparing food in a small dark room. On an impulse, I gave him something for the monastery and told him about my love for this land, how I felt so much one with this land, and that I felt an inexplicably deep interior sadness about having to leave Tibet the following day.

At that moment the white haired man came into our dark room. He was tall, and while he stood there silently in the doorway he looked at me lovingly for quite some time, with warm dark eyes, full of understanding, full of compassion. Then he left. OM namah Shivay.

I thought this white haired man was a friend of Nic, but six weeks later, and with Shastriji's help, I learnt who this man was and what a blessing had been bestowed on me.

When I returned to the courtyard, together with Nic, it was empty. Everybody had left.

A glorious orange-red golden evening greeted me outside, and while going back to our camping place, accompanied by several children, I realized that all my sadness had vanished! I was filled with happiness and profound gratitude. Adieu beloved Tibet!

Then the trek began again, up and down through Nepal's green mountains and valleys which are so completely different from the majestic wideness of the Tibetan highlands.

Towards the end of our pilgrimage, exactly one day before the end of our trekking adventure (it was Monday, June 26, 2000), I was walking alone. The others were at some distance behind me when a young man of about 20 years of age came towards me at great speed. Even from a distance, I was aware that this was a being who could see in all directions at the same time. He had very unusual eyes, large, very fiery, with a great deal of white around them. His whole being appeared to be made of fire. He was incredibly alive!

He came straight towards me and took firm hold of one of my mountain walking sticks. In so doing he looked directly at me, laughing, as if he knew me intimately, and with a joyfulness that seemed to have many dimensions.

"What? Does he want my walking stick?" I asked myself, and was very puzzled by his spontaneous and challenging behaviour. For some time we stood eye to eye without saying anything.

"Who might you be?" I asked myself.

His whole being was so familiar, and still I did not know who he was.

While he was holding on to my walking stick and I likewise, I asked myself: "Should I give him the walking stick?"

I knew we still had a very steep and long part of our trek in front of us, and these mountain walking sticks were a great help, an important part of our equipment, and so I decided not to give the walking sticks away yet.

Then I saw two noble-looking, very slim and unusually tall men who were following him. As he now let go of my stick, he turned to these two men, who looked like brothers, and said something to them, apparently about me. One of them looked at me very intently and deeply for a few moments. Then the three of them went on.

"Who were they? And who was he?"

It puzzled me greatly.

"Was it Baba Goraknath, whose presence I had felt so strongly the day before? – No. – But who was it then?"

One thing was clear to me. He was not a being of this world.

For quite some time, I was unable to speak with anyone at all about this encounter.

When we got back to Katmandu, happily all in good shape, Craig said: "Never again in our lives will we strain our bodies like this!"

And I added: "Except when we go again to Kailash!"

In the evening I called Shastriji and the next morning Muniraji, to report how deeply blessed this pilgrimage had been, and how grateful I was for all their encouragement, inner support and their protection.

And of course in my heart I thanked my friends in the west for their good thoughts and prayers every day.

Throughout all, I knew that it was Babaji who had guided every step of my journey.

So my deepest gratitude always goes to him and to the infinite God.

My fellow pilgrims and I had often felt that on an inner level there were many beings accompanying us on our way. We had not been travelling alone.

On the phone, I told Shastriji about the radiant child who had come down the hill at the beginning of the Kora around Kailash.

Shastriji immediately said: "This was Babaji!"

And by that he confirmed what had already become clear to me in the meantime.

After several days, when I called him up from Germany, his first words were: "You met the true Babaji!"

Only after several weeks was I able to tell Shastriji about the encounter with that beautiful, fiery young man who had come towards me at such a great pace and, laughing, had held onto one of my mountain walking sticks. "Who was he?" I asked him.

"That was Herakhandi Baba!" said Shastriji. Babaji in his earlier appearance. "Herakhandi Baba in his young form!"

How wonderful! Until then I had only experienced Babaji within me in his previous form as the Old Herakhan Baba.

I asked Shastriji: "Is the one I met the same as is described in Yogananda's biography as the immortal Babaji?"

"Yes!" was his answer. And later Shastriji said: "Herakhandi Baba is Bhairav Baba as well!" – This is the great protector of truth and love.

When I told Shastriji about the powerful communication with Kailash which I had experienced in the night below the northern face of Kailash, he said: "You met Kailash! And you met the Lord of Kailash!"

In answer to my question as to who these two slim tall men were who were with him, Shastriji said: "They are his guardians. They are always around him as his guardians."

What a grace!

When, with Shastriji's help, this all became clear, I heard Babaji within me saying: "And I met you three times!"

Finally I realized when that was:

It was on my final day in Tibet, when I was so sad about having to leave Tibet and the white-haired man came and looked at me with such love and compassion. "Who had he been?"

Shastriji said: "This was Mahendra Maharaj!"

Mahendra Maharaj, a great scholar of scriptures, a prophet and an adept, had foretold Babaji's return. He was the highly respected teacher of Shastriji and a being full of love. Although in the form of a man, he was an expression of the Divine Mother.

At this point I have no more words!

Those people to whom Babaji has revealed himself are aware that Babaji can appear for us anywhere and in any form.

He has control over the five elements and can manifest whatever and whenever he wishes.

He can assume a physical form for just a few moments in order to give someone his blessing, or he can remain for a longer period in a manifested body.

How can I know whether he maintained the form of the wonderful child for just the short time that I met him, or for a longer period? That lies entirely with him. – The same also naturally applies to Babaji's appearance as the young Hera-khandi Baba, together with his two companions.

When I set off on this pilgrimage, I was free of thoughts and expectations and had only the wish that it would go well for all of us.

OM namah Shivay!

"God is love and love is God," Babaji said to us repeatedly. I understood this as: when we are in the space of love, we are in God.

One could also say: Kailash, this "holy seat of the Divine upon Earth" is love, even though he looks severe, appears to be dangerous.

Babaji could also look severe, appear to be dangerous for our ego, but – he was – and is – Love.

Tibet II –
The second pilgrimage to Tibet
in 2004

In honour of Gurla Mandhata

The inner call to come to Tibet again reached me in January 2001: "Come again – this time in order to honour Gurla Mandhata."

For thousands of years Mt. Kailash has been honoured as the seat of the Lord, of the highest Divine Being and Consciousness, while Gurla Mandhata is regarded as the female counterpart of Kailash, the seat of the Divine Mother. It is still a wild and rather untouched mountain.

Babaji had always stressed, how important it is in our time to honour the Divine Mother, to connect with her.

Inspired by this call to honour her and her holy mountain, I found three other friends who were thrilled to come with me.

My plan was to be in Tibet again in May 2002, for the Sagadava celebration. But as the situation in Nepal worsened dramatically following the Maoist rebellions, and remained bad, at the last moment we had to postpone the pilgrimage.

Therefore our joy was all the greater when we were finally able to set off in 2004, making a party of three with my friend Marielu and Adrian, a friend from Ireland.

The question: "How can we honour Gurla Mandhata?" had stirred within me for a long time. The prophecies said that this mountain would become as holy as the Kailash and that now the time for this was ripe.

Already in 2001, I had talked with Shastriji and Muniraji about this, and it was clear to me that, beginning at Kailash and then around Lake Manasarovar, I would perform Vedic fire ceremonies (see page 216) in order to celebrate the Divine in his male and female form – in its oneness.

Our journey again started in Kathmandu and at my request Tenji was again our head Sherpa. He brought a small crew of Sherpas with him who looked after us lovingly. Imagine, even in the desert they managed to bake a delicious birthday cake!

To begin with there was an unwanted stopover: A small plane was meant once again to fly us from Nepal Gunj, a hot town on the plain full of mosquitoes and the first station after Kathmandu, up to 2,900 m at Simikot. The wind however was too strong and the small plane was unable to fly.

So we lost one day's trekking and were going to lose the second day, which would have caused problems as we had to be at the Chinese border punctually at the pre-stated time!

In Nepal Gunj we met some very nice Indians who wanted to fly by helicopter to the border of Tibet to avoid undergoing the strains of the trek. But their flight was also made impossible by the very strong winds. So we prayed from the depths of our hearts and – in contradiction to the reports at the airport, the Simikot plane surprisingly and suddenly appeared! It was liberating to be able finally to continue our journey.

How wonderful to see the mountains of Nepal, which were already somewhat familiar to me, from above and to land safely on the narrow runway of the mountain village of Simikot.

Gurla Mandhata with Lake Manasarovar

Then it was up and down through the valleys and mountains of Nepal, in order to arrive acclimatized in Tibet. Eight hours of trekking per day, for seven long days over swaying bridges where people and herds of goats met each other and the thundering River Kanali rushed beneath. Again, the magnificent steep waterfalls, jumping down from the heights in Nepal, and the experience of being at the limit of exhaustion and yet still being able to go on!

This time, thanks to God, there were no landslides and also no dramatic rainfalls, but instead a small sandstorm.

Before the endlessly long descent to the Chinese border at Sher, we had again to surmount the high pass (5,100 m).

Because on this occasion the paths were open, the Land Cruiser was able to collect us directly at the Tibetan border, with a guide sent from Lhasa who immediately seemed very strange to me.

He made one mistake after another until Tenji decided to search for another guide, and indeed found a very nice one. But the first guide nevertheless continued to follow us, like a shadow.

At Purang, the main Chinese border checkpoint, our passports, together with those of all the other Westerners, were taken away until the next day. We were forced to stay there overnight, under the worst conditions possible.

I was full of revolt against this suppression of our freedom and the loss of our precious time in Tibet!

Now that we were here, held up at this miserable spot against our will, it became very clear to us, how great must be the suffering that is systematically inflicted on the Tibetans!

My friends had been lying on their beds fully clothed, in the hope of avoiding collecting any bugs or viruses. I was wearing my nightdress, and I developed a high fever, vomiting and diarrhoea during this night.

We were the first to set off very early the next morning towards Lake Manasarovar.

What deep joy to greet Mt. Kailash in the distance, to see the gentle foothills of Gurla Mandhata in its indescribable loveliness and beauty, the sparkling Raksastal and finally the radiant smile of Lake Manasarovar!

There we all immediately felt ourselves welcomed and warmed by love after the strains of the long trek and the difficult situation at the border.

Because of the one and a half days lost at the start at Nepal Gunj, we had hardly had a day to rest and we all felt a very great need to recover.

Regarding the Devi in Gurla Mandhata, since the start of the pilgrimage we had read every day in the Sapta Sati, a book of verses of the Divine Mother in Sanskrit. What a feeling of joy now to see before us the living Gurla Mandhata, the magnificent mountain, which rises up to 7,680 m to the south of Lake Manasarovar!

Early next morning we set off in the Land Cruiser for Kailash which we reached in three hours. Praying for blessings with all our hearts, we began the Kora immediately.

At the start of the Kora, two very cheerful Tibetans came towards us. They were very colourfully dressed as if going to a wedding. They greeted us joyfully with: "Tashi delek!," as if they had already known us for a long time.

How beautiful it was to see again the south-western face of Kailash from Tarboche, to sense its grandeur and power, and above all to be able to camp so close in front of it.

Early in the morning of the day of the full moon, which was the Sagadava celebration, I started on the first of seven fire ceremonies while the others went over the hill to the Sagadava celebrations.

This first fire ceremony was in honour of Kailash, and in thought also for our deeply honoured and beloved friend Shri Vishnu Datt Shastriji, the great seer through whom Babaji had always spoken and who shortly before, at the age of 97, had left his body. Shastriji was full of a deep love and admiration for the Divine Mother. In addition to 65 other books he had also written the Sapta Sati, a book with 700 verses in praise of the Divine Mother, from which we read for the Devi every day on this pilgrimage.

After completing the first fire ceremony at Kailash, I arrived at the Tibetans' celebrations just in time for the raising of the new flagpole. We had brought with us from Germany sixty small flags, painted by friends for this celebration.

They were all tied to each other with long strings, and now, together, we hung them up. They fluttered there in the wind with thousands of Tibetan flags such as "Tibet Free."

When the wind reads the messages on the flags, then they become reality – this is the conviction of the Tibetans.

After my rebellion in Purang, which was followed by high fever and diarrhoea, I was still somewhat weakened physically. It was clear to me that I should take this as an indication that I should rather not accompany the others to Dolma La, but instead travel directly to Lake Manasarovar in order to continue immediately with the fire ceremonies.

After a short midday break, we went along the path by "Nandi's Face" towards the west side of Kailash.

My heart was bleeding from the understanding that this time I would not encircle Kailash and see its northern face. Thus, each step I took along the way became a deep inner greeting for the beloved being of Lord Shiva and Mt. Kailash.

As we settled down and read the Sapta Sati in view of Kailash and the surrounding mountains, it seemed to us as if the beings of the mountains were listening attentively and full of gladness.

In the following night there came a greeting from Kailash: As I lay in the tent at night my heart began to beat wildly in a way that I had never experienced before.

I called out: "Babaji, help me please!"

I took medication for my heart, which, however, had hardly any effect. Sleep was out of question. Instead my racing pulse grew wilder and in addition I felt an extreme pressure in the middle of my forehead.

As everything became ever more dramatic, I asked myself whether I should wake up Tenji. – "No." –

I sat upright in the tent: "Babaji! Babaji!" I attempted to breathe through this racing heart and the pain like a concrete block in the middle of my forehead. Suddenly, in the middle of this inner distress, the "concrete" opened, dispersing all the pressure that had seemed as hard and impenetrable as stone.

Through this opening, a being of light appeared, vibrating gently. It was Babaji, coming from the eternal with his hand raised in blessing.

The unbearable pressure in the centre of my forehead and the racing of my heart had ceased immediately. Now there was only this Divine Being and his sublimely gentle vibration – totally wonderful. Peace spread around and enfolded me.

I fell into a deep sleep… until the early morning called us and we parted ways.

Moved, I told my friends about the experience of the night, which held an important message for them also.

Marielu and Adrian, who were encircling Kailash for the first time, set off for the northern face of Kailash with Tenji, two Sherpas and some Yaks. The full moon had caused a change in the weather, meaning that Kailash was hidden by clouds.

I drove with our Tibetan driver and Maila, a Sherpa, in the Land Cruiser to the eastern side of Lake Manasarovar.

On arriving there, an intense light writing was visible in the sky. I had never seen anything like this. The blessing and welcoming greeting of the Divine Mother could be clearly felt: The air vibrated with joy.

To the south Gurla Mandhata showed herself in complete clarity, whereas Kailash to the north was already half hidden behind the clouds.

While the tents were being put up I bathed in the lake. Pure love embraced me. I felt no cold.

Then I assembled all the things which I needed for the fire puja the next day.

In the morning it was pouring with rain. Everything was hung about with clouds. I pleaded with God: "Please let it stop raining in good time before 12 o'clock noon!" Because fire ceremonies should always be started before 12 noon.

And indeed, at 10:30 a.m. the sun broke through the thick swathes of rain everywhere, and I went to the lake with a rucksack full of ingredients for the fire ceremony. The clarified butter, or ghee, went hard immediately as the temperature was around freezing. Using camphor and many small cotton wicks soaked in ghee, I was able to start and maintain a fire even at this height of 4,500 m. In addition I had found some dried yak dung.

It was a long and very intense fire ceremony. It was 3:30 p.m. when I was finished with all the mantras and readings from the book of the Divine Mother, the Sapta Sati.

In the evening, as I went to the lake again, the fire still smoked and glowed powerfully in the little Agni Hotra copper pot which we had brought with us. The wind kept it so alive, and the yak dung burnt for a long time.

The next morning there was thick snow everywhere. My Sherpa placed a small bowl with warm washing water by the tent. After a while he shook my tent very vigorously, apparently to free it from snow, not knowing that beneath it I was washing myself from head to toe. Then a sheep peered curiously into my tent through the little opening.

The large amount of snow caused me to worry about my friends.

"How is it for them as they make their journey around Kailash?"

A sentence from "The Way of the white Clouds" by Lama Govinda came to my mind: "If you are caught by a snowstorm on Dolma La, then your life is over."

The entire Kailash appeared to be covered with snow. As far as I was able, I gave my worry about my friends to Babaji: "Please, watch over them."

Happily the sun then broke through, the snow melted and, wonderfully, I was able to perform my second fire ceremony looking towards Gurla Mandhata.

I was repeatedly amazed how rapidly the weather at Lake Manasarovar can change.

In the afternoon, thanks be to God, my friends returned in a truck. – They had both completed the kora, physically exhausted, but inwardly very happy and they spoke of their experiences with gratitude.

Tenji had brought water from Lake Gaurikund for me – from the holy lake at the altitude of 5,570 m, below Dolma La – what a great gift!

Adrian explained humorously how he had been filming a yak which was sliding down the mountain together with the baggage on its back, until he suddenly realized: "Oh, that's my luggage!"…

The Sherpas were already in action and freeing the yak from its load, so that it could get up, be loaded again and set on its way. Everything was rescued, the yak and the luggage.

Marielu continued to rest, and in the morning I carried out the third fire ceremony, again on my own. This time in wind and rain, but it was possible – with God's help – and afterwards I felt fresh and full of energy.

Now we continued our journey together.

It was Monday, June 7, 2004, and we were on our way to Gurla Mandhata, the holy mountain of the Divine Mother and the female counterpart of Mt. Kailash.

We were driving in our Land Cruiser along a dusty and stony track from the direction of Lake Manasarovar, and were approaching the foothills of Gurla Mandhata when we saw three people walking through this wide and lonely land without any luggage at all. A very upright tall and elderly man, dressed completely in black and with a very white face, was walking with two companions. Suffering was written on his face. He emanated such an awe-inspiring dignity that I immediately asked myself: "Is this Lord Shiva?"

No – but then who is he?

His appearance struck my heart and moved me deeply.

His two younger companions looked at him lovingly, in particular the tall handsome woman, perhaps in her forties, who was also dressed in black. The third person, a younger man radiated great friendliness and he reminded me of a much-loved friend of mine.

This black clothed, tall, upright man with the extremely white face – was he an apparition of Christian Rosenkreutz?

Was Christian Rosenkreutz the guardian of Gurla Mandhata in these times?

Was it he who opened the inner portal to the holy mountain for us?

These were very holy moments for all of us, to be able to touch Gurla Mandhata for the first time in our lives.

We left our Land Cruiser and each of us began to explore the mountain, climbing some distance up it to experience it. It was utterly still. A very fine vibration surrounded us. In my heart I sensed deep secrets, which were connected to this holy mountain.

Love embraced us, and the tangible grandeur filled us with reverence. Kailash was powerfully sublime, Gurla Mandhata lovingly sublime, and both of them full of light.

And the stones that we found, extremely dense and substantial, spoke an intensive tongue.

Still greatly moved by our contact with the holy mountain of the Divine Mother we then found a very beautiful spot to camp, not far from Gurla Mandhata on the south-western side of Lake Manasarovar and completely untouched and still.

The next day was June 8, for which many astrologers had forecast a unique Venus constellation of love, by which means a great deal would be made possible and which could open many doors.

As so often, before a great light is set free, a shadow first comes as a test.

Hardly were we so happily settled when the police came, informed by mobile by our "shadow guide." We had seen him phoning on a hill. We were told that it was no longer permissible to camp here and that we had to pack up and go straightaway, at the very latest by early next morning. In addition, they wanted a "fine" from us. So we all stayed overnight and prepared for an early departure the next morning. While the others broke camp and pro forma set off with our luggage and our tents, Marielu and I remained at this wonderful spot so that we could perform the fourth fire ceremony at sunrise right on the lake shore.

The whole sky was full of light and great joy could be sensed, rejoicing, everything seemed to consist of purest bliss. Sky, lake and mountain, everything seemed to be singing. Our hearts sang with them. – It was indescribably beautiful!

The fifth and last fire ceremony performed at Lake Manasarovar in honour of the Divine Mother took place in deep concentration on the north-western side of the lake, right at the water's edge. We had camped here at the lake when we had arrived. It was very clear to me what a blessing it was to be able to perform this work of the fire ceremonies around the holy lake.

On the last afternoon at the lake we visited the Chiu Gompa, which was built high up in the mountain on a rock, where hundreds of years earlier Padmasambhava had left a physical footprint in the rock. Even today his presence can be clearly felt in this place.

We went yet higher and reached an elevated plateau, from which an expansive view opened up on all sides: in the north towards Kailash, in the south to Gurla Mandhata, in the east to Lake Manasarovar and in the west to Raksastal-Lake.

The entire sublime, divine mandala revealed itself – and we were in its centre.

A strong energy permeated this place that, from then on, I called the "Panorama Place."

The Ganga Chu, which had connected the somewhat higher Lake Manasarovar with Lake Raksastal, but which had been dried up since the Chinese invasion, used to flow from Lake Manasarovar deep down below the Panorama Place and then along to Raksastal. May the Ganga Chu flow once again so that light and darkness may reconcile with each other.

The time for departure came on June 10. We had now to leave this divine fortress on earth.

Before we set off on the long journey right across the Tibetan highlands in the direction of Lhasa, we drove once again towards Kailash.

Everything here was filled with the divine presence, highly enchanting, and I believed that all of Tibet was as beautiful.

But as we went towards the east through a landscape that was in parts like a desert, and which often was simply endlessly vast, empty and lonely, I became very aware of the difference between this and the "Kailash Fortress" permeated with its dense, divine inner substance.

There were no real roads anywhere here, just sand tracks. When someone came towards us, which seldom happened, this involved huge clouds of sand. It was a mercy that our Land Cruiser was airtight.

Our driver sometimes stopped just to exchange a few words with the other driver. Each human being here was very precious.

At one stop we got to know a bit more about the Tibetan way of life – in a nomad tent. Outside, the endlessness of a gently curved landscape of sand or rocks interspersed with a few strips of grazing land – and inside, in the tent, the gaily painted tables and benches which served as sleeping places at night, and colourfully dressed Tibetan women who shared out butter tea in front of an oven fuelled by yak dung. On the wall, there stood a half dried piece of yak meat, from which each visitor could cut a piece for himself. The grandmother of the family sat in the corner and was unceasingly moving her prayer beads and murmuring mantras.

Everything here was simple and friendly.

Then we travelled further on, over many almost unnavigable passes and through deep holes. It was a highly adventurous and dangerous journey, but our driver was excellent, and in addition a hearty man.

Luckily, we did not have a single puncture on the passes, only on those tracks that were not so dangerous. We were always in good spirits, with a great deal of humour, warmth and understanding for one another.

Throughout this journey, which seemed to be never ending, we not only experienced the expansiveness of this land, but also its tremendous loneliness.

Again and again, a man would appear as if out of nowhere with a herd of sheep or yaks.

We experienced the Tibetans as very welcoming. They shared the little they had, their tea, their salt, their tschampas (roasted barley flour mixed with butter tea and formed into little dumplings, which taste delicious) even with us foreign pilgrims.

Once, during a picnic in some greenery, a Tibetan came up to us with butter tea, served it to all of us and gave us some of his salt – and we gave him some of our provisions.

Adrian said that it was better here than in the Ritz hotel.

There was one boy I will never forget who came running up to our car with a lamb in his arms and pleaded us to help his lamb, which had one blind eye. – In retrospect, I found myself often thinking about this scene. Christ, through this boy with his lamb in distress, had shown us the need in Tibet and had asked us to help.

We were on our way through the Tibetan Highlands for five days and in our tents at night-time we could hear yaks breathing nearby.

Then our camping time came to an end. We now approached the towns of Shigatse, Gyantse and Lhasa with their really very moving holy places.

The moment came to bid adieu to the Sherpas who had accompanied us in the truck, with the tents and all the other materials, since we had arrived in Tibet, and who had lovingly cared for us throughout the entire journey. We had really developed a heart connection with them. Now they would be driving back to Nepal in the truck.

Tenji always sat with us in the Land Cruiser and he accompanied us to the last. But now we had to take the "shadow guide," who had always travelled in the truck, into our vehicle with us.

To make space for him in the rear of the car we had to put our luggage on the roof. After 18 days in tents, we went into a hotel for the first time in Shigatse – it was a luxurious Chinese hotel – and as our luggage was carried in, sand trickled out of our pockets and rucksacks. The men and women at reception looked shocked. I said to them: "You call yourself the Manasarovar Hotel, but we have just come from Lake Manasarovar." That broke the ice.

After the wonderful camping experience we felt totally foreign in this, our first hotel, which was so luxurious. Before, we had been able to talk to each other through the tents, but now each of us was shut in a large double room and surrounded by the most modern technology.

The "shadow guide," who was accommodated in a wing of the hotel, had fortunately disappeared the next day. He had found a bus to Lhasa.

In Lhasa the matter relating to him was cleared up by Tenji and our second, very nice guide at the appropriate office, and it turned out that, apart from all the mistakes he had made which we knew about, he had also held back a great deal of money. And our "fine" was returned to us.

Inwardly, we bore the treasure of the six fire ceremonies, of the first at Kailash and the further five at Lake Manasarovar, within the consciousness of our hearts, and we carried it all with us now to Lhasa and via Lhasa to Samje.

I had always known that our last, our seventh fire, would take place in Samje. Samje is called the soul of Lhasa, and is where Buddhism originated in Tibet. It consists of a temple complex and a monastery. At first it seemed almost impossible to get to Samje. One had to obtain an extra permission, but we succeeded in getting it.

Lhasa was very moving. We were overcome by the powerful charisma of all the treasures in the Potala. What hidden wisdom, which is penetrating earth, cosmos and mankind, stands behind all of this! – We were likewise moved by the continued prostrations of all the Tibetans who daily surrounded the Potala.

We lived in an enchanting Tibetan hotel, lovingly painted from top to bottom: the "Dood Gu Hotel" close to the Chokan monastery. Everywhere in the Tibetan part of Lhasa the streets and paths were full of people walking around with prayer malas, immersed in mantras.

Tibet is the land of prayer.

With all these impressions, we were finally on our way to Samje. After 4½ hours of bumpy tracks we arrived there and straightaway were filled with a sense of how it had been here beforehand when Tibetan Buddhism started from here in the year 775 after Christ.

The main building represented the centre of the four worlds. Four further temples symbolized the four continents and at that earlier time there was also one temple for the sun and one for the moon, which however we could no longer locate.

In the temple itself, each of us had a deep experience with a four metre high golden Buddha. Very alive, he immediately entered our hearts. We felt Babaji's presence very intensely through him.

In Shigatse, Gyantse and Lhasa we had seen many impressive statues of Buddha, lamas and world mandalas, but we had never before been so deeply moved as by this statue of the golden Buddha in Samje.

Everything was a bit run down, but nevertheless wonderful. We slept in a four-bed room in a hostel for pilgrims, which was clean and simple.

I wanted to start the fire ceremony straightaway the next morning. We found a suitable place, too, a little outside of the monastery, for our seventh and last fire ceremony.

To begin with we connected ourselves with the light and the energy of Kailash, Lake Manasarovar and Gurla Mandhata, and we prayed from the depths of our hearts for blessing and healing for Tibet and thereby for the whole world, because Tibet is the heart in the heart of the world.

Then it began to pour with rain and we were all kept busy, trying to protect our fire, and succeeding in it. Marielu held a rain cape high above it while I made the offerings. It was very intense, this closing fire through which we formed the bridge to the "Kailash Fortress."

After completing the fire ceremony we were soaked through and totally happy.

The fire was burning magnificently, despite the rain. Tenji collected us and drove us to a very cosy Tibetan restaurant a couple of minutes away by car, where we were able to change our clothes. What a hearty welcome we received here!

The owner brought us warm blankets, tea and tschampas.

Deeply grateful for having made our closing fire in Samje, this ancient and very familiar holy place, we went back to Lhasa. We spent the last day there, mostly at the lake behind the Potala. It is shrouded in legend, and in it the whole Potala was reflected.

There we celebrated our leaving thanksgiving for the whole Tibet journey, reading both at the lake and in front of the Potala the verses for the Divine Mother from the Sapta Sati.

May Tibet be happy again, and with it the whole world!

About the Vedic Fire Ceremony

The father of fire is light – the mother of fire is love.
Fire is the medium of transformation.

The Rishis, the saints and the seers knew that it would bring about great blessings if something from the abundance of creation was offered back to the creator. This gave rise to the Vedic fire ceremony.

How it is performed, the accompanying mantras and the offerings are precisely described in the Vedas, based on what the Rishis saw.

During the recitation of the mantras with the names of divine beings, offerings are made to the fire of Rice (a mixture of rice, sesame, barley and sugar), ghee (melted clarified butter), flowers, fruits, incense and coconuts.

In order to carry out a Vedic fire ceremony it is necessary to get the permission and the blessing of a master.

Shastriji once said, "The fire is like the mail. It brings that which you send to the desired address immediately."

What we offer is received by the divine beings upon whom we have called in that moment. – This is a particularly beautiful way to make contact with them.

There are two kinds of sacrifice in the created world:

The horizontal – one gives to another who has less.

The vertical – we give something from the fullness of the creation back to the Divine. Thus a circle of giving is brought into action: A little rice is sacrificed, an abundance of rice will flow back down.

The great masters perform fire ceremonies in many locations to relieve famine, among other purposes.

Babaji emphasized the great importance of the Havan, a fire ritual: "The creation originated from it."

There are many reasons for carrying out a fire ceremony: in order to invoke rain and fruitfulness; for protection against disasters or in order that wishes may be fulfilled. Not just for the cleansing of the atmosphere, but also of feelings and thoughts; and for the healing of the elements within us and in nature. The harmful is transformed; the good flourishes. Likewise, fire ceremonies are also performed for wealth and abundance, and for peace, love and happiness.

Tibet III –
The third pilgrimage to Tibet
in 2006

The Mystery of Raksastal

The first pilgrimage to Tibet in June 2000 was filled with the joy of being able to see Tibet again, to take in this expansive country in its resonating infinity, to experience the drama of Raksastal, to dive into the love of Lake Manasarovar and to encounter the majesty of Kailash.

For me, the whole was a great celebration of remembrance – and finally: to be touched deep in the heart by Gurla Mandhata.

In May 2004, following the second call to Tibet, the theme was to honour Gurla Mandhata, the mountain of the Divine Mother opposite to Mt. Kailash, and to stretch the bow of love from there across the Tibetan highlands to far distant Samje, the soul of Lhasa.

On this second pilgrimage, arriving at the "Panorama Place" where one can see all four surrounding majesties, Mt. Kailash to the North, Gurla Mandhata to the South, Lake Manasarovar in the East and Lake Raksastal in the West, it was important to realize that together they form a divine fortress on Earth. I call this the "Kailash Fortress." It seems that the essential powers and hidden keys for the entire creation are held there – and from there, moved into action.

The science of Geomancy[13] views our Earth as a living being, which has Chakras, or Lotus flowers, just like human beings.

Tibet is viewed as the hidden heart within the heart chakra of the Earth. Therefore everything that happens there has deep significance for the entire Earth.

Inwardly I knew that I would go on a third pilgrimage to Tibet. I would never risk making such a long and often dangerous trek through Nepal to Tibet without having a clear inner call. Together with the call comes the blessing, the power and the protection.

But what was the task?

One day during a walk at my home, I was given a vision: Raksastal! I saw that this lake came into being through the tears of Parvati, the great Goddess, Lord Shiva's wife.

When mankind separated itself more and more from the love of God – from oneness – it happened that Parvati, – while remaining in her inner being always one with her Lord – in a part of herself, out of love, descended together with mankind, which was in the process of forgetting its origin, that is its oneness with God. So Raksastal originally bears in itself the tears, the pain and the sorrow of the Great Goddess, caused by the descent of mankind and its separation from God. It was only later that the Luciferian powers took over the lake, together with other powers in opposition to the Divine. – That was the point at which Raksastal became the lake of demons. This all moved me greatly.

When I related all these intuitive insights to Muniraji on the phone, he said: "Yes, Yes, Yes," so quickly that I gained the impression that he himself had shown me all of this.

At the same moment it became clear to me that now indeed the time had come for the transformation of Raksastal and what it represents for mankind.

I also felt within me the Tibetans' deep desire: "Oh, may the Ganga Chu flow again!" – that small river which connects the lake of the Sun, Lake Manasarovar, with the lake of the Moon, the Raksastal – which is connecting the light with the darkness, "then Tibet will be happy, and thus the world too."

How can all this come true?

I recall that in 2004 an Indian Guru came from Bombay with 120 devotees in order to carry out a twelve-day puja for Raksastal at about the same time as we were performing our fire ceremonies to honour Gurla Mandhata at Lake Manasarovar.

At that time I felt very touched that someone had the impulse to do something for this frequently so radiant but lonely lake.

From the north, Mt. Kailash with Lord Shiva and from the south, Gurla Mandhata with the Divine Mother look over these two sister lakes which lie directly between them.

Lake Manasarovar, full of life and love, the lake of the Sun – and beside it Raksastal, lonely, the lake of the moon, which is the expression of our separation from God and our freedom of choice. We can either choose love and open again ourselves to oneness with the Divine and be happy, or remain separated, experiencing loneliness and fear and exposed to all the "crocodiles," such as envy, jealousy, pride, frustration, rage, hate, and the entire range of unhappiness.

Lake Raksastal

Raksastal is rugged, of long shape and has three islands, while the Manasarovar-Lake is round and has no islands.

What could be done to assist this work of transforming Raksastal? The clear answer was: to perform nine fire ceremonies in all of the four parts of the "Divine Fortress." Fire is the great transformer.

I will relate a small incident which helped us understand a lot: While we were asking ourselves where it would be best to perform our fire ceremonies, we were visited by a very talented friend who carries out radiesthesia in an ingenious way. I showed him photos of Raksastal, including one with an island on it. He expressed the opinion, "Oh, this island radiates an astounding light."

We then puzzled over where this island could be found on the map of Raksastal. After some research we discovered that the only possibility was the island in the south of Raksastal, called Lachato Island. Our friend proposed that we hold our fire ceremonies at Raksastal very close to this island in the south of the lake. But I was not entirely convinced.

I called up Muniraji, our great, radiant friend and deep inner teacher: "Is it true that there is an island full of light in Raksastal?"

"Yes", he said.

I questioned further: "Does Parvati live there, surrounded by demons?"

"Yes" he replied.

"On which island is she?" I wanted to know.

"On the map there are three islands: One is the Lachato Island in the south of Raksastal, in the southwest is a smaller island without a name and there is a larger island much further away in the west of Raksastal, called Topseroma Island." "Parvati is always on Topseroma Island." This was his clear answer.

OM namah Shivay!

This story helped me to better understand the myths about demonic powers and their ability to deceive, in which they show themselves in a brilliant light.

But it was only because we were led in the wrong direction that we got wind that in Raksastal there really is an Island of Light and, thanks to Muniraji's clarity, we found the true Island of Light.

What a profound revelation, that the great Divine Mother herself – Parvati – lives on this island as a pillar of light in the midst of all the negative forces, exposed to the demons and their attacks. Her purity and the light of love, her oneness with the Lord, are her protection.

Like the Yang in Yin she maintained the presence of the light in the darkness – and that over eons.

In this, she clearly expressed the state of mankind, in which the Divine has to work in the midst of many dominating powers of darkness.

What can free her? Surely, when love on the Earth increases and also, when the Divine Mother and her love are again remembered.

I had sent Muniraji a map of the "Kailash Fortress," with the precise plan of where we wanted to hold the nine fire ceremonies. We intended to start this work on June 11, 2006, the day of the full moon, the Sagadava festival. I asked for his blessing on everything and asked him also if he would accompany us inwardly. –

Which he did in a wonderful way.

At the end of May 2006, we set out for Tibet once again. This time I only went with Marielu, a small crew of Sherpas and with Tenji as our guide again. We were already a well-tried team.

My preparation for this third and deeply moving pilgrimage to Tibet had unrolled in the prior eight months when I had often painted the whole day long and half the night. – I simply had to paint that which had been revealed to me deep within. I followed my inner intuition, knowing this was "my Kailash" before Kailash. So 100 oil paintings were created.

Some 14 days before the start of the journey a small incident happened. As I was going to say good night to our garden of heaven, I saw, standing in one of the beds, a post which really did not belong there.

It was visually disturbing and I spontaneously decided to pull it out – that was at about 11 p.m. – but the post had been hammered in hard and while pulling it out, I cricked my back, really badly as I later discovered. I had a great deal of pain, but my doctor friends really did everything they could to put things right again and make me fit for the journey – and were finally successful.

We flew via Thailand to Kathmandu. In the airport in Thailand, where we had a wait of some hours, I was able to walk quickly and lightly, much to my relief. But, when disembarking from the plane in Kathmandu, as I lifted my heavy rucksack down out of the baggage locker – and I had even had an inner warning to allow myself to be helped – people were crowding around and jostling so much – I again totally disabled myself.

I spent the following three days in bed in the "Nirvana Garden Hotel" in Kathmandu, with a hot water bottle at my back and deeply immersed in prayers for healing.

I phoned Muniraji and told him of my bad condition. I knew I would go on at any price, even if I had to take a helicopter to the border. I asked him: "Do you see me walking?"

His answer was: "Yes."

From deep within I asked him for healing, and I also asked why this had happened to me. He simply said: "This can happen." And then, full of energy, he said, "Say, I am alright."

This then is the mantra that he anchored in my spine – "I am alright." – It was truly powerful.

Marielu asked me to make a short visit to the shops with her, as she wanted to show me something. I was so weak and in such pain that after just a few minutes I had to take a rickshaw back to the hotel immediately.

For me it was a matter of being or not being. There was only the inner path of healing, since in Kathmandu there was no chiropractor to be found anywhere.

I knew that there would be tests before starting on such a pilgrimage with these intentions, but had no idea that they would be so hard.

I remained in faith.

So we flew to Nepalgunj where we met Tenji, our beloved Tenji, who, with his "Primeval jungle method" did his best to set me right. – It helped!

The next morning we were immediately able to fly from Nepalgunj to Simikot, where the trek began. As predicted by Muniraji, on that first evening of the long trek I felt neither pain nor stiff muscles, even though it had been unbelievably strenuous.

OM namah Shivay!

What a grace and encouragement, not just for me but also for the others. But the matter was by no means over and done with. Seven days, each with about eight trekking hours through Nepal, were lying ahead of us, and the pain soon started up again. While Marielu often happily walked on ahead, this time I had to stay a good way behind the others and I made only very slow progress with my mountain walking sticks.

On the second day of the trek someone came towards me, radiating a wonderful charisma full of warmth and goodness. He was dressed in Nepali fashion, had on a hat with a rim and wore a grey-white moustache. The look of his bright eyes penetrated deeply into my heart like a greeting.

"Jay, Jay!" he said to me quietly as he passed.

I was deeply touched by the light and the depth of his glance, and from the warmth and the love that he radiated.

I asked Tenji shortly afterwards whether there was such an expression in Nepalese as "Jay, Jay!" He said, No, he did not know this word. However, I knew it from Sanskrit. It means, "Victory!"

Later on I became certain that this was Shastriji.

I had also had highly astonishing experiences with him earlier, through which I sensed that he could also physically materialize himself.

How thankful I was for this encouraging encounter!

On the third day of the trek the pain was again so bad that I performed a focussing with Marielu during a stop by the Kanali river. I perceived that I was surrounded by beings full of pain, who apparently were accompanying me on the way to Kailash. I decided that I would just sing Hallelujah with each stab of pain, so that each step was made for the joy and celebration of God. I knew that through this transformation within me, I would no longer attract any beings of pain, and respectively, that their pain would be transformed along with mine.

The Kanali river, which rises in Kailash, was repeatedly a source of strength, even when it was only audible from a distance. Its powerful rushing sound seemed to be filled with mantras and full of the glory of Kailash.

But then, in addition to the pain which was increasingly transformed by the Hallelujahs, I developed diarrhoea and vomiting. Tenji was very worried.

A day of rest helped, but I still had serious diarrhoea. Especially, early in the morning before the last day of the trek, faced with a pass of 5,100 m in height, I was terribly weakened by diarrhoea.

Tenji, full of compassion, had the bright idea of setting me on the horse which we had with us for emergencies and which was otherwise loaded with some of the luggage.

With the horse's help I managed the climb. It carried me right up to the top, even though half way up the mountain it had to stop and was breathing so hard that I wanted to get off it straightaway.

For the others, too, the climb was difficult, and we were very happy that we had all made it.

After that we faced the long and steep descent, and a hike along a ridge. I dismounted from the horse and together we made the seemingly endless descent right down to the Chinese border at Sher. This is the first border post, the second then follows at Purang.

In the meantime a large group of Indians had landed by helicopter at the border. Still, even the path up to the customs post proved to be very difficult for many of them. Later, we heard that only 15 of the 60 Indians who had come were able to make the Kora.

We again had a guide from Lhasa assigned to us, but this time it was a wonderful Tibetan, called Tako.

We were filled with a deep happiness to be in Tibet again. This time, as if by magic, everything went well at the border in Purang. Tako undertook everything in order to get us through all the formalities with lightning speed. Whereas on the last pilgrimage we were held in Purang like prisoners, this time, as if on wings, we were on our way to Lake Manasarovar in the very shortest time.

What mercy God showed us there!

The first one to be seen now was Raksastal. The cleft lake was lying there in enrapturing beauty, the lake of the Moon and the demons, on which Parvati has her island. – Again and again I had to ask the driver to stop in order to get out and to take photos of these very stirring movements of light and shadow on Raksastal.

I sensed it as a mighty greeting from the power of light, which operates here dynamically and sovereign over the forces of darkness.

Shortly afterwards we reached Lake Manasarovar, our so familiar and beloved lake, which immediately bade us welcome:

In the sky I saw something that was supernaturally bright and came from a totally different dimension than the beautiful light-filled clouds, some of which looked quite angelic.

This totally unearthly radiance appeared to be a great ark of light, which hovered shining in the heavens like a horizontal lingam. Inside there were many light beings. They waved…!

I was filled with bliss.

We felt ourselves completely at home at Lake Manasarovar, the lake of the creator, of life and of love, and we were deeply grateful that we had succeeded in coming here again, into this perfect beauty, simplicity and stillness.

What a heartfelt inner joy it was to see, on this first evening in Tibet, the mountain of the Divine Mother, Gurla Mandhata, bathed in light, so close and just in front of us to the south of the lake!

And then how wonderful to watch the awakening stars in the twilight, so large and twinkling, until the moon appeared radiant in the darkness!

I reminded myself that only sixteen hours ago we had still been on the great 5,100 m high pass in Nepal – me totally weakened and exhausted by diarrhoea – then facing the long, long descent,… and now we had arrived at Lake Manasarovar, so happy and grateful that we really did not notice that our bodies were tired. Through pure happiness I felt totally fit.

Amazingly, now that we were in Tibet, my pain and likewise my diarrhoea had disappeared – OM namah Shivay – and so it remained for the whole of the rest of the pilgrimage.

Naturally, I now felt the responsibility to remain fit in order to be able to perform the forthcoming work of the fire ceremonies. In order to avoid getting diarrhoea again, I instinctively ate almost nothing but rice, plus all the good vitamins and minerals that I had with me.

The next day, luckily, we took a day of rest at Lake Manasarovar, having gained a day by not being detained at the border.

Strengthened on all levels, we set off on June 10, 2006 to Kailash via Tarboche. What a big joy over the reunion!

On Sunday, June 11, 2006, which was full moon, we performed the first of the nine fire ceremonies. We were facing Kailash, while on the other side of the hill the Sagadava festival was being celebrated with trumpets and the erection of a new flagpole.

It was not easy for Marielu and me to get the fire started, despite using dried yak dung and the ghee-soaked cotton wicks, which we had brought with us. But with a great deal of patience we finally succeeded.

We prayed for blessing on the impending work, which this time was mainly for Raksastal.

We had brought an extra rucksack with us to contain everything needful for the fire ceremonies: the Agni Hotra copper pot, the daily rice-sesame-barley-sugar mixture, the ghee, the dried flowers in all colours, dried fruit, incense, perfume, many yantra symbols, the Shiva lingam, a water container, etc.

For this first fire ceremony, as for all others, we spread out our holy cloth, the red twelve-leaved lotus flower cloth of velvet, which had lain on the fresh earth of Babaji's Mahasamadhi. We set up pictures of Babaji, of the Divine Mother and our divine friends, in prayer for their protection and blessing. We asked Babaji that he might do everything through us…

Each time we celebrated our fire ceremonies, we gave the place one of the various yantras we had brought with us, burying it in the earth at that precise spot where we had held the ceremony. Mostly the fire burned full of energy and smoked for a long time afterwards – and so we placed carefully selected protective stones around it, with a plea to God that it would be protected from then on.

After our first fire – it was a clear, sunny, crystal day – we went to the other side of the hill to greet the Sagadava festival with its new flagpole.

In the afternoon we searched for the right place to make the gift to Kailash of a large Shri Yantra plate, which we had brought with us.

This time we did not bury it directly beside the place of the fire, but instead went a long way along Kailash. At a special place, which could only be reached by clambering, I laid it between two flat rocks. It was a deeply cheering energy there and I did not want to leave the place again.

OM namah Shivay!

The next morning, it was Tuesday, June 13, 2006, we drove back to Lake Manasarovar in preparation for Raksastal.

Throughout the entire journey, but especially in Tibet, the sense of Muniraji's presence was ever present and alive, which filled us with deep gratitude.

With our awareness and hearts full of love, respect and compassion for Parvati, which left no place for fear, we approached Raksastal in the Land Cruiser.

Tenji had great respect for Raksastal with all its demons, and following his advice we performed our fire ceremony, not where I had planned it, directly on the lake front – in any case it was too windy there – but at some distance from the shore, in a small hollow protected from the wind, but with a view over to Topseroma Island, which we could see in the misty distance in front of us.

And all the time, the sense of Babaji's presence was very intense.

Tenji and Tako got the fire started for us, which was a masterwork because of the strong wind and thin air. It was a strong and radiant fire. At our desire, Tenji participated in the fire offering.

The fire ceremony was clear, deep and strong. Obviously all other unsettling or disturbing elements were kept away from us.

At Lake Manasarovar I had found a large stone that looked like a dove. After the fire ceremony I laid this stone on the bank of the Raksastal, directly at the lakeside, as a bringer of peace and also in order to connect the sibling lakes to each other. We gave the Raksastal lake a Shri Yantra and buried another Yantra in the sand by our fire. After this fire ceremony at Raksastal we all truly had a deep feeling of happiness and gratitude that it had been made possible, guided and protected by Babaji.

This was followed the next day by the third fire ceremony, at Lake Manasarovar. It took place to the north west of the lake, on the side where the Chiu Gompa is situated, higher up. Here, all the Sherpas wanted to help get the fire started. Again, we gifted a Yantra to the lake.

The fourth and following fire on the east side of the lake, close to the Seralung Gompa, was also very beautiful.

Here there came a great gift from God – the red girl: It was Thursday, June 15, 2006. Before we were to set off for Gurla Mandhata, the mountain of the Divine Mother, I went once again to Lake Manasarovar, close to the place where in the morning we had performed our fourth fire ceremony. I sat on a sand dune and was filled with thankfulness.

I looked towards Gurla Mandhata and spoke with the mountain of the Divine Mother. I felt the melody of the mountain and at the same time saw its awe-inspiring majesty. I asked for blessing and protection.

Soon we would be there. This time not only to touch the feet of the mountain, and thereby also the Devi, but also – for such was our hope and plan – to remain there for three days, and on each day to perform a fire ceremony at a different place on her huge mountain – in her honour and as a blessing for Raksastal.

While I was sitting there deep within myself, a red girl suddenly appeared in front of me. She was dressed in red from head to foot, a most beautiful child of about ten years of age.

Gurla Mandhata

She sat down in the sand next to me, quite still, and drew something in the sand. — Then she suddenly sprang up, looked into the distance towards the north-east and whistled highly impressively, simply between the tongue and the teeth, a whistle that could certainly be heard a long way off. — This led me to think that she was perhaps a shepherdess.

Then she sat down next to me again, now very close. I showed her my note-book and searched in my pockets for sweets to give her. We communicated without words.

She began to strew sand on my trouser legs, again and again. Finally, in response, I also strewed sand on her trouser legs.

Only later did I discover that this strewing of sand is an ancient method of healing.

It was enchanting. Such spontaneous openness, closeness, intimacy – what love there was between us!

Until it dawned on me: "Oh, I must get back to the others! We want to set off for the holy mountain!"

I searched for something that I could give her as a present. In the meantime some Tibetans had come along the lonely shore. An elderly man passing by spoke to us. Shortly afterwards the little red girl jumped up and was gone. After a few steps I could no longer see her.

The face of the girl in red did not look Tibetan; the expression of her bright eyes was wide awake and her face was fresh, lively and, at the same time, very finely cast. She looked just enchanting, and in such a simple way there was so much love expressed between us.

In my heart, I was driven to think of her over and over again. I wanted to give her so much more and wished very much that I would meet her again.

I looked out for her, but I didn't see her again.

But I could see her in my heart.

Over the days, weeks and months, then through the years, it became increasingly clear to me that she was an expression of the Divine Mother who had appeared in this form and gave her love so deeply, and blessed us for our further journey…

Perhaps she maintains this form as the red girl for a while, or appears repeatedly from her holy mountain in this form, to help the Tibetans, to bless and protect them!

June 15 was also the day on which, six years earlier, I had met Babaji in the form of a child when I was about to go around his holy mountain, Kailash. He had also appeared to be about ten years old, just like this girl.

Maybe he also maintains this form in the Kailash area for a while, to help, to support and bless the Tibetan people.

My heart is full of gratitude for the sweetness of this love, and my wish is that every person on this earth could experience this love.

After my encounter with the red girl we set off together for Gurla Mandhata, the mountain of the Divine Mother. We were very concentrated.

When, on Friday, June 16, 2006, we wanted to light our first fire on the holy mountain, our driver led us somewhere completely other than originally planned. He drove us on a small upward path to the forward part of Gurla Mandhata and told us to disembark. Tenji, Tako, Marielu and I went further up the mountain until we had a broad view over Lake Manasarovar as far as Kailash, not knowing that beside us there was a ravine.

Tako looked down and, shocked, said very quietly: "There is Chinese military!"

In the shortest space of time they came up to us, their faces expressionless like masks, and told us that under no circumstances could we remain here, but must leave immediately.

It was clear to me, that any resistance would be senseless, and Tako said with low voice: "If you resist, they will strike you down."

So, with our treasures, we made our way back down again, and then, intimidated, started our fifth fire ceremony below at the foot of Gurla Mandhata, praying for mercy and protection from the Divine Mother. The shock still sat deep in our bones. Later we discovered that this ravine was one of the Tibetans' escape routes. It was really a very strange feeling, to be confronted by the presence of the Chinese military on this most holy mountain.

In the afternoon we visited a small Gompa close to the earlier Tashi Gompa. It was modest and quiet, but filled with a deep spirituality.

When we got back to our tents we heard about a visit from the Chinese police, who came with four men and explained that we were camping here "illegally." But Tenji and Tako managed to arrange for us to remain there for a further two days, since apparently there was no place at all on Gurla Mandhata where one was officially allowed to camp. For that, they took Tako's identity card and his permit to work as a guide, which we were later able to redeem on payment of 70 dollars.

At the next and sixth fire ceremony, on June 17, 2006, in the middle of the lower area of the great holy mountain, we again felt much freer. Every time we made offerings we did so with Tenji, whose heart was filled by it.

Later, on the way to Kailash, we met a tall German who does a lot for the monasteries, and who had been told, during his circuit of Lake Manasarovar,

"There, up on the hill, (namely there where we were camping on Gurla Mandhata), there are three nuns." – The third nun in this case was our Tenji…

Apart from meeting the Chinese military on the mountain it was wonderful to explore the lower region of the holy mountain. The vibration was substantial and intense.

The seventh fire ceremony on June 18, 2006 was deep and clear and even freer. It was the third to take place on the holy mountain, right at the backward side, from where one can very clearly see Raksastal with Kailash as well as Lake Manasarovar.

With precious stones, which we had found on the mountain of the Divine Mother, we drove on, now along Lake Manasarovar towards the north. Halfway, we made a stop at a mountain and climbed up to a most enchanting Gompa, which was set high up on a rock and offered a marvellous view over Lake Manasarovar.

It is called Gossul Gompa, Gompa of the Stars. Truly a Gompa of the heavens, where each one of us was filled with a deep sense of happiness. Here one was really closer to heaven than to earth.

I felt the lake breathing to the heavens, heaven and lake resonating with each other, so deep and so pure – and our souls were resonating with them…

Once again we camped close to Chiu Gompa. During the circuit of Lake Manasarovar it struck me as well as others, including Tenji, that in the last few years the lake had continually withdrawn, all around its shores. I had first seen it in the year 2000 – and now there was a broad sandy beach where earlier there had been water. If Lake Manasarovar continually receded, the Lake of the Creator, what did it mean?

Was it a sign that the creation will be drawn back again to the creator? – In our hearts we felt this. This question occupied others, whom we met, as well.

On Monday, June 19, 2006, we performed our eighth fire ceremony on the "Panorama Hill," in the centre of the great divine mandala, with Kailash in the north, Gurla Mandhata in the south, and the two lakes to the left and right.

In the morning, it still snowed heavily! But we trusted that as soon as we attempted to light our fire, the weather would co-operate. And indeed, that is how it happened. Suddenly the sun came out, and we had brilliant weather.

By and by a whole row of Tibetans were assembled around our fire, including an old lama who was the head lama for all the Monasteries in the region, with a beautiful Tibetan nun, who accompanied him. They were very interested in what we were doing, and when we read the Sapta Sati, as we always did, the lama, standing behind us and supported by a staff, looked with great attention at our texts, astonished that they were Sanskrit and not Tibetan.

During the Arati, all of a sudden a Tibetan youth dressed all in black, eyes wide open and a black hat on his head, appeared at the front. Through him at that moment came the sense of a strong bright presence there. I knew that it was not Babaji. Only later was it revealed that it was Kakbushundi.[14]

The fire ceremony on the "Panorama Hill" was particularly intensive, and we were very happy that it had been possible to hold one fire directly following the other.

On the next day, June 20, 2006, we took off for Kailash. It was snowing heavily. We left our vehicle standing at the foot of Kailash and set off. There we met up with a group of 54 young Russians who all wanted to make the Kora around Kailash. Wiry young people, full of élan and hope. They were accompanied by a lama. We saw them make several stops, gathered around the lama who made one puja after the other, again and again.

Later we heard that of the 54 Russians, 53 had managed to complete the Kora! Of 45 Indians who were on the route in parallel, almost all of them turned back. Only a very few were able to complete the Kora.

As we trekked to the north face, this incredible joy overcame me again. I ran ahead as if I had wings, while Tenji, with Marielu and the Sherpas went on slowly and carefully a good way behind me. Tenji was worried about my pace and called me back repeatedly – but I was so full of joy and happiness to finally see the north face that I felt totally fit.

It snowed and snowed. A thick fog began to shroud everything. It got totally dark and unpleasantly cold.

"So, where is the north face anyway?"

In a tent below, all those following this path around Kailash had gathered and were trying to get warm and find a place to pitch a tent for the night.

"Dear Kailash, would you please show yourself!" I implored him – as certainly many others were doing.

As if by a miracle the fog parted, and it happened that Kailash suddenly showed himself through the dense fog, as if born of light and spirit. In complete and transparent beauty, he surprisingly stepped forward out of the clouds.

Mt. Kailash appears through the clouds

What love was felt there, all of a moment! The sun came out too, pleasantly warming after all the snow, fog and cold, and now very special views opened up to display the majestic dignity of the mountains all around – what a great gift for all of us!

On Wednesday, June 21, 2006 we performed our ninth fire ceremony – the wonderful fire which was our thanksgiving to the north face of Kailash. Afterwards we donated to Kailash all the yantras which remained and buried them in the earth by our fireplace.

Then, together with Tenji, we climbed up towards the north face of Kailash, as far as we could, right up to 5,400 m. Tenji then said: "Don't go any further!"

How moving to be so close to the mighty dome.

And there, at this height, we made the gift of our crystal lingam and our white festive Tibetan scarves, which we had been wearing at each of the fire ceremonies, to Kailash.

"It is accomplished!"

In the night of Wednesday, June 21 to Thursday, June 22 something overwhelming occurred: I had stepped outside my tent, and there stood Mt. Kailash as if shining from within in the night. Marvellous stars were grouped around him, stars like powerful diamond lights!

I have never before seen such huge stars. They formed a real bow of stars close around Kailash.

Most exciting was that the star high up in the centre of this star bow was positioned precisely on the sublime point of Kailash's 1000-petalled lotus. It appeared to sit there and was the most radiant of all! How can a star sit on the top of Mt. Kailash?

This star twinkled and twinkled, it sent out real waves of light. It spoke – so it seemed to me – as if Lord Shiva personally was sitting there. I could not avoid thinking like this because they were so vivid, the light and the love, the speech emitted by this star went directly into my heart.

I was deeply moved, full of awe and bliss. I stood there for a long time, forgot the cold – stood there in a long warm white nightgown, with only my blue fleece jacket over it, and I felt no cold.

The other stars, powerful, luminous and large, were silent, but this one, the highest, was speaking.

After a while, deeply happy from experiencing this celebration of the stars around the Kailash, I went back into my tent.

The next morning I related this to the others and asked if they had also seen it. But no, they had slept.

I then sealed all this in my heart.

Only months later, when I related this to a small circle of friends at home in Germany, did it become clear to me that, from an astronomical point of view, such a thing cannot occur. The stars cannot stand in a circle around Kailash, like the crown of stars around the Madonna.

That is completely impossible – but I had really seen and experienced it.

Following this, I called Muniraji. I had already sent him a photo book about this pilgrimage and had also written him about this star bow around Kailash. And I asked him: "Muniraji, the star on the top of Kailash which twinkled so, was that Darshan?"[15]

His answer was a powerful: "Yes!"

I asked further: "Was that Lord Shiva, Babaji, sitting there as a star on the top of Kailash?"

Again, his answer was a powerful: "Yes!"

Overwhelmed I put the phone down. The next day I called him again to ask about the other stars. Naturally, I was interested to know what were the other stars that had stood in the bow around Kailash. They were eight stars and a ninth hidden behind them. "And the other stars? Were they also Darshan?" I asked. And again Muniraji's answer was a radiant: "Yes!"

OM namah Shivay!

Thereupon I was completely still.

The celebration of the stars around Kailash! "What a sign for our times!," a friend said to me later, "that the Divine reveals itself like this, that divine beings appear as stars!".

"Who knows?" I asked myself. "Are there other people who had similar experiences at the same time? How wonderful that would be."

Fulfilled by the appearance of divine beings in the form of stars around Kailash, I constructed a great bow of stars in our garden, with eight stars made out of metal and a ninth hidden behind them.

What remains amazing is that through this bow of stars, the presence of the divine beings around Kailash is intensely perceptible even here in Germany. Each time in the garden that I look up high, it is almost as if I am standing on that midsummer night directly in front of Kailash, surrounded by his crown of stars. Happily, other people with open hearts and spirits also feel this.

Again and again I bow, filled with deep gratitude and joy, before the radiant light and love, the absolute power of the Divine Being.

Next morning we had to say goodbye to the beloved northern face of Kailash. Our path led us back along the western side of the mountain. Great "guardians" flanked the path to the west. Kailash appeared "armed," looking to the west.

His south-western face expressed sovereign power. But in contrast to this, his eastern face, which we could see from some places near Lake Manasarovar, looked gentle and full of devotion, like a lamb.

We arrived in Darchen, formerly a tent village at the foot of Kailash, where the Chinese are now systematically building small rectangular stone houses. There I was lucky enough to meet again the beautiful Tibetan woman whom I knew from my second visit to Kailash.

I had Shastriji's words in mind: "If you perform nine fire ceremonies around the area of Kailash, then you have to, as with Navaratri, adorn and give food to nine little girls in honour of the Divine Mother and celebrate them as little Devis." At that time I had asked Shastriji: "How should I find nine little girls at Kailash?"

It was made possible thanks to the beautiful Tibetan woman. She arranged it all for us. In her small shop we selected beautiful scarves and malas for the nine little girls, and I left her with the money to make a wonderful meal for all of them on the next day. I was very grateful and happy that this was made possible in such an easy way.

From Kailash, it was a jeep journey to the eastern side of Lake Manasarovar, near Seralung Gompa. I went to the lake shore where the red girl had appeared, close to the place of my fire ceremony. Wherever I looked, there was no little red girl to be seen. But Gurla Mandhata was magnificent to look at.

We then had to take our leave of that which we loved so deeply. Marielu had tears in her eyes. Once again we asked the Divine Mother for her blessing on everything. In looking towards Gurla Mandhata, which we held so close to our hearts, we asked ourselves whether we had done everything right.

There was still sadness in us resulting from our meeting with the Chinese military. Only later did we come to realize that this is a reality in Tibet, and that we had to meet them so that this, too, could be transformed by the fire ceremonies.

All of this work in the "Kailash Fortress" was our contribution for Tibet, the heart in the heart of the planet, which has taken so much upon itself, and this time especially for Raksastal, which longs for freedom.

Early on Friday, June 23, 2006, we had to depart. On this, our last day in Tibet, it was suddenly clear to me that I definitely had to make a tenth fire ceremony.[16]

It was the nine little girls, who would now be celebrated at Kailash, that brought this to my mind. But then I decided to perform this tenth ceremony – it had to be an inner fire ceremony – for all the people in Tibet, not only for the little girls. I wanted to start straightaway but the Sherpas were pressing to set off. Sadly there was no time left and we set off. – Shortly afterwards the vehicle came to a halt. The problem first had to be identified. All of a sudden there was time!

Sitting in the sand, concentrated and full of joy, I started this tenth fire ceremony, which was meant not only for all the people in Tibet, but for all the people of this earth. – When we were able to continue on our way, I continued with the work during the journey and was filled with a deep concentration, over and above all the potholes. It was entirely wonderful!

I was amazed — suddenly I knew it — it was Gauri[17] herself, the Divine Mother from Gurla Mandhata, who through me performed this last tenth inner fire ceremony. What a gift! What a blessing!

Then our journey began through the wide and vast solitude and stillness of Tibet back to Nepal.

Particularly on this return trip, a deep melancholy and sorrow overcame us because of the whole situation in Tibet. Only now and then was there a shepherd with his flock to be seen, in the distance a few nomad tents, over and over monasteries that were completely destroyed, where one could only see ruins, but where, in despite of this, the spiritual presence could still be felt very strongly.

We were filled with deep compassion for the Tibetans who have had so many of their places of devotion destroyed.

When people are no longer allowed to honour the Divine as their hearts wish, how in the long run can a person and his life have meaning and energy?

Having arrived in green Nepal, with its steep canyons and waterfalls, we immediately felt a yearning for Tibet, its vastness, its stillness and the sense of its being, penetrated by infinity.

OM namah Shivay!

Finale:
The Rider of the Apocalypse

It was Friday evening, February 19, 2010; I sat in meditative mood in our snow-covered garden and inwardly I saw this:

A light-filled rider on a white horse came from a higher plane, the plane of life that never dies, descending, in wide spirals and in deep concentration, down to the physical plane.

In his hand, fluttering in the breeze, he held a white flag. On the flag there was a sign in red: OM with a cross – Babaji's sign.

His form was slim and full of light and he was as majestic as he was unassuming. He wore a Tibetan cap made of innumerable tiny diamonds of the greatest purity. His robe was beautifully embroidered on the breast and appeared to bear a hidden Yantra on the inside.

A sign from Shambhala?

The rider was Babaji.

Having arrived on the physical plane, there was no longer a white rider to be seen, but a black one.

Now I was able to see Babaji very clearly and close up, in his form as Bhole Baba, exactly as we had experienced him. He exuded great power, was wearing a black cape and a large black hat with a very broad brim. He was dressed in black silk from head to foot.

I knew that underneath he was pure, radiant gold.

Right at the start of this inner vision, at the spot in the garden where I was sitting, an enormous cone had formed reaching into the depths of the earth; it was a funnel-like opening with the sides consisting of trickling loam sand scree with a few small nuggets of gold dotted here and there. In this funnel-shaped opening into the depths there were anchor points, hidden way stations, which had been made by all those who serve the Divine, mankind and the Earth.

Babaji as the black rider now rode on a dark horse down into this funnel, in spirals and at great speed, freeing innumerable souls for the other dimension as he went. While doing this, he poured forth his wonderful divine fragrance, thus raising the human souls into a new state of consciousness. As he arrived at the bottom, the power of his gaze caused a spring to arise at the deepest point of the funnel.

Life itself effervesced upward from the depths, forming a truly beautiful fountain, pink-orange-ananda-coloured: It was the great Goddess who streamed upwards in it, representing Life that never dies.

Nothing black was visible on Babaji any more; he was pure radiant gold. His awareness poured into the Devi.

Then I saw Muniraj sitting up above on the rim of the funnel, in light-coloured clothing. He caused a light-filled plane to form above the deep cone on which there became visible buildings of light with radiant beings in a state of bliss – that is where the New Life, the New World arose like a living giant Meru Shri Yantra.

Stern Babaji giving a blessing

Notes

1   See Wosien, Maria-Gabriele: *Babadschi. Botschaft vom Himalaya (Message from the Himalayas)*. Publisher: Reichel, 1990.

2   Oscar Marcel Hinze (1931–2008), a great man, full of Light, full of Love, with deep inner visions. He is the founder of the Academy of Phenomenology and Integral Science. In lectures of unique pregnancy, radiance, liveliness and depth, he connected natural and spiritual science, Eastern and Western spiritual paths and was a great inspiration to many people in Europe. I lived for twelve years together with him, first alone, then in a group.

3   OM namah Shivay: I bow to you, o Lord.
I surrender to you, Lord, or: I take refuge in God.
Your will shall be done – or simply: I love you, Lord.

4   A little metal vessel with a handle was used for the Arati ceremony. It was filled with one or several balls of cotton wool, pointed on the top, which had been plunged in liquid, cleansed butterfat. These are lit and give off a beautiful living flame. The metal vessel with the flame is passed clockwise in front of a picture or a statue of the Divine.

5   OM Hariyakhandi is a reigning mantra, which if it is repeated again and again, opens all the chakras in the body, starting from the crown chakra.

6   Oscar Marcel Hinze, *Tantra Vidya*, Motilal Banarsidass,1979.

7   In August 1981, Babaji had given instructions for a new Dhuni to be built down below on the riverbank, where the holy fire should burn continually; he had given some of the people from the West, who wanted to remain in Herakhan, a yogic initiation, and made them guardians of the holy fire.

8   For example, in the night of February 24 to 25, 1957, in the ashram of
     Kathgaria while the people were singing, an enormous three-meter-high
     flame appeared over a Murti of the old Herakhan Baba that was to be con-
     secrated the following day. Herakhan Baba was visible in this flame. After a
     few minutes it diminished and entered into the Murti.

9   According to Rudolf Steiner, the Mars period of human history ended 600
     B.C., followed by the Mercury period.

10   Kali is the Divine Mother in the aspect of her power.

11   Saraswati is the Divine Mother in the aspect of her wisdom.

12   Lakshmi is the Divine Mother in the aspect of her love, friendship, beauty,
     wealth and abundance.

13   Geomantic: According to Peter Dawkins' researches, Australia, with Ayers
     Rock for example, is viewed as the root chakra or as the 4-petalled lotus of
     the planet. Africa, especially South Africa, is seen as the sacral chakra or the
     6-petalled lotus. South America, with Middle America, is viewed as the solar
     plexus chakra or the 10-petalled lotus. India forms the heart chakra, the
     12-petalled lotus. Europe is seen as the throat chakra, the 16-petalled lotus.
     North America forms the brow chakra, the 2-petalled lotus. Asia with Sibe-
     ria is viewed as the crown chakra, the 1000-petalled lotus. Tibet is viewed
     as the heart in the heart chakra, the expression of the soul, as the hidden
     8-petalled lotus in the 12-petalled lotus of the Earth.
         Peter Dawkins, Architect (M. A. Cambridge) is an internationally
     renowned geomancer, philosopher, author and teacher of the Western
     tradition of wisdom. He is the founder of the "Zoence Academy," a cosmo-
     logical science of life and the living, director of the "Francis Bacon Research
     Trust," which has specialized in research relating to Bacon, Shakespeare, the
     Rosicrucians and other philosophers of the European Renaissance, and is
     co-founder of the "Gatekeepers Trust."
         His researches substantiate the unity of the cosmos, the earth and man-
     kind and led to the rediscovery of the ancient science of landscape temples
     and of the subtle interplay of the spiritual and material world. His work
     serves perception and healing in the holistic sense, in particular as related to
     landscapes. For the work of healing for the body of the earth, he leads geo-

cosmological pilgrimages worldwide. He calls it planetary garden work.

14 Kakbushundi – a great enlightened being which, according to Babaji, lives in the form of a crow on the peak of a hill in the Himalayas. Shastriji achieved self-realization through Kakbushundi.

15 Darshan – face to face with the Divine, being seen and blessed through the presence of the Divine – for example in a master, to have the insight in the Divine – experience of the view of the Divine.

16 After each Navaratri, which is concluded with nine fire ceremonies, there takes place as a general rule a tenth fire ceremony, which celebrates the victory of light over the forces of darkness: historically, the victory of Lord Rama over the demon king Ravana.

17 Gaura Devi, also called Gauri (pronounced Gori), is the name of the wife of Lord Shiva, here also the name of the Divine Mother of Gurla Mandhata, the female equivalent of Kailash.

Glossary

ARATI
Ritual devotion, a service of worship in which light is offered to an image of God

ASHRAM
Place of retreat and shelter nearby a temple or monastery

AVATAR
A great divine incarnation in human form

BABA
Revered Father, generally used for a holy man, an added term of respect and reverence

BABA GORAKNATH
Avatar of Lord Shiva at the beginning of the Kali Yuga, about 3100 B.C., famous because of his miraculous powers

BHAIRAV BABA (BERU BABA)
Main power of Lord Shiva, his right hand,
Shiva's form as a destroyer of the evil on one side,
and as great healer and protector of the good on the other side

BHOLE BABA KI JAI!
Praise to Bhole Baba, to the Father, who is simple!

BHAJANS
Songs of reverence and praise to the Lord

DARSHAN
Face to face with the Divine, being seen and being blessed through the presence of the Divine – for example in a Master; insight into the Divine, experience through the view of the Divine

DHARMA
Law, order, eternal law, which rules the creation

DHUNI
Fire pit

FINDHORN FOUNDATION
The Findhorn Foundation in the north of Scotland, co-founded by Peter Caddy 1962, developed into an international community, whose workshops and programmes have been visited by more than 100,000 people from all over the world. It is also recognized by the UNO.

GAUTAM GANGA
Holy river by Herakhan, named after one of the seven Rishis;
its source in Lake Manasarovar in Tibet, it flows underground until rising to the surface near the Herakhan-Kailash.

GHEE
Clarified butter, which is offered to the divine beings

GAURI
With light golden skin; name of Parvati

GURU
Spiritual teacher

HANUMAN
One of the immortal beings; king of the monkeys; hero of the epoch Ramayana; who is serving to the Divine

HAVAN
Also Yagna, ritual fire ceremony

HERAKHAN
Also: Haidakhan

HERAKHAN VISHWA MAHADAM
Shri Babaji's ashram, supreme holy universal place

HIMALAYA
Place of Snow

KAILASH
Name of two holy mountains, one in the Kumaon area of Northern India, and one in Tibet

KALI
"The Black One"; name of the Great Goddess

KALI YUGA
Time era named after Kali, which started 3100 B.C.

KIRTAN
Singing of religious songs

KRIYA-YOGA
Spiritual teaching-method of Babaji, which serves the renewal of life

KUTIYA
Hut, hermitage

LAHIRI MAHASAYA
Disciple of Babaji in Kriya-Yoga in the 19th century

LILA
Divine play, drama

LINGAM
Phallic cult symbol

MAHADEVA
"Great God", name of Shiva

MAHENDRA BABA
Disciple of Babaji, died in 1969; he prepared for the Reappearance of Babaji as Shiva-Avatar

MALA
Prayer rosary of 108 beads

MANTRA
Prayer formula, of itself an active vibration of sound, which through repetition quiets the mind and helps to realization of the Divine

MUDRAS
Meditative hand gestures

MUNDAN
Tonsure

MURTI
Form, statue

NAVARATRI
Religious celebration of the "nine nights" in honour of the Divine Mother in springtime and in autumn; celebrates the victory of light over the darkness

OM
Primeval sound of creation, symbolizes the All-oneness of the Divine

OM NAMAH SHIVAY
I bow in front of you, Lord
Lord, Thy will be done
I dedicate myself to you, I surrender to you
God, I love you

PARVATI
The Great Goddess: Lord Shiva's wife; daughter of King Parvata, the Lord of the Himalayas

PRALAYA
Dissolution of the world

PRANAM
Gesture of reverence, falling on one's knees,
Or bowing down to the feet of a holy person

PRASAD
Purity, Lightness, blessed food

PUJA
Religious prayer service in connection with a special ritual

PURUSHA
Immortal being

SADA SHIVA
Eternal Shiva, name of Lord Shiva

SANATANA DHARMA
The eternal original law, source of all religions

SATI
The Great Goddess in her first appearance; wife of Lord Shiva; daughter of King Daksha

SHIVA
Mahadeva, the Great God; the one who brings happiness; Hindu Godhead; the Self of all beings, one of the trinity "Brahma, Vishnu and Shiva." Shiva brings destruction, and through this the purification and renewal of the creation; his home is eternity.

SHIVARATRI
Shiva's night; once a year in February or March this great festival is celebrated; during the day people fast, and during the night they stay awake, singing and meditating or performing ritual worship.

SIDDHESHWAR
Vishnu's holy mountain by Herakhan (or Haidakhan)

SIDDHIS
Supernatural powers

TRISHUL
Shiva's trident

YAGNA
Vedic fire ritual, offering, fire pit

YANTRA
Cosmic magic diagram;
SHRI-YANTRA: supreme yantra of the Divine Mother
MERU-SHRI-YANTRA: Sublime, three-dimensional Shri Yantra

PARAMAHANSA YOGANANDA
Indian Yogi, who was sent to America by Babaji and Shri Yukteshwar to teach Kriya-Yoga; author of the *Autobiography of a Yogi*; he made the name of Babaji well known in the west.

YOGI
One who is following the path of union with God

Acknowledgements

When I asked Babaji in 1979: "Please give me your hand," he replied: "Not one hand, all hands." This is how it has been with this book.

My deepest thanks therefore go to Babaji himself who has guided and inspired me, given me courage and strength to write as openly as I have been able to, and who worked through those who have helped me on different levels.

From the bottom of my heart I thank:

Shri Muniraj Maharaj first and foremost; my deepest thanks for having been able to check important questions with him and for supporting everything with the light of his love.

Shri Vishnu Datt Mishra Shastriji, who has accompanied me on the inner levels right through to the last page. Both are men whose inner vision, knowledge and love are total.

Peter Caddy, my husband, who with his sun power and absolute faith has been at my side from the inner levels throughout this process.

Peter Dawkins and Marie Louise Jung, who have been very active in waiting for me to start writing this book for which Babaji gave his blessing as far back as 1983.

Petra Bunke, who was a loving, perceptive sun and marvellous inspiration for the book.

Gisela Behrendt for her love all the time.

Evelyn Lajwanti for her joyful assistance, and later: her wonderful loving help with the English corrections.

Mohini Brigitte Hoffmann for her absolutely selfless devotion and great help, for her total application.

Uma also for jumping in to help at the last minute.

Edit Bernhardt-Herr for her supportive work in all friendship.

Barbara Hubricht for the sensitive and loving help and application, and for time and again clearing space for me.

For the English translation my deep thanks go first to Richard Freeman and to Krishna Viswanathan who out of the love of their hearts helped me in this work.

How can I thank Madhuri Margret C. Falter for her total selfless engagement with the correction of the English translation, just as if it was her own book.

And then Uschi Dickenson, sent as a loving, correction and translation angel at the end.

A loving Thank You also to Martin Bichler for the digital imaging. Also to all the spontaneous helpers Babaji sent me just at the right time.

And, last but not least, to Ruth Maria Kubitschek heartfelt thanks for taking the time to write the foreword.

They all did it out of love. May Babaji bless them deeply.

Vita

Renata Caddy, born in 1941 into a loving family that was culturally and spiritually very open, experienced an early childhood overshadowed by war. Later on though she had a radiant youth in her parent's home in Munich, through which she also came into contact with Zen philosophy.

After her A-Levels she studied painting, graphics and sculpture in Munich, Berlin and Paris. She completed her studies with Professor Alexander Camaro in Berlin who at that time was her marvellous teacher in painting as well as in life. While studying, she took inspiring trips to Greece, the Sahara, Egypt, Russia, Spain, Provence, Brittany and Tuscany.

In 1967, she married Dr. Peter Zürn and did several exhibitions of her oil paintings with readings of her own texts and poems in Frankfurt. Zen became more and more important both for her work and in her life.

In 1968, she met the « Mother » of the Shri Aurobindo ashram on the inner planes who then became her inner spiritual teacher. In 1972, she went to India to meet her in person.

From 1973, she lived and worked with Oscar Marcel Hinze, the founder of the Academy for Phenomenology and Integral Science. She deepened her knowledge of graphology in the context of depth psychology (for which she received a diploma), of art therapy on the basis of anthroposophy, astrology and spiritual healing with various healers, especially with Harry Edwards in England.

In 1975, she first met Peter Caddy, the co-founder of the Findhorn Community in the north of Scotland – now recognized by the UN – whom she later was to marry.

In 1977, she moved to Lake Constance.

In 1978 came the inner call from Babaji – she immediately flew to India to meet him.

Following that, she regularly visited Herakhan up until Babaji's Mahasamadhi in 1984, when he handed everything over to Shri Muniraj. After that, she regularly visited Babaji's ashram to be in the presence of Shri Muniraj and

Shastriji and participate in the healing festivals (navaratris) for the world.

In 1979, she began transforming a wild garden next to her home on Lake Constance into a living healing garden.

Since 1980 she has been giving intensive seminars and workshops on subjects fundamental to life: path to our centre, finding our Self, self-development, mandala weeks, partnership workshops, planetary yoga weeks, healer trainings and very frequent painting weeks on themes like "Painting on the Path to the Self."

In addition to the seminars, regular weekly meditation evenings in house and garden were also held from 1982 onwards.

In 1985, the name for the whole place revealed itself: *Quell des Heilens (Source of Healing)*.

In 1987, she married Peter Caddy. She went on giving talks and seminars, some also jointly with him. They travelled much together. Peter was a planetary being, open to all cultures and countries.

At home on Lake Constance, Peter worked in the garden intensively and with great love, anchoring the Light in its soil.

From 1992 onwards Renata has been organizing the solar festivals in her centre *Quell des Heilens (Source of Healing)* with fire ceremonies and sacred dance.

In 1994 Peter died suddenly – in a car crash. That meant that Renata Caddy had to complete the last part of his autobiography. *In Perfect Timing* has been published in several languages.

Through all these years, she has kept up her painting at great depth; in addition to individual pictures, there are also series of paintings: the Caravan series, the Resurrection series, the Mystery of the Blue series, the Scotland series, etc. They have all been exhibited repeatedly.

In 2000, 2004 and 2006, Renata Caddy went on pilgrimages to Mt. Kailash in Tibet. This resulted in a further series of paintings: "The Tibet Series" and "Humanity's Journey through transformation into a new Life," comprising 100 oil paintings.

She is currently working on her three-volume opus, the first of which is *Encounters with Babaji – Master of the Himalayas.*

FINDHORN PRESS

Life-Changing Books

For a complete catalogue,
please contact:

Findhorn Press Ltd
117-121 High Street,
Forres IV36 1AB,
Scotland, UK

t +44 (0)1309 690582
f +44 (0)131 777 2711
e info@findhornpress.com

or consult our catalogue online
(with secure order facility) on
www.findhornpress.com

For information on the Findhorn Foundation:
www.findhorn.org